Waterways of Bangkok

Waterways of Bangkok

Memory, Landscape, and Twilight

Michael Hurley

NUS PRESS
SINGAPORE

Published by:
NUS Press
National University of Singapore
AS3-01-02
3 Arts Link
Singapore 117569

Fax: (65) 6774-0652
E-mail: nusbooks@nus.edu.sg
Website: http://nuspress.nus.edu.sg

print ISBN 978-981-325-278-3 (paper)
ePDF ISBN 978-981-325-279-0

National Library Board, Singapore Cataloguing in Publication Data
Name(s): Hurley, Michael, 1978-
Title: Waterways of Bangkok : memory, landscape, and twilight / Michael Hurley.
Description: Singapore : NUS Press, [2025] | Includes bibliography and index.
Identifier(s): ISBN 978-981-325-278-3 (paperback) | 978-981-325-279-0 (ePDF)
Subject(s): LCSH: Chao Phraya River (Thailand)--Social conditions. | Waterways--Social aspects--Thailand--Bangkok. | National characteristics, Thai.
Classification: DDC 306.09593--dc23

Cover image: Bangkok Yai Canal, by Michael Hurley
Photography: All photos in the book are by Michael Hurley

Typeset by: Ogma Solutions Pvt Ltd
Printed by: Markono Print Media Pte Ltd

Contents

List of Images

Introduction

This is an ethnography of the Chao Phraya River in Bangkok, Thailand—a study of life along the river and canals, of the culture of water in a modern metropolis.[1] Waterways provide an empirical starting point to explore and try to better understand "Thai" society. The Chao Phraya River is the binding thread of the Thai heartland, the realm of a traditional way of life, and also enshrined in the state-promoted Thai national story. But waterways can also inspire new ways of seeing. Based primarily on fieldwork undertaken during intense political turmoil, as the long-reigning king was dying, this book offers alternate perspectives on the Thai past, present, and future. It is deeply engaged with places, and the cultural patterns and peculiarities of places, and thus written in conversation with communities of scholarship formed by area specialists, including those who study Thailand or other countries in Southeast Asia. At the same time, this book is a study of the relationship between memory and landscape—far reaching aspects of human existence—and thereby overflows national, regional, and disciplinary boundaries.

Rivers everywhere gather stories and images, reflecting broader patterns of society and culture. In ancient Sumeria, along the Tigris and Euphrates, dwellings and temples were built from alluvial mud, and floods of fertility raised fields of grain. Egypt was and remains centered on the Nile, and even the gods traveled by boat along that gentle, life-giving artery. The Indus flows with archaeological tales of irrigation, planned cities, and the collapse of a society. The Yangtze flows from afar, as if descending from distant clouds, giving rise to an enormous patchwork of cultivated landscapes, and is now dominated by monumental hydroelectric dams. According to the sinologist Karl Wittfogel (1957), massive irrigation projects entailed the emergence of despotic power. Rivers have also been

[1] Setting aside tones, the colloquial Thai pronunciation of the river's name can be approximated as *jow* (rhymes with "now") *p'ya*.

realms of oblivion. In Greek antiquity, souls crossed the Styx and shed their memories in the Lethe. As told by Buddhist folklore in Thailand, the tortures awaiting the impious include a burning river of thorns (Tsuzuki 2010: 4). In the late 19th century, the novelist Joseph Conrad sent Marlow upstream along the Congo to witness the vile truth of colonialism and the ivory trade, a story remade in the 1970s by director Francis Ford Coppola as a journey along the Mekong into the savage heart of American empire. In Hindu tradition, the maternal Ganges flows from the matted hair of Shiva, and still today numerous pilgrims bathe in the sacred waters. In the 1960s, during pogroms that accompanied the rise of General Suharto, Javanese rivers turned the color of blood. Rivers emerge from rain and snow, slithering down from highlands, connecting past, present, and future. Rivers evoke mud, motherhood, and life, the sacred and profane, mythology and militarism, beauty and horror.

Peter Boomgaard observes, "In the study of Southeast Asia, there has always been a strong emphasis on everything terrestrial with a concomitant neglect of aquatic aspects" (2007: 1). This book is a study of Bangkok's aquatic culture, but waterways are always engaged with land. Rivers and canals have banks as well as terrestrial beds. Although the river is still used for transportation—and Bangkok dwellers do sometimes jump, wade, or fall into the water—people generally return to land. Waterways do not exclude the terrestrial, but rather provide ways to explore it. The Chao Phraya River flows through the center of Thailand's national body. The river is both a blood-line and time-line within the body, winding through and binding the terrains of great city-kingdoms. She is also Thailand's nurturing mother, though poisoned and ailing. Furthermore, the river is one of the most prominent internal aspects of what Thongchai Winichakul calls the "geo-body" of Siam (1994). In his analysis, the Siamese geo-body was brought into being through encounters with the British and French imperialists, and especially through the imperative to define the limits of Siam's territory. A national body, both material and imaginary—hard, tangible, and immediate, but far exceeding anyone's line of sight—was brought into being through the process of mapping. Once born, the geo-body becomes an orienting and enclosing structure, the "life" of which, in Thongchai's rather sinister phrase, "is diabolically generative" (1994: 135). Maps impose shapes in solid colors with bold border lines, uncorrupted, distinct from adjacent shapes in other colors. As instruments of nation-building, maps have changed the forms, scales, and conventions of memory. Clifford Geertz writes, "The suffusive mists of cartographic identity—even the sheep seem Moroccan, even the volcanoes seem Indonesian—make it difficult to remember that places are accidents and their names ideas" (1995: 22). As the Siamese borders were established in black, internal features of the terrain were also gathered, including rivers and mountain ranges. The Chao Phraya River was drawn and named. The riverine landscape is a product of erosion, deposition, and the brute labor of digging and building, but also a product of imagination, the ongoing evolution of the geo-body.

Water defines Bangkok's geography. Bangkok is a tropical port-city, 13.7 degrees north of the equator and subject to the monsoon cycle of the Indian Ocean. It receives abundant rain, as befits a city of Indra, god of storms. Wolf Donner, examining the economic geography of Thailand, describes Bangkok as follows: "Situated upon a very low-lying plot of land in the immediate vicinity of the sea, traversed by the largest river of the country [the Chao Phraya River] and covered by a network of natural as well as man-made channels, the area is shaped by water, depends on water and is threatened by water" (1978: 765). Born of confluence, the maternal river flows from north to south, winds her way around Ayutthaya and through Bangkok, and drains into the Gulf of Thailand. The central plains, known as the "cradle of rice and water" (อู่ข้าวอู่น้ำ), consists of a densely populated terrain of agriculture and extensive urbanization, flanked to the west by the Tennaserim Range, and to the east by three bodies of mountains: Phetchabun, Dong Phaya Yen, and Sankamphaeng. Along these plains, the river's course sweeps from side to side, turning in wide arcs, but over the past several hundred years has been repeatedly modified by shortcut canals, and the flow is now partially controlled by dams.

The landscape is saturated with meaning and connections. This makes waterways a highly generative focus of ethnographic study—we begin with water, but soon engage broader socio-cultural realities: ghosts, royalty, ancient cities, the rural hinterland, and so forth. In the opening pages of *Pai Daeng*, Kukrit Pramoj guides us along the waterways from Bangkok to Red Bamboo, the village where the story

A view of the Chao Phraya River

will unfold. We go upstream along the Chao Phraya River, some 90 kilometers, turn off into a canal, travel some additional distance along the water, and finally arrive at a quiet village with a rundown monastery (Kukrit 2009: 7). Waterways enable travel, connecting city and country.[2] Gaston Bachelard, writing of rivers, observes, "Water flows and leads life elsewhere" (1983: 8). As we will see, water also gathers other times and places, bringing, so to speak, elsewhere to here. The past becomes present and the faraway arrives in Bangkok. In the course of fieldwork, one finds patterns. People raise, again and again, certain themes, questions, and observations. Such repetition is significant, even if perspectives do not converge on a single point of view. Culture may be multiple, strange, or fragmented, but patterns do emerge. This book explores patterns of memory along the waterways of Bangkok.

---

[2] Blaise Pascal, an innovator of public transportation, writes: "Rivers are roads that move, and carry us where we wish to go" (Abbey 1991: 3).

Many in Bangkok perceive a bond between waterways and a "way of life". This holds true for those who live along the waterways, as well as those who do not. It is said to be an old, original, and authentic Thai way of life. Some of the features of this way of life include: fishing, houses on stilts,[3] boats as a primary means of transportation, canoe races, floating markets, itinerant merchants paddling through the canals, calling out the names of their fruit or wares, the use of canal water for cooking and cleaning, dramatizations of royal power, such as the royal barge procession, and the annual festival in which people set afloat banana-leaf boats, make offerings, and apologize to the spirit of the water-mother. This is all enmeshed in collective memory—how Thais see or imagine the Thai past and present, and how the collective is imagined by its members. Thais are often said (by themselves) to have a special relationship with water. Many said, "We (Thais) have long been bound [ผูกพัน] to waterways." But this way of life is also perceived as outdated and declining, and according to some, has mostly vanished, implying that what one sees today, between the riverside hotels and shopping complexes, is merely a tangle of decayed remnants from a once thriving aquatic past.

The Chao Phraya River is also part of a national time-line, or what can be called the progression-of-centers narrative. Since the 1930s, the Thai past has been periodized as a series of city-kingdoms: Sukhothai, Ayutthaya, Thonburi, Bangkok. In a sense, this reflects a traditional cultural logic, widespread in Southeast Asia, in which polities are named after their urban centers, but this particular configuration is closely tied to a more recent process of nation-building. Sukhothai is a city, but also a time period: the Age of Sukhothai. Ayutthaya is a city, but also a time period: the Age of Ayutthaya. And so on. Notably, these cities are linked together by the Chao Phraya River. Ayutthaya, Thonburi, and Bangkok were built directly on its banks. Sukhothai is further north, near the Yom River, one of the four rivers that flow into the Chao Phraya. Children are taught to sing the names

[3] Stilt houses also appear in Thailand's non-riverine landscapes, including the highlands. Thus, some scholars argue that there is no strict or fundamental connection between these structures and waterways. They have other uses: storage, shade, a play area for children, and so on. Nonetheless, such houses do offer protection against flooding.

of those four rivers: Ping, Wang, Yom, Nan. The Chao Phraya proper, beginning at the confluence of the Ping and Nan in Nakhon Sawan, is less than 400 kilometers in length.[4] Nonetheless, in the national context, it is a great river. As one informant so concisely said, "It is the most important river in Thailand." Teeraparb Lohitkun, an award-winning Thai author and documentary filmmaker, calls the Chao Phraya River the "nation's bloodline" (Teeraparb 1993: 145). The river ties together the centers of the official royal-national past and present. This progression-of-centers narrative has sometimes been challenged, but it remains prominent and still organizes most books on Thai history. It has become a ready-made structure—a simple, durable outline for collective memory.

This project began by observing the river as a tangible, structural element of the Thai national story. During fieldwork, however, knowledge sometimes falls apart. Established assumptions are shaken and dislodged. Thus, arising from the discordance and surprises of fieldwork, this book takes a critical view of the progression-of-centers narrative. At the same time, creative opportunities arise: the landscape can inspire new perspectives. An American missionary named William C. Dodd, who died in 1919, argued that Thais originated in the Altai Mountains, an icy region north of Xinjiang. This theory, although demolished by scholars, is still widely taught in Thai schools. Thais are said to have migrated south, beginning around the time of Siddhartha, eventually settling in Sukhothai, where they overthrew an oppressive Khmer regime. In subsequent generations, as the story goes, Thais migrated further south through the river basin, cutting vast networks of canals, remaking the landscape. There is indeed a deep past of Khmer sovereignty along the river, which has always been a terrain of contact, exchange, and mixture. In addition to Sukhothai, Angkor had outposts along the lower reaches of the Chao Phraya, including Lopburi, formerly a center of the Mon civilization of Dvaravati (Wyatt 2003: 17–25). Any attempt to trace Thai origins inevitably finds entanglement with Mon, Lao, Chinese, Malay, and

---

[4] By comparison, the Mekong is over 4,000 kilometers in length, and the Yangtze is even longer at over 6,000 kilometers. Srisak Vallibhotama has proposed a more limited definition of the Chao Phraya, arguing that the river should be seen as beginning at the confluence just south of the ruins of the Petch Fortress of Ayutthaya (2017a: 54).

countless others. Mon, for example, among the region's oldest peoples, adopted and spread Theravada Buddhism; Chinese brought vegetables and sailing ships; and the Thai language would disintegrate if half the words adopted from Khmer were repatriated to Cambodia.

This book works against reification of Thai identity, especially notions of "True Thai". The latter implies a unity of blood, physiology, culture, and nation. Such myths and reductions are dangerous and damaging. Sujit Wongthes writes, "The matter of race and ethnicity [เชื้อชาติ] has for a very long time been like a devil's shadow cast over the study of Thai history and archaeology" (1991: 140). It is not, however, only in academia, rather this shadow is cast over the whole of society. I take inspiration from Thomas Blom Hansen, who writes, "My own view is that the task of the social scientist is to produce knowledge and writing that defies ethnic closures by documenting and exploring the richness, diversity, and multivocality of the social world of even the smallest of localities. Good scholarship is usually unsettling to established or widely held ideas, and scholars, to my mind, should strive to make their work as useless as possible for those who promote ethnic closures" (2001: 17). Benedict Anderson (1978) pointed out that the reification of "Thai" is a serious problem in Thai studies. Scholars in Thailand such as Charnvit Kasetsiri, Sujit Wongthes, Srisak Vallibhotama, and Kasian Tejapira have long worked against closures, ethnic and otherwise, of the national imagination. More recently, Ong Bunjoon (2010, 2009, 2006), a scholar of Mon descent, has written several excellent books that reflect on the ethnic terrain of Thailand. Ong grew up south of Bangkok and spoke a heavily accented, monotone Thai in primary school. His book about the many peoples of Siam (Ong 2010) offers a series of person-centered studies reflecting the country's ethnic complexity. By the end of the book, the reader suspects that "True Thais", if they do exist, are anomalous. Once during a celebration for Mon National Day, Ong was confronted by a senior police officer, who chided him for writing so much about Mon people. The officer asked, "Why don't you do something for Thai people?" It was a wounding question. Ong reflects, "I didn't know what to say. I am Thai. I live in Thailand.... People who have different ethnic backgrounds—Mon, Khmer, Lao, Chinese, Vietnamese, Malay, and so on—each is one part of Thai society" (2008: 85).

The words Thai and Thailand are still encrusted with exclusionary politics, but entirely avoiding them is difficult. This book is oriented toward a re-opening of "Thai" and based in a hope for Thailand, or perhaps a new Siam, to become shelter for both Thais and non-Thais. Moreover, this structure of ethnic opposition itself should be cast into uncertainty. The Thai nation was defined in Bangkok, the urban center, but the center has never been so True Thai as the nation-builders imagined. The Chao Phraya River has for many centuries been the meeting place of many different peoples, and today the region is even more of a melting pot than ever before. This brings us to the work of Edward Van Roy, who has examined ethnic multiplicity in the creation of Bangkok. Although he describes a division between Thai rulers and mostly non-Thai subjects, he begins dismantling this distinction, observing that, aside from perhaps Buddhist monks, "the ruling elite, traced to its ancestral roots, was actually the kingdom's most ethnically diverse social group" (2017: 15). Furthermore, among the lower strata of society, as non-Thai groups have become Thai, the latter category has absorbed formerly external cultural traits (ibid.: 39–40). Van Roy's depiction of early Bangkok suggests that ethnic groups were rather isolated from one another; the process of melting was later driven by state policy. The matter of pre-national entanglement is still being explored, but what can be discerned in the emerging picture, at least in my view, is not a southward-migrating tribe, gradually absorbing other peoples, but rather that "Thai" is a relatively recent concept, which has obscured the multiplicity of Siam.

Notably, the word Siam has been found in ancient Khmer, Mon, and Burmese inscriptions (Preecha 1988: 69–70). Portuguese merchants later acquired the word from Malays (Jit 1981: 26) and it soon spread throughout and beyond the emerging colonial world of Southeast Asia. However, the origins of the name are still rather mysterious. Jit Phumisak, in his last book, an enormous philological study, observes that in dynastic chronicles from Mongol-ruled China, peoples of the southern lands were referred to as *san* (ส่าน), a word (said to come from Nanzhao) meaning river basin or, one may infer, water-side societies (เมืองริมน้ำ). In contrast to the nomadic peoples of the forests and mountains, who did not control water, the *dtai* (ไต)—a word he carefully distinguishes from *thai* (ไทย) (ibid.: 4–6)—practiced agriculture, used plows and other tools, such as hoes and rakes, and, crucially, built dams and cut drainage ditches (ibid.: 236–9).[5] Jit proposes a well-founded hypothesis that the name Siam might originate from the word *sam* (ซำ), still found in Lao and other languages, which refers to a kind of water spring (ibid.: 288–95).

Scholars have illustrated the exclusionary nature of the Thai nation-building process by showing that when the name Thailand was adopted in 1939, most of the population was not Thai (Streckfuss 2012). This is a crucial point, based in strong evidence, but it should also be emphasized that even those identified as Thai were of mixed origins. In the course of nation-building, this multiplicity of origins, the centuries of mixture along the river—far more ancient than any national consciousness—was to a great and disturbing extent forgotten. Long before the age of nations, Thai became the language of commerce along the Chao Phraya River, much as Malay had been in maritime Southeast Asia. That is, it was used for trade between peoples who spoke other languages (Nidhi 2016). But one should also be wary of emphasizing the singularity or fixity of this language in the distant past, especially before the introduction of the printing prcss (by Doctor Bradley) and the subsequent process of nation-building. As Eric Hobsbawm warns, "National languages are … almost always semi-artificial constructs" (1990: 54). Even today, with countless forces of standardization, there is considerable diversity within the Thai language, and the past was likely characterized by even greater variety and a wide-ranging scale of mutual intelligibility. Speaking Thai has never been a guarantee of Thai identity.

The question of what it means to be "Thai" is deeply implicated in ongoing fears, attachments, and conflicts. Much of this book was drafted near the end of the Ninth Reign, before the death of Rama IX on October 13, 2016. After the main period of field research, as writing was underway, the military seized power. The coup in May 2014 was carried out in the name of the monarchy, described in the official announcement

[5] The category *dtai* is an analytical construction designating numerous dispersed ethnic groups, past and present, both within and well beyond the borders of Thailand. Jit Phumisak (1981) argues that, since ancient times and in multiple languages, the words *dtai* (ไต) and *tai* (ไท) have meant person or people (คน). In his analysis, with the emergence of slave-based societies, the words evolved to designate free people in the sense of non-slaves.

as the institution that unites the "heart-spirit" (จิตใจ) of the Thai people (*Thai Rath* 2014). In the discursive ecology of Bangkok, Thais are often described as royalists by definition. In recent years, especially since the overthrow of Prime Minister Thaksin Shinawatra in September 2006, a fierce conflict has ensued between Red Shirts and Yellow Shirts. Although the political situation continues to evolve, this conflict illustrates some of the country's most central and persistent fissures and tensions. The Yellow Shirts, a conservative, royalist movement, have spoken in the name of "Thai", denouncing Red Shirts as traitors, king-topplers, burners of the country, while the Red Shirts have spoken in the name of "the people" (ประชาชน), denouncing Yellow Shirts as promoters of dictatorship, as a backward movement driven by the exploitative upper strata of society. Both sides claim to defend democracy. However, they often disagree on the meaning of the concept, as well as how it should be implemented in Thailand. Yellow Shirts have been scorned as agents of authoritarianism—or more precisely, "power-ism" (อำนาจนิยม)—while condemning Red Shirts as slaves of "vile capital" (ทุนสามานย์). This conflict shows that definitions of the nation have everything to do with belonging, freedom of expression, and the distribution of power.

The name of the river invokes the royal institution, especially the monarch-dominated "field power" (ศักดินา) system, in which Siamese society was divided into four categories: royalty, nobility, commoners (or *prai*, those subject to cycles of conscripted labor), and slaves.[6] Land, or power over fields, was allotted according to rank. If one examines the distribution of field-power in the early Bangkok period, one sees that the dominant categories of royalty and nobility were intermeshed. Royalty held the highest degrees of power, but the system also included lower royalty with less field-power than high-ranking nobles (Akin 2017: 130–1). *Chao Phraya* was a high noble rank and a man of this rank could control 10,000 *rai* (approximately 4,000 acres).[7] *Chao*, depending on the context, means lord, king, or royal figure. Scholars in Thailand have

[6] The field-power system began in the Age of Ayutthaya. Nidhi Eoseewong argues that absolute monarchy came later, and was short-lived in Siam, beginning in the late 19th century and ending in 1932 (2014a: 105–13).

[7] For further study of the field-power system, see Jit Phumisak (1998) and Akin Rabibhadana (2017).

gathered evidence that the river was named in the 19th century after a village named Bang Chao Phraya at the mouth of the river, but the identity of the noble figure after whom the village was named remains unknown (Sujit 2005: 64–7). In addition, it is worth noting that the man who became Rama I—prior to seizing power in the late 18th century, initiating the Age of Bangkok, and founding the current dynasty—was a general of the rank of Chao Phraya. He was not royalty by descent, but rather a strong figure within the field-power system who overthrew the king of Thonburi and established himself and his descendants as royalty.

Releasing a boat from a dock. The sign says "Long Live the King" beside pictures of Rama IX commanding a small boat.

Although absolute monarchy officially ended in 1932, the royal institution persists and royal power remains deeply and widely etched in the broader Thai landscape. Notably, the Thai word for king (กษัตริย์) is closely related to the word for cultivated land (เกษตร) (Sulak 2016: 8). Royal images are extremely abundant in Bangkok and beyond. Many roads and bridges are named after royalty, and many temples were built or modified under royal patronage. The tallest dam in Thailand, which crosses the Ping River, was renamed in 1958 after Rama IX: the Bhumibol Dam, a concrete reflection of Field Marshal Sarit's resuscitation of the monarchy. It has eight turbines and is the country's largest hydroelectric dam, with an official capacity of 779.2 megawatts. It was ceremonially sanctified by Rama IX, who opened the first turbine. During fieldwork, news circulated about the construction of a "monkey cheek" (แก้มลิง), an example of the progress of the royal landscape. In brief, a monkey cheek is an area that receives excess water to alleviate floods. The system includes marshes, basins, and canals, scattered around Bangkok, both east and west of the river, with storage areas by the sea that can be drained by gravity or pumps. In some depictions, the river flows down the middle of a monkey's face. Rama IX recalled, as a young boy, watching a monkey eat a banana, observing that it stored the banana in its cheek before chewing and swallowing. After the severe floods of 1995, the king proposed the application of this principle to regional water management.

Key Words

The central theme of this book has a meandering lineage in anthropology, traceable back to Sir James Frazer's *The Golden Bough*, an enormous, twelve-volume study of "memories enshrined in a landscape" (Fernández-Armesto 2002: 126). Notably, Frazer's book opens with a discussion of a painting by J.M.W. Turner of Lake Nemi. Frazer sought to explain a tradition in the encircling forest, captured in the image of a priest-king waiting for an assassin. Tradition, a perennial theme of anthropology, sustains collective memory. The word *memory*, in my usage, refers to recollections of events, people, and places encountered in the course of mortal life, as well as recollections of the collective past. This includes shared facts or stories. It also includes images. Photographs, for example, can evoke a sense of life in the old days along the river. Scholars distinguish between "episodic" memories, based in experience, and "semantic" memories, or memorized facts (Corkin 2013). We can also distinguish between learning about the past from storytellers in a village and learning through mass media. This book focuses on cases wherein the experienced, received, or imagined past is "our" past. For example, in 1767, Burma destroyed the ancient city of Ayutthaya. In Thailand, this is not merely a learned fact, it is a definitive part of "our" national past, a broader existential framework. This makes it difficult to separate memory from imagination. Memory shapes imagination, and conversely, imagination shapes memory. Memory can include distortions, or even events that never happened. This holds true for memory in the skin-bound, personal sense, as well as the broader collective sense. Such groups are also limited, contained, and defined by boundaries. Memories are often particular to places. As a place-bound person, one has claims to such memories. One is not, however, necessarily limited to a single collectivity. People of a place are often members of a nation, a far more expansive community, and a nation's culture of memory always transcends place. Other forms of collectivity, such as those bound by religion, can be even more expansive.

Collective memory does not necessarily mean that everyone remembers the same things, but rather that memory is part of collective life, including society and culture. Memory is never merely storage in detached individual minds. At an organic level, memory depends on neural networks. But minds cannot survive in isolation. Humans engage the world, objects, and other beings. Memory is outwardly entangled. Furthermore, cultures of memory precede birth—thus one is engulfed by pre-existing patterns. Culture, however, as anthropologists have long known, is always internally differentiated. Thus we will observe some of the differences, complexities, and boundaries, including boundaries that are crossed, within Thailand. On the other hand, one sometimes finds remarkable convergences. The destruction of Ayutthaya is an example—a tragedy of national scale built into Thailand's education system. Most people in Thailand know something about it: first of all, that Burma was the perpetrator. And crucially, it was "ours". It was "our" city-kingdom. Its destruction was "our" national tragedy. Memory is central to the self-understandings of a people. But the aquatic landscape of memory in Bangkok is deeply conflicted. As patterns of memory change, so does society.

Collectivity is not limited to human beings. Students of anthropology are, of course, concerned with people and their ways of life. Waterways offer a starting point: exploring the Chao Phraya River in Bangkok, one finds the water and terrain full of meaning, stories, and fragments of the past. The river is a defining figure of the Thai landscape, and given her shape, extension, utility, and temporal depth, she gathers a culture of memory. Hugh Raffles, in his study of the Amazon River, writes, "Slowly, through months of talking, a biographical landscape, at once material and fantastic, one born from the politics of history and molded out of everyday life, began to take shape" (2002: 4). Life is written into the terrain, while the terrain also shapes life. The landscape is a realm of interaction between the living and non-living. Notably, Maurice Halbwachs, a path-breaking figure in the study of collective memory, also included non-human elements, especially topography (1992) and urban space (1980), in memory's framework. Such research has been further developed by Jan Assmann, who explores intersections of place and memory in formations of collective identity. Memory congeals in tangible sites and cyclical practices. In one suggestive passage, he describes the repetitive ceremonies of non-literate societies as "the canals or arteries along which the elements that form identity flow" (2011:124).

Landscape studies is an eclectic field that crosses disciplines. The present work delves into the cultural aspects of landscape. The possibility of exploring this theme was greatly developed by Yi-Fu Tuan's (1977) study of experiences of space and place, in which he considers openness and closure, motion and stillness, the gradient from abstract to concrete, and above all, an enormous range of engagements with geography. More recently, Tim Ingold (2011) has explored the life of landscapes, gracefully weaving together ethnography and philosophy. Such work influenced my attempts to write experience-near accounts, but my descriptions have also been pushed by an atmosphere of discord. Landscapes have sensory and emotional aspects; they are also under various forms and degrees of control. *Landscape* is a surprisingly complex word. John Stilgoe, a prominent figure in landscape studies, offers a useful definition: "Landscape ... designates the surface of the earth people shaped and shape deliberately for permanent purposes. Oceans, polar ice, glaciers, [etc.] are properly wilderness" (2015: ix). However, before any settlement, the earth is already shaped. Any landscape, no matter how urban or engineered, still involves non-human materials, forces, and agencies. The word *landscape* predates the English language and has an extensive past in the Germanic world. Some readers will associate it with painting, perhaps quiet scenes of countryside. Indeed, it has carried such associations for centuries. Early landscape painters drew inspiration from the Roman poet Virgil, mixing empirical detail with evocations of a gilded age (Clark 1979: 109). Images and stories give meaning to landscapes. Moreover, in the wake of the industrial revolution, romanticism energized the genre of landscape painting—earth became a source of spiritual renewal (Paglia 2013: 85). This idea is worth preserving. The maternal river is not merely a construct—she is also a source of life. The word *landscape* also has associations with agriculture, and this predates formal practices of landscape painting. J.B. Jackson, an independent scholar and lifelong explorer of landscapes, observes that in medieval Europe the word *land* referred to "a defined piece of ground". He then adds, "We can assume that ... it was most often used to indicate a patch of plowed or cultivated ground, that being the most valuable kind" (1984: 148). The Chao Phraya River has a long, productive past and remains vital to agriculture in Central Thailand. That matters, even though this study was carried out in urban Bangkok. There is a sense that the river leads back—for the landscape is soaked in temporality—into a world of rice fields. Conversations about the river often traveled upstream, into the rural hinterland, even when talking to people with no rural experience. Furthermore, on the subject of land, it must be emphasized that in 1939, a few months before the outbreak of World War II, Siam was renamed, thereby becoming *Thai-land*, the land of Thai. The model was likely imported from Germany (*Deutsch-land*). As is well documented, Nazi Germany, viewed from afar, was a source of inspiration for the Siamese leadership, who, with much enthusiasm, constructed their own racial myths and aimed explicitly for territorial annexations.[8]

[8] Charnvit Kasetsiri, who has advocated changing the name of the country, gives a fine overview of this period in Siam/Thailand, including a discussion of racist nationalism, in a book titled *Siam or Thai* (2008b). The Victory Monument—an enormous concrete bayonet in the center of a traffic circle—provides a glimpse of broader territorial ambitions. The monument celebrates military bravery, fallen soldiers, and territories ceded in 1941 to Thailand. The Thai military occupied provinces in French-ruled Cambodia and Laos, namely Battambang, Siem Reap, Champasak, and Sayabuli, all of which were returned to France after World War II. After the invasions, the Ministry of Fine Arts released a series of nationalistic songs, an example of which is the memorable track "Across the Mekong" (ข้ามโขง),

The word *landscape* existed in Britain more than a thousand years ago, but seems to have fallen out of use for several hundred years until reintroduction (Jackson 1984: 148). The word came back to Britain by way of trade: "It entered the English language, along with herring and bleached linen, as a Dutch import at the end of the sixteenth century" (Schama 1995: 10). In the Low Countries, the landscape included its human inhabitants and their works: "The human design and use of the landscape ... *was* the story, startlingly sufficient unto itself" (ibid.). In recent centuries, the word has been encrusted with notions of pristine nature, or otherwise some kind of idyllic rural life. In this ethnography, however, one enters an urban landscape, and hopefully the reader will see, hear, and feel the city. Conceptually, landscape enables us to move through scales. We can zoom out, consider the national terrain or the regional map, but often we need to get closer to the surface. An experience-near approach, applied with proper care, can deepen our understanding of landscape, this domain in which people move and breathe.

Scape, the latter part of this compound, once denoted a "collection", and thus a landscape might be seen as "a 'sheaf' of lands, presumably interrelated and part of a system" (Jackson 1984: 148).[9] One need not, in principle, appeal to a word's origins or earlier meanings, but the etymological depths can provide perspective or inspiration. Let us for a moment consider landscape as a collection, sheaf, or system. How are the patches or parcels held together? In many cases, there is a boundary. National boundaries are certainly of great significance. Stilgoe writes, "River itself derives from the same roots that produced and nurture riven and rivalry. Both connote division and separation, trouble with fords, bridge-building expenses, slippery, placeless people, even

---

which carries the message that land across the Mekong River (namely, Laos) is Thai territory. This song even inspired the name and label of a popular Thai liquor: Mekhong (established in 1941). Luang Wichit Wathakan, credited with writing the song, argued that Lao and Khmer were actually Thai people.

[9] According to Tim Ingold, scholars who write in English often confuse scape with scope (2011: 126). This, he argues, introduces a distortion, whereby one imagines prior separation from the landscape, with the observer standing outside, looking from afar, projecting maps, fantasies, and constructions.

trolls" (2015: 173). The Chao Phraya River, however, is not much of a boundary, and the Thai word for river suggests, not rivalry, but rather a maternal being. The river has banks, of course, and one might wait for a crossing. There are also differences, real and imagined, from one bank to the next. The western bank, or Thonburi-side of the river, is seen as less developed, relatively quiet, and said to be more rough or "savage" (เถื่อน). Disparity between the two banks widened for decades, especially from the Fifth Reign (1868–1910) forward, when modernization efforts heavily targeted the east bank. However, during the Sarit dictatorship (1957–63) convergence became increasingly visible, with a notable turning point as older, slow-going vessels—row boats (เรือแจว), and so on—were replaced by motorized long-tails, which accelerated aquatic travel between the east bank and garden-based settlements along canals across the river (Srisak 2017a: 146). The Chao Phraya River does more to connect than divide. And in connecting, she collects. She binds, but not so much in the sense of a boundary.[10]

The geographer Denis Cosgrove has a very different approach, but his analysis is highly relevant. He focuses on Europe and North America and he considers landscape as a very particular, historically specific mode of seeing and representing the cultivated earth. In his analysis, landscape emerges during a transition from feudalism to capitalism. Landscape, he argues, is a "controlling composition", an objectification of the earth by outsiders (Cosgrove 1998: 270). It is both a reflection and instrument of power. Insiders, by contrast, he argues, do not objectify the earth as landscape. This study of waterways, differences aside, is similarly concerned with how people perceive, remember, and imagine. Cosgrove shows that power and historically specific processes shape perceptions and representations of the earth. This brings to mind a startling observation by Srisak Vallibhotama, a senior archaeologist in Thailand: prior to the late 19th century, there was no Chao Phraya River. That is, she was not yet defined as a totality. Rather, she was divided, so to speak, into segments, and each segment had a unique name given by the

---

[10] An interesting comparison would be between the Chao Phraya and the Mekong. The transformation of the latter into a border—separating Thailand and Laos—has certainly changed and in some ways restricted its connectivity. The Chao Phraya has never been a national boundary, thus no checkpoints or border police.

local community (Srisak 2008: 37). Under Rama V, the primary river of Siam was named Chao Phraya, perhaps after a village in the present-day province of Samut Prakan. Other rivers were also named, and thereby brought into being. Mountains were gathered into ranges, and each range was given a name (ibid.). This elucidation of royal-state geography, an ambitious new composition, appeared in parallel with new kinds of control, including the 1892 centralization of state administration, the groundwork for subsequent top-down nation-building. Here this study diverges from Cosgrove, for this composition has had a definite and powerful impact on the worldviews of insiders. One can now imagine the entirety of the river, even if one knows intimately only a small segment. The riverine landscape has been nationalized.

The word *landscape* is sometimes borrowed from English. Srisak, for example, uses it, but the word is not widely used in Thailand. There are also words in Thai that capture aspects of landscape (ภูมิประเทศ, ภูมิทัศน์, ทัศนียภาพ, etc.). Notable among these is Srisak's (2008) expression *pumi-wathanatham* (ภูมิวัฒนธรรม), or "cultural landscape". A cultural landscape, in his usage, centers on a community; it includes the built environment, nature, and supernatural beings. People in such a community have lasting attachments to the landscape. Srisak, a fierce critic of state centralization and a long-time proponent of in-depth studies of local culture, history, and geography, argues that cultural landscapes in Siam or Thailand (he prefers the former name) are being destroyed by capitalism and industrial society, which produce instead "inhuman landscapes", wherein people exist in a reduced, corrupted, and brutish condition—a stark contrast to life as communal beings (Srisak 2013: 47–56).[11] People increasingly live in communities of strangers. Newly constructed residential quarters, often with imported place-names, rapidly deteriorate. The Chao Phraya Dam—Thailand's first, financed by the World Bank and used especially for agricultural irrigation—opened in Chai Nat in 1957, coinciding almost exactly with the beginning of Field Marshal Sarit's aggressive, industrializing regime. Srisak writes, "Dams have reduced biological diversity and nearly eliminated the natural cycle of high and low waters,

[11] "Inhuman landscape" is my translation of นิเวศเดรัจฉาน. The word นิเวศ suggests an ecology, landscape, or housing development. The word เดรัจฉาน literally means animal, but in this context is better translated as "inhuman".

and above all, have ended over a thousand years of riverine society" (2017a: 147).

Fieldwork

This ethnography is based primarily on 12 months of fieldwork in Thailand, mostly Bangkok, between 2012 and 2013. This period was preceded by approximately four months of preliminary research during summers off from the University of California, Irvine. In the course of my subsequent stays in Thailand, notably several months between 2016 and 2017 (and frequent returns since), as well as extensive reading and correspondence, material has continued to accumulate. In the preliminary period, I explored Bangkok, meeting people, getting to know the city, and also traveled around the country. I began taking notes and committed time to language study. Later, during the central 12-month block of fieldwork, I resided in several locations, mainly in a Thai-Chinese neighborhood in Bang Rak, a short walk from the Chao Phraya River.

Skyline seen from a riverside district

Fieldwork entailed frequent movement within Bangkok, often by boat, but also by foot, bus, car, motorcycle, and train. Informants were scattered around the city, and thus the reader will meet people from a variety of communities. Transit in Bangkok was sometimes exhausting, and more than once I was overtaken by nostalgia for an old ethnographic ideal: working in a village, or on some island—in other words, in a single, bounded community. This project was different: I might, for example, go out in the morning, talk to people in the alley, order soup and coffee, buy a bag of sliced mango, then go to the nearest pier, board the boat, go upstream, stop, stay for a while, then go upstream again, spending time at several sites in one day, then returning to the alley in the evening. One positive result of this method is that it offers contrasts, different points of view from people who live in different communities. We will also see convergences.

Data collection entailed a variety of methods, including participant observation and interviews. Here the word *interview* generally applies to "taped" conversations (the device was a hand-held digital recorder). For the most part, interviews came late in fieldwork because it seemed appropriate for them to follow participant observation. In the course of research, one gets a better sense of what and how to ask. But interviews can sometimes be an effective way to establish relations. For example, the sword-maker gave an interview shortly after our first meeting. His responses were concise and the interview was over in about 10 minutes. Not wanting to impose further, I shut off the recorder. But he continued talking for a long time. Indeed, one must learn to listen. And then something remarkable happened. People grew curious and wandered out of the hovels. Some hovered over us, and a group gathered in the alleyway. This meeting changed my status. People had never heard of anthropology, so it was necessary to explain that, although I was studying the river, I did not intend to take water to a laboratory. Sitting down with the recorder to conduct an interview made it clear that I was trying to learn about their community. This encounter also demonstrated approval from an older, respected member of the community, and thus people became more comfortable with my presence.

Some people, however, were reluctant to be interviewed. They would insist they had nothing to say or did not know anything. This was partly based on a misunderstanding. The Thai verb for interview (สัมภาษณ์) is rather official sounding, conveying notions of fact-gathering. One interviews experts or authorities. Some voiced concern that they would be unable to answer the questions. Others recoiled, saying they were unable to speak "academic language". Fortunately, some informants offered guidance and suggested alternate ways of wording the request. One said plainly and helpfully, "Don't call it an interview." However, as is usually the case, most conversations were not taped. More often, fragments were collected in my notebooks.

Research also entailed audio recordings of events and ambient noise, which later helped to reconstruct scenes and places. I took photographs and hand-written notes while traveling around the city, trying to capture the gleam, grit, and momentum of modern Bangkok. Informants sometimes drew maps, sometimes upon prompting. Others did this without being asked. It was simply a convenient way to explain the layout of the waterways. This material was valuable because as they drew maps they also described places, connections, and memories.

Let me add a brief note on language. There is too much secrecy about field languages among anthropologists. Many of us work in places in which we are not natives, but language proficiency is rarely discussed openly. What are the implications of an ethnographic record flooded with works written by authors who are dependent on English-speaking informants? I recall seeing a transcript from a seminar at which Benedict Anderson presented his essay "Studies of the Thai State". Sulak Sivaraksa, a leading intellectual in Thailand, was present and offered his thoughts on foreign researchers. He had likely known many such individuals. In response to Anderson's provocative and pivotal essay, Sulak (although praising the author) suggested that foreign researchers should dedicate more time to studying the Thai language. My study of Thai was mostly self-directed. I also took a short, informal course in Bangkok. During research, I did not have an interpreter or field assistant. For about two years prior to full-scale fieldwork, I studied Thai almost every day for at least three hours. I also met a hired conversation partner, usually twice a week. Upon arrival in Bangkok in 2012, I was conversational in Thai, able to discuss a wide variety of topics, and also able to read newspapers and books, including novels and academic literature. The imperial dominance of the

English language presents a formidable challenge, which, for an aspiring ethnographer, requires conscious and consistent resistance. Otherwise, the ever-growing record of ethnographic research will be impoverished. During that year and later periods of fieldwork, English was mostly eliminated from my day-to-day life, the main exception being that my fieldnotes were in English mixed with Thai words, phrases, and quotations. All interviews were in Thai. All conversations, unless otherwise noted, were also in Thai. Aside from a few small exceptions, I have done the translations myself.

Chapters

Chapter 1 is about origins, travel, and Chinese predominance at the center of the Thai nation. Origin stories are explored as part of collective memory, including how origins are situated in the landscape. Sukhothai, near the banks of the Yom River, which flows into the Chao Phraya, is regarded as the first capital of Thailand, and thus, from the standpoint of Bangkok, origins lie upstream. The narrative alternates between ethnographic vignettes, some about the Chinese, others about Loi Kratong, an annual festival. On the day of Loi Kratong, Thais gather at the water's edge to release banana-leaf boats and apologize for polluting the river. This tradition, said to originate in Sukhothai, is bound to a story of national origins. According to the progression-of-centers narrative, time flows downstream. But the river, as an aquatic passage, and with the grace of the monsoon, also enables movement in the other direction, bringing us to a celebration of Loi Kratong at the Temple of the Ship, centered on a large concrete replica of a Chinese merchant ship.[12] Two stories of origin meet: one floats downstream from the ancient "Thai" capital, the other sails upstream from China. I propose a reframing, suggesting the Thai nation began not in Sukhothai, but in Bangkok, a city shaped by people who sailed upstream.

[12] Wat Yannawa, a Buddhist temple renovated during the reign of Rama III. Walter F. Vella calls it Temple of the Everlasting Ship (1957: 47–8), but "everlasting" seems to be an embellishment. ยาน = vehicle; นาวา = ship.

Chapter 2 is about continuity, change, and loss. It explores the complex patchwork of memories, melancholy, and decay in the aquatic landscape, against an invasive background of turmoil, including the Red-Yellow conflict and the ailing monarch. The narrative begins with a paradox: Thais are said to have a primordial relationship to waterways, but now, especially in Bangkok, water manifests as a frightening, destructive force. The Chao Phraya River signifies both a way of life and life-destroying floods. Upon my arrival in the field, floodwater in Bangkok was still receding. Floods had not always been destructive; in the past, floods were part of the seasonal cycle. Loi Kratong was once a celebration of the flood season. But as floodwater spread through Bangkok, filling streets, alleys, offices, and houses, it became a harsh reminder of dramatic changes in the way of life. I explore the river as a poetic landscape, a realm of contradictions, lingering memories, and a persistent sense of loss. Along the waterways, between the high-rises and shopping strips, reside stories, images, and ghosts, traces and figures of the past, as well as communities facing eviction, struggling for a place in the culture of memory.

Chapter 3 turns to forgetting, the erasure of a violent past from the landscape. It begins with the destruction of Ayutthaya, an event central to official history of river and nation. People in Bangkok often observed that "upstream lies Ayutthaya", a city destroyed by the Burmese. By contrast, no one mentioned Vientiane: decades after the fall of Ayutthaya, the Siamese invaded Vientiane, reducing it to ruins, and transferred most of the population to the basin of the Chao Phraya River—a forced migration of perhaps more than 100,000 people. Lao from Vientiane were among the builders of Bangkok. I argue that landscapes undergo canonization, whereby power shapes collective memory and, as a corollary, what can and cannot be seen in the landscape. The chapter offers an experience-near account of the royal barge procession, with golden barges based on originals from Ayutthaya, but builds tension around the event with an analysis of the power dynamics of presence and absence, reframing it against a shadowy background of invisible events and bodies: the massive transfer of Lao from Vientiane.

Chapter 4 is a study of belonging, centered on an Islamic community at the edge of a notoriously corrupted canal, a trench of black water lined with ramshackle slums. Muslims occupy a curious and difficult position, both socially and spatially, in Thai society. Buddhism is enshrined by the state, and Thais are often assumed to be a Buddhist nation, yet around one-tenth of Thailand's population is Islamic, with the greatest concentration in the southernmost provinces, near Malaysia. The chapter depicts an Islamic community at the center, showing that memory is vital to the formation and persistence of places. Memory connects, forming lines, intersections, centers and peripheries. I take a geographical approach to the question of belonging, tracing how place is woven into national and transnational geographies.

Chapter 5 considers memory in relation to the future. Memory creates linkages across space and time, enabling people to imagine the trajectory of society. The river is a lively terrain of ongoing construction, with bridges, buildings, piers, and markets, but informants often drew a contrast between two kinds of development: one centered on material, the other on heart-spirit. This was usually framed as an imbalance, whereupon people observed the comparative backwardness of heart-spirit, a lament with an almost proverbial quality. The chapter contains four water-bound case studies, each a reflection on trajectory in relation to collective memory. Thailand is often said to be distinctive from other countries in Southeast Asia because it was not formally colonized. This celebrated narrative, deeply ingrained in the national story, has been used, especially by enforcers of the old order, as a political weapon. I argue for an inversion, reframing Thailand as a country that has evaded decolonization. The chapter takes a tragic turn with the seizure of power by the military, an arrest of Thailand's trajectory, and ends with an emic metaphor of canalization: the slow, hard work of redirecting the river.

Water is a curious element, a primary constituent of life. Water drips, flows, and evaporates, forming gray skies over Bangkok. In ancient Southeast Asia, bronze kettle-drums summoned rain. Water erodes the earth, forming trenches, creating habitats for humans, crocodiles, and poly-headed serpents. Water reflects and absorbs. It can carry life-giving soil or poisonous waste. Oxcarts in old Siam struggled along muddy, rain-ravaged paths, while boats traveled with ease by wind and current. Water provides peculiar forms of connection and distinctive experiences of movement, and thus, even if you live in Bangkok, it is possible, and so one hopes, you will find in this ethnography a city that is both familiar and strange.

Chapter 1
Origins

It was the day of Loi Kratong in Bangkok in the Buddhist year 2555, the Year of the Dragon.[1] The festival is celebrated annually in the 12th month of the lunar calendar, which falls in November. People gather at the water's edge to ask the river for forgiveness. Small candle-carrying boats, traditionally made of banana leaves, but now more often of foam, are released on the water's surface. This popular festival is said to be an instance of "original Thai" culture, passed down from the upstream ancient city of Sukhothai. Indeed, as the day approached, many informants suggested a visit to Sukhothai to see the (ostensibly) preserved ancient form of the festival. But I remained in Bangkok and observed Loi Kratong at the Temple of the Ship, a riverside Buddhist temple, at the center of which stands a large concrete replica of a Chinese merchant ship. An image emerged: Loi Kratong, as a cultural practice, travels downstream, while the merchant ship travels upstream. In the twilight by the river's edge, punctuated by candles and fluorescent bulbs, two stories of origin, each moving in a different direction, came into contact.

Sukhothai, according to the dominant narrative of Thai history, with its progression of centers downstream along the Chao Phraya River, is a cultural point of origin.[2] Children in public schools learn that Sukhothai was the first capital of Thailand (Thongchai 1994: 163; see also Sunait 2009). And yet many Thais in Bangkok trace their origins to recent

[1] The full name is *Wan* Loi Kratong (the day of Loi Kratong) or *Ngan* Loi Kratong (the Loi Kratong festival), however it is often simply called Loi Kratong. See, for example, Phya Anuman Rajthon (1954).

[2] Sukhothai was built near the banks of the Yom River, which flows into the Chao Phraya. It lies just north of the confluence at Nakhon Sawan, which is generally regarded as the starting point of the Chao Phraya.

immigration. Many tell stories about Chinese parents or grandparents who came upstream by merchant ship. Origins are not only a matter of time and place, but also of direction. As we will see, memory incorporates the riverine landscape—not as shapeless space, but as a passage.

Landscape is absorbed in all nations into cultures of memory (Smith 1986, 2010), and perhaps, as one historian suggests, "national identity … would lose much of its ferocious enchantment without the mystique of a particular landscape tradition: its topography mapped, elaborated, and enriched as a homeland" (Schama 1995: 15). Winding her way through Bangkok, the Chao Phraya does have a certain presence. She also allows practical engagement, such as travel by boat, and even today, with the spread of road and rail and extensive connection by air and fiber-optic cable, the river remains an important element of Bangkok's infrastructure.

Center of Origin

In Thailand, all rivers are mothers, but the Chao Phraya is the mother of the nation. She is thus vital to the Thai origin story, but also sets a contrast to the still young national form. The word *mae nam* (river or water-mother) is made from the words *mae*, which means mother, and *nam*, which means water. The word has likely descended from an animist, pre-Buddhist culture, in which women led ceremonies at the center of social life (Sujit 2016: 42–3). Today, the Chao Phraya River has a special significance in the official national story because she links together the royal capitals. These cities are conceived as the centers of the Thai past, with Bangkok as the center of the Thai present. History goes downstream. The story of the Thai nation—its official version, at least, as promoted by state institutions—is divided into ages, with each age named after a different royal capital: Sukhothai, Ayutthaya, Thonburi, Bangkok. This biographical outline of the nation, traceable to the eminent historian Prince Damrong, was standardized in school textbooks in the 1930s (Peleggi 2002: 15). It remains current and powerful, and continues to circulate widely in everyday life. For example, one morning a fruit vendor from Ayutthaya, now a resident of Bangkok, said, "There are only a few cities in Thailand that have anything to do with history: Sukhothai, Ayutthaya, Thonburi, and Bangkok." In such a view, history is a narrative of concentrated power and excludes most cities, villages, and people.

One afternoon—the month is October and Loi Kratong is weeks away—I find a book about the Chao Phraya River, borrow it, and walk to a copy shop. The shop is dark, with aged, brown walls, and shelves lined with framed photographs of Thai royalty. The woman who works and lives here is Chinese, with very white skin, but has never been to China. She points out a picture of the reigning Thai king's Chinese grandmother. Rabbits are rooting in the debris strewn on the floor. Floodwater arrived in Bangkok from up-country last year. A friend, whose house had flooded, brought the rabbits, putting them in care of the woman and her father. No one came back for the rabbits. "You should go to Sukhothai for Loi Kratong", she says. "The vessels are made from coconut shells instead of banana leaves. This is the way the original Thai did things. Sukhothai is the ancient capital. If you want to see the real thing, go to Sukhothai."

Loi Kratong at Sukhothai, said to be very beautiful, attracts mostly Thai rather than foreign tourists (Peleggi 2002: 67). Instituted in 1987, it is a fine example of "invented tradition" (Hobsbawm 1983). Sukhothai was once part of the Khmer empire, but is now claimed, delineated, and approved as Thai national heritage. In Southeast Asian studies, the relationship between center and polity is an important theme, one that concerns culturally specific notions of space and power. Ancient kingdoms in Siam, as in other parts of Southeast Asia, were often named after their urban centers. An artifact of this pattern is present in contemporary Thai language, wherein the word *muang* (เมือง) works at two scales: it means city, on the one hand; it also means country, in the sense (nowadays) of a bounded national territory. Bangkok is a *muang*. Thailand is *muang thai*. And although the name Thailand does not incorporate the name of the metropolis, the current age, in which the entire country is absorbed, is the Age of Bangkok. In the ancient kingdoms, power was concentrated at the center and unstable at the periphery, where it overlapped with fields of power radiating from other centers. Stanley J. Tambiah (1976, 1977) referred to this configuration as a "galactic polity", wherein each center holds a multiplicity of satellites in its orbit, and each satellite is a lesser center with satellites of its own. Tambiah saw the galactic polity as persisting in contemporary Thailand—now locked into its most extreme polarity: the "radial polity", wherein all roads lead to Bangkok and the latter has become an overgrown monster, "a mammoth [of] uncontrolled urban growth" (1976: 273).

Sukhothai, a ruined and mostly forgotten city, became an object of antiquarian attention during the reign of Rama IV (1851–68). In subsequent years, the ruins were cleaned, transformed, and resignified. Sukhothai is now a manicured national park and World Heritage Site. Under Rama IV, Siam signed the Bowring Treaty of 1855, a trade agreement that transformed the Siamese landscape. Rice production expanded in the basin of the Chao Phraya River, and Chinese-owned rice mills, with brick chimneys visible from afar, sprouted along the waterways (Srisak 2017a: 26–7).[3] This also entailed an increased need for irrigation and transport, and thus further canalization (Tanabe 1977: 24). Exports of rice, mostly to China, had been expanding since the previous reign (Sujit and Puwadon 1999: 128). Rice was transported to and from the mills by water-going Chinese merchants. Chinese-owned lumber mills also multiplied along the river (ibid.). Today some Bangkok residents remember the Bowring Treaty, observing that "(we) Thai people" were disadvantaged. Siam ceded extraterritorial rights: British subjects would be immune to Siamese systems of trial and punishment. Rama IV was intensely aware of powerful outsiders—British, French, and Dutch—who were taking control of neighboring lands. This time precedes the birth of the Thai nation, but forms a crucial part of its generative background. When Sukhothai was rediscovered, the city's remains enabled new claims of antiquity—not for the nation, but for royal power. In 1833 a monk named Mongkut, the half-brother of Rama III, visited the ruins and reportedly found a block of siltstone inscribed with an archaic script. Mongkut later ascended the throne as Rama IV. The stone inscription, known as Inscription One, dated (controversially) 1292, and now installed in the National Museum, indicated the kingdom's expanse and claimed royal rule over many

[3] Rice was the long-standing staple crop of lowland Southeast Asia, but the Bowring Treaty entailed an enormous increase in production for export. According to one study, in the period between 1850 and 1935, rice exports from Siam multiplied by about 25 times, a pattern that resembled colonial Burma (Batson 2017: 10).

ethnic groups.[4] With the later advance of nation-building, this emphasis on ethnic variety was replaced by a politically motivated imagination of Thai homogeneity—a natural, racial unity beneath only superficial differences of name and custom among the peoples of Siam (Barmé 1993). Rama IV, however, a pre-national Siamese king, perceived rule over a multiplicity of peoples as an index of royal power. Not only did this resonate with his vision, but it could be used in negotiation with the imperial powers of Western Europe (Dhida 1982: 13). Furthermore, the inscription is said to represent the earliest instance of the Siamese writing system. According to the inscription, the king of Sukhothai had invented the script. Since Sukhothai was a great, prosperous, and ancient kingdom, with an upstream center that could be claimed for Siam, the ruins expanded the spatio-temporal image of the Siamese royal polity. Later the ruins were subordinated to the origin myth of the Thai nation. That myth, however, remains deeply entangled with the royal institution—as encapsulated in the well-known slogan (from the 1910s) of Rama VI: Nation, Religion, King.

Sukhothai and Ayutthaya were both accepted in 1991 as World Heritage Sites by the United Nations Educational, Scientific and Cultural Organization (UNESCO). Maurizio Peleggi argues that this "amounted to the ultimate validation of their central place in the national historical narrative" (2007: 180–1). According to this narrative, Ayutthaya is successor to Sukhothai. This linear arrangement, however, as Dhida Saraya (1982) explains in detail, is considerably flawed. To begin with, the two city-kingdoms existed simultaneously; there was a definite temporal overlap of hundreds of years. Dhida writes, "Sukhothai was a city [*muang*] with its own historical evolution, independent from that of Ayutthaya and Bangkok" (1982: 12–13). When Sukhothai collapsed, parts of it were absorbed into Ayutthaya, but the latter did not sprout from Sukhothai. Consider also the people of ancient Ayutthaya, whose

---

4 The authenticity of the inscription is contested. According to the archaeologist George Coedès, the inscription was carved in 1292. However, the art historian Piriya Krairiksh and others have challenged its authenticity—and even attributed the forgery to Rama IV (Peleggi 2017: 67–8). For an extensive review of the controversy, see Sujit (2003). The inscription stone was added in 2003 to the registry of UNESCO's Memory of the World Program.

narrative traditions—oral storytelling as well as royal chronicles—associated the "birth" of their city-kingdom "with myths and external forces beyond human control" (Charnvit 1979: 165).

True Thai

A Chinese zodiac diagram was taped to the shop wall. I asked if she was Chinese. "Of course", she said. "Everyone around here is Chinese." She continued, "There are no True Thais [ไทยแท้] anymore. People have mixed together. Let me tell you something. When I was a schoolgirl, I had a friend who was True Thai. She lived in an old-fashioned house made of wood. We were afraid to visit her! If we went to her house, we'd have to crawl. It wasn't like this—we had to keep our heads low, especially around older people. Who would be brave enough to visit?" She described the family as "four-reigns Thai". Her childhood friend, she said, was "suppressed".[5]

A few days later, an informant across the river, a native of Bangkok, offered a different perspective. Upon hearing this story, she pointed to herself. "I'm True Thai", she said.

"How do you know?" I asked.

"My family is from Central Thailand", she replied. "Everyone in my family has a Thai face. And there are no strange names."[6]

It was an intriguing expression: "four-reigns Thai". This often refers to someone who has lived through the reigns of four kings, thus one

[5] I recorded her words by hand as follows: แม่งเก็บกดว่ะ (she was suppressed). The first word (แม่ง), a vulgar expression—literally, "your mother"—arguably reflects two aspects of Thai society: hierarchy and respect for motherhood. The word is a compression of the word for "mother" (แม่) and a vulgar second-person pronoun (มึง), but here it referred to her childhood friend. Motherhood is widely honored, and thus a non-deferential reference to a "mother", plus the harsh closing particle (ว่ะ), gives the expression a certain bite. Coarse pronouns are used among friends, but can also express contempt or dominance. According to Jit Phumisak, the most common of these (กู and มึง) have been disdained since the age of slavery, as social class came to be expressed in language (1998: 134).

[6] A few years later, this informant told an amusing story: recently, at a convenience store in Bangkok, the clerk, upon seeing her face, had identified her as a foreigner and spoke to her in English instead of Thai.

who remembers the culture of a past age. The expression also invokes a literary work: *Four Reigns* (2011) is the title of a thousand-page historical novel written by Kukrit Pramoj.[7] Kukrit, some say, is still unmatched. In addition to being a polymath, former prime minister, and actor, who once appeared on screen with Marlon Brando, he is also the towering figure on the skyline of Thai literature. *Four Reigns*, written in the early 1950s, is his masterpiece, still among the most highly regarded novels in Thailand. It follows the life of Ploy, an upper-class, Bangkok-born Thai female, from her childhood to death. A changing kingdom is seen through the eyes of Ploy. The story begins during the reign of Rama V (crowned in 1868), one of the most revered kings of the Chakri dynasty. Ploy, still a child, is delivered by her mother into the care of a royal woman in the palace. She learns the values and practices of the palace, including self-conduct, but this was a time of transformation, and even palace dwellers had difficulty keeping pace with the forward-looking king. Rama V visited and carefully studied nearby colonial states, including Burma, India, Singapore, and the Dutch East Indies, and began rebuilding the Siamese state on similar lines. Customs also changed. At the beginning of the reign, for example, subjects kneeled or crawled before the king, but he declared such obsequiousness unfit for a civilized people. Henceforth, subjects would stand in his presence (Sulak 2016: 16). Ploy represents pre-modern Siam, the Siam that Rama V sought to transform. As the story unfolds, she is increasingly disoriented by a rapidly changing world.

Kukrit worked relentlessly to define and promote Thai identity. Ploy is now seen as a representation of authentic, True Thai culture. Although few Thais seem to have read this novel—it is more often a decoration—the vision has been influential, putting down roots in everyday life, as seen in the shopkeeper's expression: "four-reigns Thai". Most people in Bangkok, it seems, recognize the title. Even those who have not read it might sense that the book is about True Thai culture. Renditions for television have certainly extended its influence. *Four Reigns* has been filmed many times, and easily runs over twenty hours, a drama overflowing with scenes of an idealized past and noble grace. I found bootleg copies

[7] *Four Reigns* is the conventional English translation of the title (*สี่แผ่นดิน*). The word translated here as "reign" also means earth or kingdom.

for sale by a dock on the river. Like popular soap operas, or "sewage dramas" (ละครน้ำเน่า), stories like *Four Reigns* are taken in pieces. Knowledge of the past is acquired through fragments, through images and scenes, but fragments are easily gathered into frames, or outlines of time, such as those drilled by the public school system.

What is True Thai? It is an obsession in Bangkok. The vignettes above reflect broader patterns: one view is that True Thai vanished in the recent past, whereas the other self-identifies as True Thai. Both agree, however, on a model of ethnic, cultural, and national authenticity. Notably, in the second case, she lamented the loss of her ancestors' way of life, a theme to which we return. One day, while crossing the river by train, she explained that life in the city was not her true way of life. "It's not that life in the city is fake", she said. "It's just not appropriate for me. My ancestors didn't live like this." As a self-described True Thai, her identity and way of life were mismatched. Like Loi Kratong, her origin was upstream in the basin of the Chao Phraya.

But rivers flow into other bodies of water. The Chao Phraya drains into the gulf and has always connected Siam to a wider world. Chinese, among others, have arrived for centuries by water. In the study of ethnic categories, one group of scholars have argued for a focus on boundaries, practices of boundary maintenance, and for the empirical value of cases in which people "*change* their ethnic identity" (Barth 1998: 6). In Thailand, the boundaries between Chinese and Thai are often permeable. Simple distinctions deteriorate. Behind the images of True Thai are stories of confluence—of contempt, desire, and mixture, arrival and emergence.

Boundaries and Entanglements

People in Bangkok, if asked, can generally offer a comparison of Thai and Chinese. One hears often-repeated stereotypes: Thais are lazy and self-indulgent; Chinese are hard-working, frugal, satisfied with a single bowl of rice. Strangely, it does not matter much whether the person one asks is Thai or Chinese, one usually hears the same thing either way. But there is also a tradition of scorn for the Chinese, commonly expressed with the pejorative word "*jek*". One informant said, "Whatever you do, don't call a Chinese person a *jek*. If you use that word, you'll be boxing."

This is part of the terrain of positions. Some people insisted from the beginning on being Chinese; others identified as Thai, until one day shifting self-definition, becoming, so to speak, Chinese. Sometimes this reflected the development of our relationship, or sometimes a situation arose, such as the death of a relative, which entailed the practice of an ethnic funerary tradition.

Sometimes one can be both. Ruth Benedict, studying Thailand from afar, claimed that Thais "have an indestructible conviction that existence is good" (1952: 34). During a taxi ride in Bangkok one evening, a radio talk show plays in the background. The interviewer interjects, "Hey, are you sure you're Thai?" Rain pelts the windshield. The interviewee responds, "I do have a bit of *cheua jin* [Chinese germ or substance], but I'm Thai. I'm happy every day." Vikrom Kromadit, a well-respected capitalist, owner of industrial complexes, and self-made public intellectual, once stated on Thai PBS, "I might look like a *jek* but I still consider myself Thai." Scholars have pointed out a shift in the status of the Chinese in Thailand during the boom-years of the 1990s (Baker and Pasuk 2009: 204). In the glow of economic success, the status of the Chinese improved. In the process, they became more Thai, and thus began to self-identify as Thai, and of equal importance, others began to recognize them as such. Yet the examples above show the persistence of a dividing line, even if it is porous and people make daily crossings.

Social class plays a role, even if not absolutely decisive. This is depicted in *Four Reigns*, when Ploy's closest friend, a woman of the palace, discovers that her brother is going to marry a "*jek*". She is horrified and deeply ashamed. Her brother's wife-to-be is a Chinese merchant who makes and sells curries, a low-prestige occupation. Later, however, Ploy also finds a Chinese companion, Bprem, a state-worker from a wealthy family who lives in an opulent house with an entourage of servants. He proudly displays his Chinese ancestry. As a man of status, his ethnic background brings no shame. It is not even discussed until a later point in the book, when Ploy balks at the discovery that her daughter's suitor is Chinese. "*Jek*", she mutters. Ploy's son quickly reminds his mother that her children, including himself, are also part Chinese. The contrast is seen again following the death of Ploy's husband. She holds a *gongtek* (กงเต๊ก) funeral, as still practiced today by many Chinese in Bangkok.

Paper objects are burned, sent thereby to the deceased. Ploy's brother, a close friend of the deceased, suggests rather deviously the addition of a small troop of minor wives—delegating the task to the attending "*jek*" (Chinese servants).

Pagoda in Thonburi

Jit Phumisak, near the end of his book from 1957, writes about the Chinese in Thai society: "Ever since the old days, the feudal lords have misled and intoxicated Thai people, encouraging them to hate Chinese [*jek*]. The anti-Chinese messages get stronger, heavier every day. It is all to divert the eyes of the public away from the feudal lords" (Jit 1998: 275). Contempt for the Chinese persists in Bangkok. At the same time, characterizing the Chinese as a besieged minority is problematic. In a geographical study of Thailand, the author observes, "Estimated at 14% of the population, [the Chinese] probably control more than 80% of the capital" (Kermel-Torrès 2004: 40). In addition to prominence in business, Chinese occupy numerous positions in government. Charles Keyes points out, for instance, that "in 1999, according to one estimate, two-thirds of the members of parliament [in Thailand] were of Chinese descent"

(2002: 1192). Furthermore, affluent Chinese have often formed ties with royalty. As one careful observer has noted, many royal descendants have Chinese family names (Nidhi 2021: 195) This is striking, especially if we consider, not only centuries of prejudice, but the centrality of anti-Chinese sentiment to the nation-building project in Thailand. The Chinese were among the "others"—perhaps even the primary other—against which the myth of True Thai came into being. Kasian Tejapira writes, "This imagined nation of pure Thais had from the beginning been positioned by the Thai royal and subsequent military rulers primarily not against the western colonial powers, nor its colonized and hence pacified neighbors, but against Chinese immigrants and their descendants who … dominated the modern sector of its economy and urban society" (2001: 189). Urban society in this context means Bangkok. What would "Thai" mean today without Bangkok, a metropolis in many ways formed by the Chinese?

One morning I crossed the Bangkok Bridge, which spans the Chao Phraya River, and went down to inspect a Chinese shrine on the river's edge. The Bangkok Bridge opened in 1959, during the dictatorship of Field Marshal Sarit, and now runs parallel to another bridge, a taller, more dramatic structure. Between the bridges, across the river from Bangkok's oldest paved road, stands the Father of Fire Shrine.[8] A man invited me inside. Shoes were left at the door. The interior was full of golden effigies and burning candles. He pointed to the central figure of the temple, the statue of a paternal deity with black whiskers and glossy, red flesh. This deity, he explained, offers protection against fire. There was a framed black-and-white photograph on the wall, a picture of the original shrine, which had been demolished to make way for the bridge. Donations, mostly from Chinese-owned companies, had funded the reconstruction. He walked to a small platform overhanging the river. Incense smoke billowed from a small shrine. He gestured with his hand, first to the shrine, then to the sky, saying, "This is for the spirits of sky and earth [ฟ้าดิน]." These beings are always honored in Bangkok's

[8] Construction of Bangkok's first paved road, Charoen Krung, began in 1861. Reportedly, the original brick surface was rough, often muddy, and quickly eroded. It was hard-going for wheeled transport like horse-drawn carriages and Chinese hand-pulled rickshaws (known as รถเจ๊ก). Bangkok's first tram appeared on the same road in 1888.

Chinese shrines. Visitors enter and depart with their permission.[9] He then pointed to the water, a sunlit expanse of the Chao Phraya River, and said, "We will *loi kratong* in the 12th month to honor Mother Ganga [แม่คงคา]."[10]

On the morning of Loi Kratong, a shopkeeper in Bang Rak was talkative. She was born in Bangkok, but her father came from China. Her mother was Thai-born Chinese. I asked if she would *loi kratong* in the evening. "No", she said, "I don't really like it. I never *loi kratong*." When she was a child, her father did not want her to participate. "It's dangerous", he would say. "You could fall into the water and drown." Indeed, as reported by media in Bangkok, every year children die of drowning on Loi Kratong. The shopkeeper opened every morning. Her only regular holiday was Chinese New Year. I sometimes suggested to informants in Bangkok that Thais celebrate New Year three times a year: Thai New Year, international New Year, and Chinese New Year. They quickly corrected me: Chinese New Year is not Thai.

On the back wall was an image of Rama V. He is remembered in Bangkok as a modernizer, the king who saved Thailand from the British and French "colony hunters". He is especially popular among merchants. A woman of Chinese descent explained, "For anyone who is a merchant, it will be good to worship Rama V. He helps in matters of commerce. He brings prosperity. As you can see, in many shops there's an image of Rama V. He's sacred, very powerful." She made routine offerings of flowers, cigarettes, and liquor. Unlike his successor, Rama V saw the Chinese as a benign presence, though not always. Much of this, if examined closely, is rather strange. If Chinese New Year is Chinese, not Thai, one might infer that the Thai king is Thai, not Chinese. But George William Skinner, in his meticulous study of the Chinese in Thailand, demonstrates that Rama VI—an architect of Thai nationalism, who wrote anti-Chinese pamphlets—was

[9] Onghokham, a historian from Indonesia, writes: "People visit Chinese shrines [*klenteng*] to request help from supernatural forces for their daily needs, such as business, career advice, finding a mate, sustenance, and recovery from illness" (2017a: 118). My translation. Ong was also G.W. Skinner's research assistant in Java.

[10] Here the emphasis is on the action of setting afloat, thus *loi kratong* appears in lower-case.

himself "over one-half Chinese by ancestry" (1957: 26). Consider also Luang Wichit Wathakan, who, following the Siamese Revolution of 1932, worked relentlessly to create a Thai national identity. He was born with a Chinese name (Kimliang), but later denied his Chinese heritage, claiming that in the Thai village of his birth, Thai children traditionally received Chinese names. According to Wichit, this curious naming practice was simply part of local Thai culture (Barmé 1993: 57).

The shopkeeper continued telling stories. Children wandered in to buy ice cream. A middle-aged man requested a shot of whiskey. I asked again, "So you're not going to *loi kratong*?"

"I prefer Chinese traditions", she said. "Many of us in this neighborhood are Chinese. I was born not far from here, but now I live here with my mother. This is our house. I cannot speak Chinese. Hardly anyone around here can speak Chinese. I traveled once to Shanghai, just for a couple weeks, but I can only visit China as a tourist. I cannot communicate with those people. Now everyone wants to learn English. There used to be many schools where children could learn Chinese, but the government closed those schools. Why did they close them? I don't know, but if they hadn't, all these people would speak Chinese. They'd be clever." Another informant, much younger, a music teacher of Chinese descent, had also mentioned the closure of Chinese schools, claiming that many had been converted into apartment complexes. One might wonder if the shopkeeper was referring to a previous era, a time of more severe anti-Chinese sentiment. "No", she said. "It was this reign. It was the current reign." Forced closures of Chinese schools, as well as newspaper presses, have been documented during the rule of Field Marshal Pibulsongkram, among the reasons being a program of assimilation (Kakizaki 2014: 161). The shopkeeper's comment suggests that the school closures have shaped her social reality, her sense of being Chinese. But when I asked on another occasion how Chinese and Thai are different, she said, "They aren't really different anymore. For the most part, the Chinese have already become Thai."

Chinese Metropolis

An express boat chugged upstream. It was early afternoon, the day of Loi Kratong, and a friend had agreed to meet near the Temple of Dawn.

With its imposing gray spires, the temple is one of the defining features of Bangkok's riverside skyline. It is a *wat luang*, a temple under royal patronage, most of which are built along the Chao Phraya. I sat in the park across the water from the temple.[11] Express boats and long-tails were still running, as police prepared to take control of the river. Some officers were on jet skis, others commanded inflatable rafts with outboard motors. In a few hours, with the onset of evening, the police would close the river to traffic. The water was turbulent, people were buzzing with anticipation, and then the tropical sky began to change. Loi Kratong follows the monsoon rains, but rain still encroaches. Shadows thicken. Droplets fall on the page of my notebook. Umbrellas open. The pineapple merchant, hunched over his cart, amulets swinging from his neck, shouts, "The deities are furious!" People flee.

Weeks later, a Thai informant sat down to discuss Loi Kratong. She was also Chinese. We met on an upper floor of Central World, a giant shopping mall. She spoke Thai with a college-educated, Bangkok-born accent. "Thai people still feel gratitude toward the river", she said. "They really do apologize. This is tradition." Thais depend on the river, or water-mother, and in the course of this dependence, often pollute the water. On Loi Kratong, they ask for forgiveness. She described the riverside dwelling of her grandparents, both immigrants from China. It was a wooden stilt house. One arrived through a nest of twisted, narrow alleys, but the house was open to water and sky.[12] It was very small. Even as a little girl, she felt squeezed by the walls. She drew a picture of the house, discussing its features. "Here's the toilet", she said, "just a hole cut in the floor, with river water below." She drew an arrow through the hole into the water. The story was also an expression of Thai feelings. When her Chinese grandmother (*ama*) swept the house, all the detritus went into

[11] A major eviction was once carried out here. Following the execution of King Taksin, a large community of Taechiew, numbering perhaps around 15,000 people, was evicted from the environs of the new palace, whereupon they moved downstream to the muddy district of Sampheng (Van Roy 2017: 176).

[12] Onghokham, in an article from 1958, observed a wide pattern of settlement in Southeast Asia, where Chinese migrants built communities along rivers or seas, with houses and shrines facing the water (2017b: 24).

the river. "Oh, *ama* swept the house", she said, recalling her childhood visits. "Where did it go? And so I felt bad. I felt bad for the river."

"If *ama* had moved to Bangkok today, she would live along Sukhumvit." Sukhumvit is a long, energetic road at the heart—or what is becoming the heart—of Bangkok. When *ama* migrated, the main road, so to speak, was the Chao Phraya River: the socio-economic center, where the Chinese had been settling for hundreds of years.[13] Chinese already had a long-standing presence in Siam when Bangkok became the royal capital in the late 18th century. King Taksin, who established Thonburi, the foundation of later Bangkok, was of Taechiew descent. The subsequent dynasty began with Rama I, whose mother was Hokkien (Van Roy 2017: 178). Chinese were among the builders of the city, draining swamps and digging canals, and also brought vegetables and gardening techniques from southern China. The vegetables sold well in the markets, but some people saw them as "dirty" because Chinese gardeners used animal dung and "rotten fish" as fertilizer (Walailak 2017: 187). Later their numbers multiplied, driven by policies of the royal-Siamese state. Chinese migrants, even if they bought passage through indenture, had distinctive potentials of mobility. Whereas Mon and Khmer migrants became *prai* and received a tattoo on the wrist, migrants from China were not place-bound or subject to labor conscription (Akin 2017: 216).[14] Once free of contract, they could move. Kasian writes, "Since the early nineteenth century, it had been a deliberate and consistent policy of successive Chakri monarchs to encourage the immigration of Chinese coolies into the kingdom to serve as an increasingly needed and taxable pool of wage labor" (2001: 10). As the Qing dynasty deteriorated—ravaged by famine, wars, and especially the Taiping Rebellion—so-called coolies, many of

[13] Migrants from China to Bangkok in the 19th century were highly diverse. As Anderson observes, they were "illiterate people speaking mutually unintelligible languages" (2006: 190). We should not assume identification with "China". Furthermore, Chinese ethnic groups were often in competition or conflict with one another (Van Roy 2017).

[14] *Prai* were tattooed with their master's name and the name of the place (เมือง) to which they belonged in order to prevent them from escaping or changing masters (Akin 2017: 103). However, many *prai* tried to flee. Some escaped into the forest or evaded capture by ordaining as Buddhist monks.

them indentured, poured into Southeast Asia (McNeill 2003: 245–7, 257). Most of them arrived by water. Until the second half of the 19th century, Bangkok had few roads, none of which were paved. Patterns of residence were shaped by waterways. Aside from the lanes inside the palace compound, the most prominent road ran through the "Grand Bazaar", a ganglion of shops, all Chinese owned and operated, built at the river's edge (Skinner 1957: 106). Most people lived along the water, either in stilt houses, raft houses, or on boats. Ross King, drawing from Sumet Jumsai, suggests that in the second half of the 19th century, 85 percent of Bangkok's population lived in raft houses—it was "mostly a floating city" (2017: 147). In the same century, "On arrival at Bangkok, most of the Chinese junks were converted into retail shops" (Skinner 1957: 106). The immigrants accelerated the transformation of riverine Bangkok into a marketplace.

Bangkok, birthplace of the Thai nation, had a surprisingly large Chinese population. Skinner writes, "The Chinese probably constituted over half the population [of Bangkok] throughout the first half of the nineteenth century" (1957: 81). More recently, a prominent anthropologist in Thai studies recalls, "one of the most dramatic differences between the Bangkok of today and the pre-World War II city lies in its present 'Thai' flavor. In the prewar period … the city had a strongly Chinese character" (Keyes 1987: 172). Notice the quotes, prompting us to question the content of "Thai" as a category. William Warren, a long-term resident of Bangkok, suggests the metropolis is largely the creation of immigrants from southern China. To this could be attributed the city's lack of "visual charm": the immigrants, concerned more with functionality, have ignored the Thai cultural emphasis on beauty (Warren 2002: 105).

But beauty has other expressions. As observed in many Southeast Asian societies, "the body itself was the first and most important medium of art" (Reid 1988: 75). Among the highlights of Loi Kratong are the beauty contests, which take place throughout the kingdom. Women, and also many of Thailand's famous, ultra-feminine ladyboys, or "girls of the second kind", compete for the title of Miss Nophamat. Lady Nophamat, a woman of the court in ancient Sukhothai, is credited with the origination of Loi Kratong. One year, as the river overflowed, she wanted to make an offering to the river spirit, so she made a banana-leaf boat and gave it to the king. Finding the idea satisfactory, the king himself released the boat, inaugurating a Thai tradition which persists to this day. That, at least, is how the story goes. The written account of Lady Nophamat, supposedly dating to the Age of Sukhothai, was long taken by scholars as factual (see Phya Anuman Rajthon 1954; Wales 1931). However, Nidhi Eoseewong has provided ample evidence that it was written in the early Bangkok period, around the reign of Rama III (r. 1824–51). It is written in the literary style of that time. Among other curiosities, the account refers to weapons unknown in the age of Sukhothai, and also includes references to Americans—in an account dated hundreds of years before the voyage of Columbus (Nidhi 2005: 229).

Lady Nophamat is likely a fiction. Scholars have protested that Loi Kratong has no historical connection to Sukhothai (Peleggi 2002: 67). The beauty contests, however, are real—an empirically verifiable fact, visible across the kingdom. Miss Nophamat is real. And she absolutely must have white skin, the primary attribute of a beautiful body. This preference is nearly universal in Bangkok. A preference for white skin is said to be an essential characteristic of Thai people. When the sun shines, women in Bangkok carry open parasols. Entire aisles of supermarkets are committed to skin-lightening creams. Traveling by boat along the river, one sees billboards with radiant, smiling models advertising these products. Clinics administer pigment-reducing injections to the already fair-skinned women of Bangkok's elite universities. Japanese and Russian tourists, sprawling on Thailand's beaches, bathing in sunlight, are viewed with astonishment, total incomprehension. Nothing is more True Thai than the attraction to white skin, as depicted in *Four Reigns*: the noble radiance of flawless white skin (Kukrit 2011: 26–7). The critical point, however, is that the standard for white skin is set, above all, by the Chinese. Beauty is defined by young females with "Chinese" skin and faces, referred to as *muai* (หมวย). An informant from the northeast offered a succinct definition: a *muai* is "a white-skinned, ethnically Chinese girl, the kind most boys like". White skin is also regarded as a desirable attribute for males. White-skinned, ethnically Chinese boys are called *dtee* (ตี๋). Thais have a strong attraction to fair-skinned Chinese bodies, and this has clearly contributed to ethnic mixture in Bangkok. Skinner writes, "The average Thai of Lower Siam and to a lesser extent of all the regions bordering on the Gulf is today fairer skinned and more Chinese in appearance than the Thai of North and Northeast Siam. Few Siamese families whose residence in Bangkok dates back more than one generation do not have a Chinese ancestor" (1957: 134).[15]

Migrant Memories

My informant sent an SMS: "I'm sorry, but I can't meet you", she said. "I have to work late. Maybe I will just *loi kratong* in my bathtub." When the message arrived, people were still sheltering from the downpour, but soon the rain stopped. Preparations for the festival were everywhere underway and the mood was energetic. Released from rain and abandoned by my informant, restlessness encroached and a destination was decided: Wat Yannawa, the Temple of the Ship. Several months before, a friend had pointed out the temple. We were crossing the river by train, sitting under an endless blast of cold air, and the temple appeared below. "Older sibling, have you visited this temple?" she asked. "Listen, if you want to write about the river, you have to go. There's a big replica of a Chinese merchant ship. Go in and take a look."

It was formerly known as the Temple of the Buffalo Corral. Rama III ordered its renovation and a new monument was built, the aforementioned concrete replica, a Chinese merchant ship. The king foretold, accurately, that the ships would disappear from the Chao Phraya River, and thus ordered the construction of a monument in their honor, enabling future generations to imagine the ships. He thereby intervened in the culture of memory, for sometimes memory requires tangible sites of anchorage. Memory creates continuity, a series of linkages that connect then and now, even if most of the intermediary links are lost. Having seen the monument, one can imagine a river full of such vessels, as it once was. But

[15] Note carefully the comparison with the "Thai" of the north and northeast. Skinner's point concerning ethnic mixture around the gulf holds, but the peoples of the north and northeast were not until recently seen as Thai. And prior to the Thai nation-building project, they certainly did not self-identify as such. Skinner worked in Bangkok only a couple decades after vigorous government campaigns to change the identity of the peoples of the north and northeast, to make them Thai (see Barmé 1993). More on this in Chapter 3 ahead.

there is more than one way to read the monument. It is also a material fixture for memories of origin, travel, and arrival. After renovation, the temple was renamed. It remains popular with the Chinese, locals as well as tourists from China. Statues of Rama III stand near the replica, along with a plaque, clearly of recent manufacture, that describes him as the "royal father of Thai commerce", who, in the aftermath of Ayutthaya's destruction by Burma, renewed the "Thai economy". The recovery, according to the plaque, was achieved by commerce with foreigners.

The concrete ship has become a device for storytelling. An old woman who had grown up along the Canal of a Hundred Thousand Stings, an old canal in Bangkok, said the language of her childhood home was Chinese. No one spoke Thai. During the interview, she still spoke with a Chinese accent—despite having lived all her life in Siam/Thailand. At the time of my fieldwork, she rarely left the house. Unlike her three daughters, she was somewhat out of place in the new Bangkok. I asked, "During what reign were you born? Was it the seventh reign?" Most Thais can answer that question, but she did not know. She knew the year, but not the reign. "We didn't think about politics", she said. "We only thought about making a living." With her thick accent and occasional preference for Chinese expressions, she was sometimes difficult to understand. Her daughters, who also identified as Chinese, but spoke crystal-clear Bangkok Thai, offered assistance. Later, they talked about their father, who had passed away. He was an immigrant from China, a fierce, hard-working man, and their memory of him had shaped their perception of the present. "Today", one said, "life is easy. In our father's time it was difficult." The other agreed. As a young immigrant in Bangkok, he survived as an ambulatory merchant, carrying goods with a pole over his shoulder. Many years later, he took his daughters to the Temple of the Ship. He pointed to the concrete replica and said, "This is how I came to Bangkok."[16]

Others told similar migration stories. Sitting in a shopping complex, an old Chinese man, born in Thailand, sipped from a coffee cup. He

---

[16] Strangely, no one ever mentioned other sorts of vessels. It was always a merchant ship, never a steamship. Baker and Pasuk write, "By the 1880s there were regular steamship services between Bangkok and the southern Chinese ports, and a regular supply of the poor and desperate ready to make the unpleasant trip" (2009: 93).

was preparing a trip to a casino on the Cambodian border. "Chinese like to gamble", he said. I asked about the differences between Chinese and Thai. "Oh, they are very similar", he said. "Thais *wai pra*; Chinese *wai jao*!" This means Thais honor monks and Buddha images (*pra*), whereas Chinese honor the lords (*jao*), spirits that dwell in places, especially shrines. But things have changed, he explained, "These days, Chinese also *wai pra* and Thais *wai jao*!" He insisted that we go immediately to the produce section of a nearby grocery store to see the vegetables that Thais received from China. He also talked about his father, who spent many days at sea before arriving in Bangkok. Prior to departure, one's eyes were examined. They would ask, "Are you healthy? Do you have any infectious diseases?" His father boarded a merchant ship destined for Klong Toey, one of Bangkok's main ports, now surrounded by a sprawling mass of informal dwellings. There were no passports. His father paid a fee to the official. He entered Bangkok and never returned to China.

Patches of the Past

Bangkok's road system is notoriously over-stressed, often choked with wheeled transport. The steadily expanding BTS (skytrain) system, which opened in 1999 on the king's birthday, has provided relief, as well as elevated views of the metropolis. Modern transportation technology offers new perspectives on old landscapes. The open-air station at the Taksin Bridge provides a wide view of the Chao Phraya River. Although road and rail have proliferated, and many old canals have been filled, Bangkok would not exist without the Chao Phraya. Much has changed in the last hundred years, during which Bangkok has developed, "reached the age" (modernized), and "stepped forward" (made progress), but an aquatic past has quietly persisted into the present.

Water is written into the name of the city: a *bang* is a village at the mouth of a waterway (Sujit 2005: 23–4). The second syllable, *kok,* quite possibly comes from *kor* (เกาะ), which means island (Srisak 2010: ix). According to a more popular interpretation, the name might originate from a village called Bang Makok, the latter being an abbreviation of *makoknam* (มะกอกน้ำ), a tree in the genus of *Elaeocarpus* that grows along the Chao Phraya and produces an olive-like fruit. Over time, according to this interpretation, Bang Makok became Bang Kok. A shortcut canal, dug in the 16th century, carved an island from an oxbow, and it has been suggested that Bang Makok was located on that island (Sujit 2005: 37–8). Wat Arun (the Temple of Dawn), also known as Wat Jaeng, soaring at the edge of the river, was previously known as Wat Makok (ibid.). However, Srisak Vallibhotama has argued for Bang Kor, citing a poetic narrative of riverine travel ("โคลงกำสรวลสมุทร") from the age of Ayutthaya, an account that, although replete with place-names, does not mention Bangkok, suggesting the name did not precede the shortcut canal, which created an island (เกาะ). Furthermore, the area's primary flora was mangrove; makok trees did not grow there originally, but came later, after the mangroves had been removed.[17] Lastly, he cites Kajorn Sukpanich, a scholar from an earlier generation, who observed that on old maps drawn by foreigners, the name of the village looks more like "Bang Kor" (Srisak 2017b: 284–5).

In either case, Bangkok was a village among waterways. Several hundred years ago, the village became a stopping place for traders, including many from afar, traveling upstream to Ayutthaya. This traffic encouraged expansion of the village into a town and trading post. In the late 18th century, with the royal command to build a new city-kingdom, Bangkok began its transformation into a full-scale port city. Notably, the Siamese were not generally a seagoing people (Reid 1993: 125). As Sujit Wongthes once said, in a characteristically colorful phrasing, "The mere sight of the sea made them vomit."[18] But the Siamese attracted foreign merchants, who mediated Siam's seagoing commerce and tribute missions. Standing on the BTS platform, engulfed in heat and humidity,

---

[17] Mangrove swamps are habitats of crocodiles, which once thrived along the river. Crocodiles were exalted in ancient times as guardians of the fertile waters (Sujit 2016: 74). Nowadays, crocodile designs are often used in magical tattoos as symbols of wild, ferocious power. Three-stringed zithers—*chakhe* in Thai—named after and shaped like crocodiles are used in traditional Siamese, Mon, and Khmer music. Chinese shrines along the Gulf of Thailand are known to keep crocodile skulls as sacred, power-laden objects (Walailak 2017: 71).

[18] This quote is from a historical video-documentary produced by Matichon, a Thai media organization.

I received a text message from a local cellphone carrier: "Put a statue of a Chinese merchant ship on your work desk—this will bring progress."

Other signs of Chinese migration can be found along the river. The statues at Asiatique, for example, are of recent manufacture. Asiatique, a riverside shopping complex, was open during my fieldwork, but still under construction. The air was thick with the smell of paint. Nail guns continued to pop. The complex is an open-air grid of warehouses and alleys, a commercialized reconstruction of an old river scene. Visitors can arrive by boat, with free trips to the complex in the evenings. Going downstream, one sees a line of national flags, marking the complex as an international meeting place. Here the past is converted into a commodity. One enjoys a sanitized version of an antiquated scene, but arguably there is more to the story. Pierre Nora, who laments the cruel erosion of place-based cultures of memory, describes memory as "a phenomenon of emotion and magic". It "thrives", he says, not on facts or dates, but "on vague, telescoping reminiscences, on hazy general impressions or specific symbolic details (Nora 1996: 3). Statues of Chinese laborers are found throughout the complex: men with partially shaved heads and long braids. Some carry sacks of rice. One pulls a rickshaw. These figures evoke not only Bangkok's past, but also a conceivable future, in which the national past will have been reimagined.[19]

Dockworkers in Bangkok are still referred to as coolies (กุลี), a reminder of a long-standing ethnic division of labor. Many of the old rice mills, mostly owned by Chinese, have been dismantled, making such work less visible. Bodies have also changed; the pigtails—a hairstyle required for men under the Qing dynasty (overthrown in 1911)—are gone. The banks of the river are no longer teeming with the figures seen in statue-form at Asiatique. However, such images quickly come to mind. A woman in her mid-forties, a migrant from a village in another province, said that when

[19] Ross King also carries Pierre Nora's ideas into the Thai context. Building on the work of a dozen Thai scholars, King explores Nora's contrast between *sites* of memory and *environments* of memory. His analysis diverges significantly from Nora's, arguing that environments of memory are still abundant in Thailand (King 2017). For Nora, sites of memory are like desiccated vestiges of once-thriving cultures of memory: "no longer quite alive but not yet entirely dead, like shells left on the shore when the sea of living memory has receded" (Nora 1996: 7).

she was a child, a new arrival in Bangkok, she saw Chinese rice-carriers working along the river near the Santa Cruz Church—in an area known as Kutti Jin, or Chamber of Chinese Monks. She saw coolies loading the ships. It was a surprising story, certainly worth investigating, but as I found, older people in the vicinity of the church all said that was before they were born, and those loading docks had long ago been dismantled.

Statues of Chinese rice-carriers

And yet her story still reflects collective memory. The Thai word *jum,* to remember, also means to incarcerate (จำคุก). It can also refer to temporary storage, such as pawning (จำนำ), or to Buddhist monks observing the precepts in a monastery (จำศีล). In short, it suggests containment, a state of being locked or steadfast in place. Images of riverside Chinese laborers are scattered, here and there, in Bangkok's ecology of images, appearing in films and television dramas, in picture books, in conversations about the old days, and now at a riverside shopping complex. The story seems plausible because the images persist and arise spontaneously in memory. She remembers, in a sense, a Bangkok that faded and transformed before she arrived in the city. This very personal memory—traveling along the river with her mother—also reflects a collective memory, in which fragments of old Bangkok remain scattered. "My mother took me there", she said. "I remember the coolies carrying sacks of rice. But I'd forgotten for many years. Then when I was older, I went back and said to myself, 'Oh! This is where my mother brought me'."

She was born in a village near Cambodia. She recalled arriving as a child in Bangkok, a strange, frenetic place, filled with unfamiliar sights and sounds. The memory of Chinese rice-carriers is part of her picture of Bangkok. Her past includes migration to the city; the city's past includes the rice-carriers. The memory convinces because of a lingering, widespread imaginary of the large and long-standing Chinese presence in Bangkok. Her memory is one piece in a partially assembled puzzle. Regarding the Chinese in Thailand, Thongchai Winichakul notes that "immigrant history is regarded as an individual rather than an imagined communal past. The past they identify with is a Thai past, but their Thai identity is a recent acquisition" (1995: 116). But perhaps there would be no Thai past without immigrants, or without the merchant ship.

Jack Goody, writing about non-literate societies, argues, "It is dangerous to speak of a collective memory in oral cultures. An oral culture is not held in everybody's memory store.... Memories vary as does experience. Bits may be held by different people" (1998: 94). Thai society has a high rate of literacy and a profusion of the printed word, but let us consider this comment on collective memory. One of the insights of Maurice Halbwachs was that even our most personal memories, memories that die with us, are always embedded in networks of social relations (1992: 38). This does not imply a simple uniformity of minds, but rather that the human interior takes shape in the context of society. Memories in the public sphere are often shared to varying degrees, but one never finds a collectivity of identical beings. The division of memory is a characteristic of all cultures. One could imagine memories as patches of cloth. Pieces can be stitched together, separated, or rearranged, as when people sit side-by-side, retelling a shared story. Each contributes, filling gaps and creating connections. They disagree about aspects of the narrative. This is all intrinsic to collective life, and the story comes to life as the patches are stitched together. More encompassing memories also form, populated by places, figures, and scenes, an ever-evolving landscape of the past—a curious image, perhaps, full of stitches and contrasting angles, in which one might see the merchant ship, not merely in an ethnically bound context, but in the emerging patchwork of a broader story of Bangkok and the Thai nation.

Banana-Leaf Boats and Merchant Ships

A police officer yells through a megaphone, "You don't have to hurry!" Passengers laugh in unison. We are suspended on the water for several minutes. People are not usually talkative on these express-boat journeys. Many doze, lulled by wind and the hum of the engine. But today, everyone is full of energy, chattering, and eager. After a few minutes, we start moving again. An urban landscape passes, street corridors open and close, a small Ferris wheel appears for just a moment. I disembark by the white, peeling hulk of the Oriental Hotel, which formerly received seaborne merchants. Tables along the street have orderly displays of *kratong* for sale, little boats made of leaf, bread, or foam. Turning onto the main road, the markets are bustling. Passing the Robinson shopping complex, one can feel the thickening crowds ahead, gathering at the cross-river bridge and the Temple of the Ship. As always, vendors in front of the department store have set up tables, piled with sandals, shirts, and belts, but the speakers by the front entrance, which usually play electronic dance music, now squeal with an old, scratchy recording of the Loi Kratong song: "On the day of the full moon, in the 12th month, water overflows the banks."

Bodies swarm at the Taksin Bridge. Students carry tambourines and donation boxes. A man announces boat trips, an opportunity to release banana-leaf boats in the middle of the river. Night has fallen and the streets, crowds, vendors, and platforms are now under artificial light. I ascend the stairs, stop at the platform, and lean over a rail. Ascending further, I step onto the bridge, which supports automobile traffic in two directions and the BTS rail. Both sides of the bridge have sidewalks for pedestrians. Many are gathered, including photographers and groups of friends. Crossing slowly, the voice from the PA system below dissolves into mush, the ambient pulse of a male voice amplified. Red lights blink just above the water's surface, signs of police presence. Some people had issued warnings. Beware of crowds. Beware of young people.

Crossing over, descending the steps, one finds a safety rail at the river's edge. Some out-of-service long-tail boats are moored. Green vegetable matter floats near the dock. On an ordinary day, fishermen perch by the rail, lines cast and poles propped. Now those gathered—this bank is far less crowded than the other—are mostly just watching the opening scene of Loi Kratong. Little candle-lit boats, just a few, begin to appear on the water. Men lean against the rail and sip from beer bottles. Merchants sell flashing mouse ears, in purple, green, and pink. A young couple arrives with their son and daughter, stopping to collect themselves by the dock. The daughter learns how to handle the *kratong*. "Hold it above your head and make a wish." The parents adjust the child's hands and arms. "Stand straight!" One can see a parallel with the ethnographic work of Margaret Mead and Gregory Bateson (1951) in Bali, where they studied the enculturation of bodies, how children learn to walk, sit, and stand like proper Balinese. Here at the river's edge in Bangkok, this is also about enacting and embodying a linkage to the collective past, for Loi Kratong is said to be an authentic and original Thai cultural practice, passed on downstream from Sukhothai, with "no break", persisting into the present. It is a kind of mnemonic performance. One must know how to grasp the *kratong*, how to stand, when to make a wish. Paul Connerton observed decades ago that scholars had rarely attended to the sedimentation of "social memory" in the body. As a corrective, he examined how "images of the past and recollected knowledge of the past ... are conveyed and sustained by (more or less ritual) performances" (Connerton 1989: 3–4). Such acts materialize and bring to life connections to the past. The collective past is woven in cycles into episodic memories—internal, flesh-bound scenes and stories.

Ferries are still in service, steadily lumbering back and forth across the river. We put coins on the table, clamber aboard, and secure places on the benches. The ferry rocks steadily, rubbing the edge of the pier—metal against water, against metal, against rubber tires. We are released and very slowly make an arc from this bank to the next. A man points and a little girl looks up. A floating lamp, one of the night's first, is making its way into the sky, a sign of renewal, carrying away someone's hardships and painful memories. It goes up and over, further and further above the hotel-and-condominium skyline of the Chao Phraya River.[20]

Activity is accelerating on the opposite bank. Some children have jumped into the water and now cling to the dock, waiting for the *kratong* to come within reach. Few people nowadays put fingernail clippings, or hair clippings, or betel in the *kratong*, but one usually drops a few coins before lighting the candle and setting it afloat. Thais say the coins represent a sacrifice. Some children collect the coins and buy snacks. Others buy glue, to be inhaled from plastic bags.

A crowd fills the temple. The massive concrete merchant ship, with masts like pagodas, stands bathed in lamplight under the night sky. One must slow down, move with the foot traffic. The complex throngs with commerce: ice cream, pork on a stick, and noodles. Not so long ago, noodles were Chinese food. This changed around the time of World War II, under the dictatorship of Field Marshal Pibulsongkram. Noodles were re-signified, the state provided recipes, carts proliferated, and the people of Thailand, a freshly renamed country, were encouraged to eat noodles. It was the age of radio; the state declared: "Noodle is your lunch" (Thamsook 1978: 236). The campaign, "closely followed" by the dictator, was successful (ibid.). Noodles have become Thai food, even though, especially when served in soup, they are eaten with chopsticks. And now on Loi Kratong, many Thais have decided, not surprisingly, to eat noodles, all happily huddling under hot electric lamps, in the shadows of the Chinese merchant ship.[21]

---

[20] Skyborne floating lamps were adopted from the traditions of the north. Rama V believed the northern lamps were a parallel of the candle-carrying banana-leaf vessels of Loi Kratong (Phya Anuman Rajthon 1954: 200).

[21] Chinese influence goes far beyond noodles and chopsticks. For example, Nidhi Eoseewong writes, "Consider what we call Thai food. Try going without a steel frying pan. You'll go without eating. And steel frying pans came from China. Before that, you couldn't fry anything (2016: 97). Chinese-style frying pans with round bottoms and two handles had arrived in Siam by the early Ayutthaya period (Sujit 2017: 186–7), and the old city had many markets known for Chinese vendors, goods, and food (ibid.: 199–201).

We approach the edge of the river. Along the way, strings extend from upper-story windows down to the asphalt, where they are fixed. Paper currency is clipped along the length of the string, with more bills being added as temple-goers make donations. The temple is noisy. Fortune sticks rattle in wooden tubes. In Bangkok, this rattling—a distinctive, insect-like sound—is part of the sensory experience of many Chinese shrines and Thai temples. Kneel, focus, make a wish. One shakes the wooden cylinder until a stick falls onto the mat. One then takes the stick, which is always numbered, and retrieves a fortune. A Thai informant, who turned out to be Chinese, offered reasonable advice: "If the fortune is good, keep it. If not, throw it away."

A steady stream of people are making their way to the dock. The water is out of reach, so people lower the *kratong* with a scoop fixed to a pole. Many sit along the rails, watching and chatting. Both young and old are present. Men, women, and children. People accumulate at the water's edge. Some toss pellets to the fish. Couples sit together and light sparklers. A monk speaks through a microphone, commenting on the donations. These are merit-making activities, and so one anticipates good fortune in the future. The monk says, "You'll be rich for sure! Just wait a few years, you'll be famous!" An abundance of *kratong* are now afloat, each with a lit candle. In the 1920s, a British ethnographer observed this festival from his riverside home in Bangkok. Thousands of *kratong* floated downstream, "on their way out to be swallowed up by the sea" (Wales 1931: 292). Now by contrast, the *kratong* cross a distance of perhaps 10 meters. Workers from the Department of the Environment wait in small, yellow boats, armed with fishing nets. *Kratong* are scooped and piled into a smoldering heap. The monk continues to comment on the donations, then guides those present through a prayer: "Repeat after me", he says. "I ask that my family and I may reside beneath the umbrella of moral authority provided by the three institutions: Nation, Buddhism, and Monarchy. Forever."[22]

[22] There are subtle variations in the wording of this slogan. In this case, the middle element was specifically Buddhism, rather than Religion. The final element is sometimes King, sometimes Monarchy.

Reimagine the Nation

Considering the influences of China and India on mainland Southeast Asia, Edmund Leach once suggested that "the influence of China has been mainly in the fields of trade and communication and has affected the Hill People rather than the Valley People" (1960: 54). The expression "Valley People" refers broadly to the peoples of the lowlands. However, in the case of Siam, the center of trade and communication has long been the "valley" of the Chao Phraya River. Bangkok is one of the biggest river-cities of Southeast Asia, and the Chinese, many of them traveling upstream, arriving by merchant ship, drove the development of the city as well as the subsequent emergence of the Thai nation.

A woman in a Thai-Chinese district of Bangkok once mentioned a serialized television drama, *Through the Dragon Design*, a reflection of her life, she said—a rags-to-riches story about a Chinese immigrant to Siam. She was Bangkok-born, but spoke Taechiew, a dialect of Chinese, at home with her immigrant father. The opening scene of the drama depicted a merchant ship at sea, with men crying, huddling together, and vomiting over the edge. Kasian Tejapira, in his study of the Chinese in Siam (1994), offers a wonderful anecdote: one evening, at a restaurant in Bangkok's Chinatown, a man sings a nationalistic song from China in Mandarin to an indifferent audience, most of whom are Thai-born Chinese, but when he sings the opening song from *Through the Dragon Design*, the mood changes entirely. The audience sings along and the performance is followed by enormous applause. The drama had a profound resonance with Bangkok's Thai-born Chinese. It told a story never before televised.

Kasian describes a Chinese experience particular to Thailand. Being Chinese in Thailand is not the same as being Chinese in China, or anywhere else. However, also worth considering are the ways in which the Chinese contributed to the creation of both "Thai" and "Thailand". Bangkok itself can be reframed as a point of origin, the nation's birthplace—a city teeming, for as long as anyone can remember, with Chinese immigrants and their children. During my fieldwork, a man said, "If you ask me if I'm more Thai or more Chinese, it will be difficult to answer." The categories Thai and Chinese are curiously entangled: bounded, but complicated by coexistence, and always prone to mixture through desire. We enter an oozing, flowing landscape in which stories meet and merge.

So easily one falls into the progression-of-centers narrative. Prince Damrong's hegemonic vision continues to orient scholarship, as well as everyday life in Thailand. The progression-of-centers narrative incorporates territory, with city-kingdoms as centers of power following the water. Yet attending closely to the landscape—looking, listening, and thinking again—one finds alternate vantage points from which to behold the nation. Banana-leaf boats, carried by the current, float downstream, but for centuries merchant ships have traveled in the opposite direction, and many never returned to their places of origin. Ships dropped anchor and formed a lively network of aquatic commerce.

The process of nation-building must have been strange and bewildering for most of the people of Siam, at least until radio, mass education, and the cultural interventions of the Bangkok-centered state took hold of day-to-day life. Around 1932, even intellectuals in Bangkok were confused by the evolving meanings and uses of the word "nation" (ชาติ) (Nakarin 2010: 414–9). Thai identity—and the obsessions with True Thai—originate not in the ancient kingdom of Sukhothai, but in Bangkok, a tropical port-city, a city of canals and commerce, a melting metropolis. Key figures who worked vigorously to define "Thai" were descended from Chinese immigrants. Even Kukrit Pramoj, who did so much to elevate Thai identity, is said to have "boasted about a Chinese element in his heritage" (Baker and Pasuk 2009: 190). As the Thai nation emerged, the Chinese were at the center of that process.

The Chao Phraya River is the primordial highway of Siam. Viewed from above, the river flows through a landmass between the Bay of Bengal and the South China Sea. Bangkok was shaped by the cyclical rhythms of the monsoon, decisive in the age of sail: beginning in October, in the cool months approaching winter, winds blow from the northeast across the South China Sea. Loi Kratong marks the end of the rainiest period; the monsoon turns and brings a new season to Thailand. Loi Kratong did not originate in Sukhothai, but it coincides well with the moment when the winds begin pushing south from the coast of China. Rebecca Solnit writes, "Part of what makes roads, trails, and paths so unique as built structures is that they cannot be perceived as a whole all at once by a sedentary onlooker. They unfold in time as one travels along them, just as a story does as one listens or reads" (2000: 72). The river evokes stories of ancient city-kingdoms, a glittering collective past, as well as stories of travel and arrival, the journeys of ancestors. Along the waterways one hears many voices. The maternal river brought these voices together, providing the basis for a vibrant port-city, a meeting place of memories.

Chapter 2

Loss

The beauty of a landscape resides in its melancholy.
Ahmet Rasim[1]

We were sitting near a fish tank, amidst masses of uniformed college students, on the ground floor of a shopping complex. A Bangkok native and self-described True Thai had narrated her ambition to move up-country and practice the way of life of her ancestors. The interview was finished, or so it seemed. She was quiet for a moment. Then she said, "I want to ask you something. I want to know: Why did you come to study the river?" She had asked this before. Only in the aftermath, or in the course of grant writing, do ethnographic projects come to appear as neat, rational trajectories. Project development is a creative process. I saw a curious connection between water and culture. Every year in April, Thais use water to wash away the detritus of the foregoing year. During Loi Kratong, Thais apologize to the river. And the river is embedded in the national story, connecting royal city-kingdoms. I noted Bangkok's elaborate aquatic infrastructure, as well as the transformation of life along the waterways, the many dramatic changes. "But that's just it", she said. "We've already turned away from the water."

This suggests, at a collective level, both connection and disconnection, the end of a relationship. To turn away is to abandon—the cause, real or imagined, of a present sensibility: a sense of loss. It is change with a negative connotation. Every landscape has its memories. Bangkok's aquatic landscape is pervaded and haunted by loss. Waterways evoke a water-centered way of life, which has been mostly abandoned and is now dying. This came to my attention during early fieldwork, in

[1] Pamuk (2005: n.p.).

Bangkok Yai Canal, part of the old course of the river

the aftermath of floods that brought destruction to life and property. It was called the Great Water Disaster (มหาอุทกภัย). Mass media and inhabitants of Bangkok lamented that Thais—river dwellers since dawn—no longer know how to live with water. The floods served as a rather unwelcome reminder. As water poured into streets, houses, and office buildings, many Thais recalled fragments of a way of life that both was and was not their own.

Sombat Plainoi, an award-winning National Artist born in the late 1920s in Ayutthaya, is known for his studies of aquatic culture. Near the end of a book titled *Life Along Canals*, he writes:

> Today, the way of life of Thai people, in terms of our relationship to water, has dramatically changed. In water previously full of fish, few fish remain. In some places the fish are completely gone. Canals once full of clean, drinkable water, are now corrupted, filthy, and stinking. Who would have thought that someday Thais would have to buy drinking water? In the future, if we continue to neglect the water, if we fail to keep it clean, we might suffer outbreaks of disease, as once happened long ago: King U Thong [said to have founded Ayutthaya in the 14th century] had to abandon his old city, which

View from a window

> was short of water and ridden with plague. What if that were to happen to us? Where would we go? (Sombat 2001: 122).

Similarly, Charnvit Kasetsiri writes, "In the old days, the river was the highway. It was at the front of the house. But now, with the transition from water to rail to road, the front has become the back. People have turned away from the river [หันหลังให้แม่น้ำ].... The river receives little attention, and it's a mess.... It has become a place of trash and waste" (Charnvit 1997: 190).

My fieldwork was during a time of uncertainty. Rama IX was in frail condition in a hospital by the river, and the Red-Yellow conflict was at high temperature. Not long before, in 2010, an enormous street confrontation in Bangkok had ended in a massacre, with dozens of Red Shirts shot and killed by the Thai military. Later, a show on Thai PBS called *Answering Questions* (*ตอบโจทย์*) invited key figures to discuss the conflict. The show then invited two controversial intellectuals, Sulak Sivaraksa and Somsak Jeamteerasakul, to debate the place of the monarchy in Thai society. Sulak is a wonderfully complex figure, bold and erudite in the extreme, an outspoken royalist repeatedly accused of royal defamation. Somsak is an academic and former political prisoner, a man who witnessed the October 6 massacre, and a critic of the institutions that promote and protect the Thai monarchy. Somsak's proposals included abolishing royal defamation laws, abolishing the Privy Council, and abolishing one-sided royalist education. Sulak promptly agreed, in principle, adding, "But for now it is still impossible." He described his ideal of kingship: not a deity-king (เทวราช), but a deity-by-supposition (สมมติเทพ)—that is, a king that would be revered, but human, fallible, and without divine powers.[2] Furthermore, he compared the monarchy to a "great tree" threatened by "parasites" (กาฝาก) and described the tree as "unsteady and tottering". Sulak said, "My duty is to care for this tree." Somsak, however, repeatedly emphasized the fundamental imbalance of the debate, constrained by laws that forbid any explicitly anti-monarchist position. The staging of this debate was dangerous, for Thailand has some of the world's most fierce lese-majesty laws. Some viewers were probably shocked. But the debate did not continue. Suddenly the host, Pinyo Traisuriyathamma, announced the immediate and permanent cancellation of the show. Shortly thereafter, he published an essay collection in which he wrote, "The primary pillars of Thai society are rotting. Year after year, this house is subjected to rain and the scorching sun. It's frightening. The house could collapse and crush the people inside" (Pinyo 2013: 53).

Continuity and change are key aspects of landscape. I find resonance in ethnographic work from the highlands of South Sulawesi: a terrain of "paths and rivers", which also provide a matrix for thinking about place, persistence, and time (Waterson 2009: xiv). In the pages ahead,

---

[2] For an overview of Sulak Sivaraksa's views on the monarchy, see Sulak (2016). In the aforementioned work, he also elaborates on the distinction between a deity-king and a deity-by-supposition (ibid.: 82–3). The latter is, first and foremost, human. The deity-king concept is widespread in Southeast Asia. For example, Nurcholish Madjid, an Islamic scholar from Indonesia, describes the "deva-raja" concept as "a source of despotism", whereas a sultan, "as God's shadow on earth", is "responsible before God to conduct a government that is righteous, just, open, and to see all people as equal in terms of dignity, rights, and duties" (Madjid 2018: 20). My translation.

the narrative moves from abandonment to eviction—loss past, present, and impending. Decades ago, Harry J. Benda challenged scholars to consider "the balance between continuity and change in contemporary Southeast Asia" (1969: 40). Colonial regimes were being broken, nations were emerging, and peasants were taking up arms in Vietnam. My intention, however, is not primarily to examine the balance-in-fact, but to shift perspective and ask: Where do people see, or sense, continuity and change? What meanings are given to continuity and change? Change is not always loss; sometimes it is perceived as progress. Loss is not merely an empirical fact, a matter of material displacement, the corollary of separation and absence. Loss is also a cultural phenomenon. In Bangkok, loss emerges in a network of associations, among the meanings, stories, images, and possibilities that reside along the waterways. Recalled with bitterness, melancholy, or nostalgia, a sense of loss persists in landscape and collective memory.

Poetic Landscape

Rivers evoke both the ephemeral and timeless. The Chao Phraya River, a realm of national myths and quotidian places, patterns and contradictions, can be explored as a "poetic landscape". The latter expression comes from Anthony Smith, a scholar of nations and nationalism, whose work provokes us to ask: how do people relate to the terrains within their borders, features of the earth that are not "mine" but "ours" as national subjects? How do these landscapes speak? While many studies have examined the material, enabling conditions of nationalism, Smith turns to the subjective. He writes, "We can hardly begin to enter into the world-view of nationalism without appreciating the profound effects of these 'poetic landscapes' on the self-understanding of many members of the nation ... an aspect that has till recently been rather neglected" (2010: 35).

In debates on the origins of nations, Smith stands opposite to Anderson, Gellner, and Hobsbawm. The latter three have built a paradigm in which the nation is a quintessentially modern construct. Anderson argues that nations emerged only with the breakdown of certain pre-modern entities, namely "sacred communities, languages and lineages" (2006: 22). Gellner takes the position that the nation appeared and persists because it fits the requirements of industrial society. He writes, "[Nationalism] preaches and defends continuity, but owes everything to a decisive and unutterably profound break in human history" (1983: 125). Hobsbawm argues that nations were "so unprecedented that even historic continuity had to be invented, for example by creating an ancient past ... either by semi-fiction ... or by forgery" (1983: 7). Smith makes concessions to these authors, but maintains that pre-modern experiences leave decisive imprints on nations. Why is one nation different from the next? Smith writes, "My belief is that the most important of these variations [between nations] are determined by specific historical experiences and by the 'deposit' left by these collective experiences" (1986: ix).

Fixed definitions of national culture are dangerous, and the notion of a deposit left by collective experiences is problematic. One might mistakenly believe the collective always existed, with the same outlines and contours it has today. This problem is taken up by Michel-Rolph Trouillot, for whom neither the deposit nor the collectivity can be accepted as given. The past is not simply piled in storage, waiting to be recalled by society. He writes, "The storage model assumes not only the past to be remembered but the collective subject that does the remembering. The problem with this dual assumption is that the constructed past itself is constitutive of the collectivity" (Trouillot 1995: 16). Moreover, the so-called deposit evolves through power-infused relations and processes. Yet there is a vast, muddy in-between, a middle range between nationalist fantasies and absolute constructivism, a place of confluence and questions: How does the landscape of the Chao Phraya River speak? What does it evoke?

It is a realm of curious harmonies and severe dissonance. One day, standing near the riverbank, a family from the northeast observed, "The Chao Phraya is so polluted. The water is black. The Mekong, which runs along the edge of our home province, is still clean." Indeed, the Chao Phraya is corrupted. The water stinks and dead things float on the surface. She evokes instability, decay and death, as well as renewal, the cycle of rebirth, reminding us that patterns of memory that define collectivity are not eternal. Patterns of memory can die. Buddhist teachings emphasize that all beings decay. In one well-known expression, life is described in a sequence: beings are born, established, and then extinguished (เกิดขึ้น ตั้งอยู่ ดับไป). The Thai word for nation (related to the Indic word *jati*) also means birth or incarnation. As time passes and society changes, national concepts might appear unsteady, and perhaps vulnerable.

Floods of Paradox

It was near the end of the Great Water Disaster. As the aircraft descended into Bangkok, the water was still receding. Thai-speaking laborers, returning from Taiwan, pressed their faces against the windows of the plane. Look! A partially inundated patchwork of rice fields, villages, and semi-urban life passed below. Damage and recovery were their first concerns. In subsequent weeks and months, floods were an inescapable topic. People heard that I was studying water, and many of them immediately added the word *overflows*—the water overflows (น้ำท่วม). Another recurring pattern was that people guessed I was studying a "way of life" (วิถีชีวิต) along the river. They said, "Oh, you're studying the way of life?" Water means flood. Water means way of life.

Floods were a reminder of change, the loss of a way of life. "In the old days", one woman said, "the Chao Phraya River was the heart of the Thai people." People in Siam, or Central Thailand, have always lived with floods, and floods used to be a celebrated feature of life along waterways. Now the meaning of floods has changed, especially in Bangkok and other afflicted urban areas. Floods bring destruction. This transformation has arisen against a background of collective memory, images and stories of an old Thai way of life. Floods, especially the contemporary variety that wreck life and property, make that background more vivid.

During the first few months of fieldwork, a television commercial—produced by PTT, the national energy company—repeated over and over. It consisted of a series of scenes, all reflecting ways that people in Thailand relate to water. The opening sequence linked water with the life cycle, from birth to death. Water symbolizes a life that is not only human, but culturally Thai: "It is the beginning. It is a friend. It is one we rely on. It is hope. It nourishes us. It is livelihood. It is the end." The screen goes black. "But today … [now the scene depicts Bangkok overtaken by floodwater] we see it as a destroyer." The voice-over then says, "Our lives have been changed, and this may change our feelings toward the waterways. But we believe, if we stay with and support nature, the waterways we love and to which we are bound will recover their beauty and remain with us." Prior to display of the company's logo, viewers see an image of the Chao Phraya River in Bangkok, a well-known symbol of life with water. The commercial reached out again and again to the cultural assumptions and sensibilities of Thai viewers. For example, the on-screen text reads, "It is the end", and the viewer sees ashes released into the water. People understand that this is a Buddhist funeral. But the floods also bring forth a paradox: Thais are closely bound and adapted to waterways. This is part of being Thai. And yet, at the same time, something has clearly gone wrong. Floods bring massive destruction to Bangkok.

"Will it flood here?" the apartment manager asked. As the wet season approached, some people in Bangkok were afraid. Mounds of white sandbags began to appear along the river. For those communities unprotected by cement barriers, sand was a primary means of defense. Previously, people said, floods did not bring such destruction. They said the "original" Thai way of life was adapted to floods. The houses were raised. Each household had a small boat. People knew how to paddle and every child could swim. Children even learned to swim before learning to walk. People could catch fish with their bare hands. The Loi Kratong festival marks the traditional flood season; the overflow is anticipated, and soon enough it will recede. Water nourishes the soil. Water is life. When the water overflows, Thais celebrate. But in November of 2011, most people in Bangkok chose not to celebrate Loi Kratong. The city was submerged and the celebration was canceled.

Along the Waterways

A brief comparison of landscapes can be instructive. The Ganges River, in northern India, and the Chao Phraya River have significant similarities. Both are seen as mothers, and during the Loi Kratong festival, the Chao Phraya is even called "Mother Ganga". Siam, like other countries in Southeast Asia, emerging within the cyclical monsoon system of the Indian Ocean, was within the expansive sphere of cultural influence from ancient India (Coedès 1968). But the Chao Phraya is also a mother of a different kind. Kelly D. Alley (2002), in her ethnography of the Ganges, discusses perceptions of the river: for many pilgrims, the Ganges, sacred and timeless, has the power to overcome urban-industrial waste. In spite of pollution and disease, the water still cleans the soul, and so the Ganges remains the center of a pilgrimage culture. By contrast, one does not make a pilgrimage to the Chao Phraya. There are many sacred places along the banks, and people travel to these sites—temples, churches, mosques, and shrines—but this is not a pilgrimage to the river. Furthermore, many of these sites are centers of community, and this is central to the "poetry" of the Chao Phraya: she evokes a way of life—real, imagined, and recollected—but as the visible corruption suggests, that way of life is deteriorating.

Tanabe and Keyes point out that "many in [Thailand] share social memories of a premodern past" (2002: 2). In Bangkok, that past took place along waterways. Some imagine those times as perfused with a golden stillness, with Thailand still untainted by the outside world. Only

Canoe with jars and plants

in recent decades does life flow, as said in Bangkok, along the "current of society" (กระแสสังคม).[3]

Some informants interpreted my project as salvage: the gathering of fragments from an antiquated, dying world. People openly lamented the neglect of Thai culture. One morning, for example, sitting at a coffee stall, an older woman described traveling by canoe during the recent floods, and then observed remorsefully, "This country elevates culture very little." On another occasion, an art gallery had displayed paintings of old canal-side houses. Children were leaping joyfully into the canals. The gallery owner said, "Nowadays, young people aren't interested in culture. They don't understand it." Some people offered causal theories. Some blamed the ascendancy of new "values", the counterpoint to culture. Others blamed the "mouth-stomach problem", the problem of satisfying basic needs. One day an informant stood at the intersection of the river and a small canal, as hammers pounded at a construction site across the water. "It's unfortunate", she said. "We only think of preservation now, when much of our culture has already vanished." But this itself is a cultural phenomenon—lamenting one's vanished or lost culture. Halbwachs writes, "[Collective memory] retains from the past only what still lives or is capable of living in the consciousness of the groups keeping the memory alive" (1980: 80). This is a reminder that most of the past is not capable of living. Yet along the waterways, an absent world, a shared past, continues—although within great limits, although faded, distorted, even actively manipulated—in collective memory. The landscape is haunted by absence. People talked about antiquated practices as if nothing had changed. One afternoon in Thonburi, aboard a bus, an informant again explains Loi Kratong: "We put nail-clippings, hair, and betel nut into the *kratong*, then set it afloat." But in actual practice, that time has passed. These days a coin will suffice. No hair. No nails. Betel is difficult to obtain. I was not doing salvage ethnography, yet such a project would resonate with obsessions in Bangkok. Thongchai Winichakul writes, "Publications on old Siam or old Bangkok flood the market. The faster Bangkok moves into the future, the greater the appeal of neo-antiquarianism. People are conscious about recollecting the past, though they would not live in it. They want to collect it for their spiritual wealth, to make the flow of

---

[3] A "current" (กระแส), that is, in the sense of an electrical or river current.

life comprehensible" (Thongchai 1995: 117). This "flood" of stories and images, a flood that shows no sign of receding, amplifies the vividness of the landscape of loss.

There is also a parallel story: the decay of organic links to the past, a process accelerated by the deterioration and destruction of communities. Packaged, mass-produced stories and images have become an alternate source material to cobble together collective memory.

Even people living along the river sometimes expressed detachment from waterways. A man described a site upstream, then laughed when asked about the nearest pier. Where do I disembark? "I don't know", he said. "I go everywhere by motorcycle." When asked about waterways, people advised me to speak to the old people. In a narrow alley, just a few steps from the river, a woman said, "If you want to learn about these things, you have to talk to the old people." I asked if there were any old people in the alley. She replied, "They are all dead."

Gray clouds arrive, heat recedes, and now a cool wind blows along the tunnel-like pathway. We sit under plastic panels, protection from both sun and rain. My informant was born in this wooden hovel, next to Wat Kalayanamit, a large riverside Buddhist temple. We are speaking through the window. One of his front teeth is broken. "Thais like to live like this", he says, "along the waterways. It's cool at night. But we are also exposed to nature, including disasters. One cannot escape; one can only protect." There is an embankment nearby, but water came over it during the flood. Residents carried sandbags and piled them on top of the cement barrier. People worked together, shared resources, and this collective self-defense brought a sense of dignity. Members of one household expressed pride in the acquisition of a case of foreign, brand-name soda during the disaster. They sold the bottles to their neighbors. No one else had it.

People in the alley were aware of the class dimensions of risk and destruction. "The floods didn't affect the rich", said one man. Then he added, with an ambiguous smile, "This country doesn't develop." If it did develop, or so he implied, communities like this would also be protected. Around the same time, downstream on the opposite bank at the art gallery, near a number of imposing, top-tier hotels, the gallery owner said, "It won't flood here. You can be sure of it. This is an economic center—it can't flood. These big hotels won't accept it."

A bird cage hangs in front of the crude, wooden structure. Inside there are three calendars, each featuring the king's face. My informant inhales through his nose. He tells me about his youth: "I only went to school for three years. I was mischievous, always getting into trouble. I didn't want to study. I was stuck to my friends. My mother forced me to ordain as a monk, so I wore the yellow robe and lived in the temple, but when I got out, I returned to my mischief. The police arrested me because I was sniffing glue. Do you know about it?" He brings out a brown glass bottle. "It's this stuff." Now he works as a messenger for a shipping company. The exports are loaded onto ships at Klong Toey, a port-slum on the bank of the Chao Phraya.

A woman in her mid-thirties sits inside on the sunken floor. Her "grandparents"—this could also mean great-grandparents or ancestors—came from Ayutthaya, where they worked in fields and gardens. They decided to live in Bangkok, left their gardens behind, came downstream by boat, and stopped near a large temple at the river's edge. They became "boat people" (ชาวเรือ, people who live on boats), and their boat was tied, among others, to the bank in front of the temple, which in those days was surrounded by fields.[4] Now those fields lie beneath concrete and tar-sealed roads. Her grandparents made a living in Bangkok buying and selling vegetables and fermented fish, thereby becoming another small knot in a thread of river-based commerce. Their children were raised here at the edge of the Chao Phraya. She says her family has been here for a long time, and she does not want to leave. But she also notes the poor condition of her surroundings: "Nothing changes here. Things just deteriorate—like these houses."[5]

In the same alley, a man sits next to a pile of wood and a can of paint. He is shirtless and has a large magical seal tattooed on his back. He offers

[4] In this context, the expression "boat people" has no connection with refugees or people escaping by boat.

[5] Note the transition from boat people to village people (*chao baan*). Sombat Plainoi, in an autobiographical book titled *Born in a Boat*, describes his recollections of making such a transition, on the same river, when his family moved from a boat into a canal-side house. He writes, "Although I left life as a boat person and became a house/village person … my life remained amphibious, a life of both water and land" (Sombat 2010: 162).

me a cigarette. Prior to our first meeting, others in the alley had praised his abundance of experience. He makes toy swords, a craft passed on to him from his father. Next month there will be a festival at the temple. His daughter will work in a booth, and the swords will be for sale. He is 50 years old, attended school for four years, and can both read and write. We sit across from his open doorway, through which can be seen a dark, cluttered interior. His grandmother was born in this house. He makes little money from his craft, but emphasizes that not many people can make these swords anymore. "I don't want to see them disappear", he said. His craft is part of a small-scale culture of memory. It is a connective and generative practice. His craft keeps him and his family—more broadly even, this small community, of which he is an important part—bound to this place and its past. The swords are not likely to be in any tourist brochure or textbook of Thai culture. Nora, writing about France, claims that "true memory ... today subsists only in gestures and habits, unspoken craft traditions, intimate physical knowledge, ingrained reminiscences, and spontaneous reflexes" (1996: 8). The sword-maker's craft is part of this place. It maintains a bond; it shows that he and his family belong here. But this place is also endangered by social deterioration, corruption, and abandonment.

"Life was easier before, in the time of my grandparents", he said. "These days we work harder, but it's not enough." Notably, second- and third-generation Chinese had often said the opposite, emphasizing the struggles of previous generations. They had, in many cases, grown up with the memories—stories of immigration and toil—of stern, disciplinarian parents and grandparents. The sword-maker saw a connection between the difficult conditions of the present and the deterioration of social relations. Competition and the "mouth-stomach" problem (the struggle to fulfill basic needs) had led to social decay. "In the old days, the younger sibling always honored the older sibling. And people helped one another. If they had extra food, they shared it with their neighbors. Today, they won't share, even if the food will otherwise rot."

The river has also rotted. "When I was young, the river was still clean", he said. "It wasn't that long ago. There were large shrimp in the river. Fish were abundant. But now many varieties are gone. The fish seen today don't come from nature—they exist only because of merit-makers at riverside temples who throw bread and pellets into the water. We used to swim in the river. These days, if we swim in the river, we will itch all over. The water is full of waste and chemicals. It's very dirty. If we swim in the river, we will have to wash our skin. It can make us sick." The community was built by a stretch of river that later became, as Srisak Vallibhotama describes, "a river of two colors", a combination of "natural sugar-brown" and "dark-black rotten mud", the latter being waste "drained and pumped" into the water from factories along canals in Bangkok, and also from upstream industrial complexes, which have sprouted like "mushrooms" along the waterways in the provinces of Pathum Thani and Ayutthaya (Srisak 2017a: 148).

As the way of life has changed, as society has changed, the river has begun to die. Nearly everyone lamented the abandonment of the Chao Phraya, noting her color and uncleanliness.

The alley leads out to a concrete platform. The pier rolls in the sloshing water. A cement path skirts the river's edge. Fishermen gather nearby and prop poles against the rail. Scavengers armed with nets and hooks pass below in waste-laden canoes. At the mouth of the alley, a hand-written sign made of green plastic is fixed to a concrete pillar. It reads: "For the kingdom, restore the river! Bring the river back to life!" The sign connects this place with the fate of river and kingdom. It draws in the surrounding landscape; place and landscape are joined. The alley—tunnel-like, with its concrete wall, wooden hovels, and plastic panels—is an enclosed place, a bounded container. But it is also open, tied to pathways, including the kingdom-crossing river. The hand-written sign is an assertion of connection, a claim that "we" also belong to this kingdom—this is our river, and her decay is our own. It suggests a time of abundance before the river's decline. People in the community found that scrap of green plastic, thought of the river, and then fixed the sign to the pillar. It was one small act of remembering. Such acts of "remembering the present" (Fabian 1996) can make connections. Edward Casey writes, "[Memory] draws the world together, re-membering it and endowing it with a connectiveness and a significance it would otherwise lack" (1987: 313). The hand-written sign creates a connection between place and waterway, and it ties the alley to a large-scale imaginary of landscape.

Culture of Water

Peter Boomgaard writes, "The role of water in Southeast Asia has changed over the years, and it will no doubt change in the years to come.... A different 'water culture' is or has been emerging" (2007: 20). Let us consider this emergent culture of water in Bangkok.

Water is associated with coolness. Coolness is related with both comfort and a centered disposition. A person with a hot heart is dangerous; one with a cool heart is composed and graceful. A Buddhist monk should have a cool heart, and thus the cooling of the heart is an objective of monastic practice. In Kukrit's book *Many Lives*, the death of a well-regarded monk by drowning is not karmic retribution but rather a fitting passage to nirvana (2010: 62–3). During a rainstorm, a passenger ship sinks in the Chao Phraya, killing dozens. The monk is not reborn. His cool heart expires in cool water. The recent floods in Bangkok, by contrast, made people "boil" (เดือดร้อน). In the absence of such destruction, the characteristics of water are also the characteristics of an ideal Thai society. So long as society remains cold, void of conflict, happiness prevails. The king said he wanted Thais to be "cold and happy" (อยู่เย็นเป็นสุข).

One cannot speak Thai without speaking of water. Water has long been associated with abundance and goodness, and numerous artifacts of these associations are found in the Thai language. Perhaps these are contributions of river dwellers, a reflection of linguistic evolution in the water-bound mesh of Siam. But similar associations are also found in the harsh, arid lands of southern India (Pandian 2009), and there are significant cultural ties between these regions. In Thailand, "heart-water" (น้ำใจ) means generosity. The distribution of generosity is uneven, curiously mapped onto the rural-urban divide. The people of rural Thailand, they say, have more heart-water than those of the cities. Hearts in Bangkok have dried up, including the hearts of people who have migrated from up-country. New arrivals are derided as stupid, like draft animals, with "water buffalo" (ควาย) being an often-heard term of abuse. People from the rice fields, unfamiliar with urban life, are said to be easily deceived. But life in Bangkok—competitive, brutal, and corrupt—will change them. People said migrants to the cities become selfish: their hearts are desiccated. According to contemporary royal-state ideology, as expressed in the concept of "sufficiency economy", rural people are the nation's backbone. Authentic Thai life is sometimes imagined to reside in rural serenity. Yet for affluent city-dwellers, the rice farmers remain too vulgar to represent the nation, and for many Bangkok natives, rural life goes hand-in-hand with liquor, laziness, and coarse manners. High culture belongs to the cities.

The influx of migrants from beyond the central region into Bangkok is associated in discourse with the decline of a water-centered way of life. The people working in the water markets are said to be migrants from other regions, and this indicates a loss of authenticity. Now, people said, the water markets are merely tourist attractions. Water markets were once part of community life. Again people lamented the decay of culture, the loss of an ancient vitality. Many of the men who command the cross-river ferries are also from up-country. I wanted to meet and talk to them, but informants were doubtful. One said, "Those guys don't know anything. They aren't locals—they're from up-country. And mostly they are just drunkards."

Perhaps the drivers of long-tail boats would also be hired hands of up-country origin, or so I had thought. Some drivers had painted the word *prai* (ไพร่) on their boats—in blood-red letters visible from the riverbank. *Prai* is a "feudal" term suggesting servitude, a low-status commoner. In the past, it designated those subject to annual labor conscription (see Jit 1998; Akin 2017). Today, self-application of the term usually identifies one as a Red Shirt, most of whom are from up-country, especially the north and northeast. One day a man was standing at the pier, waving a Red Shirt flag, calling a driver back to the dock.

The long-tail boat is a Thai icon. A panel at the Royal Barge Museum in Bangkok explains that the long-tail is an example of "Thai intelligence", whereby an engine was applied to the rear of the "original raft-boat". The term *long-tail* refers to a steel shaft, at the end of which is a propeller. The driver steers the boat by manipulation of the shaft. It has a wide range of motion; the propeller can even be raised above the water. People said these drivers demonstrate the skill and cleverness of Thais. An old man, who had never driven a long-tail, performed an imitation, taking in his grip an imaginary metal shaft. "People of other nations cannot command the long-tail", he said. Others described the long-tail as a feat of distinctly Thai mechanical skill. These boats use engines adapted from on-road

Long-tail boat

vehicles, an index of national character: Thai people are clever with tools and machines, especially in adaptation to waterways.

The long-tail drivers in Bangkok are said to be men of Central Thailand, a region long integrated by the Chao Phraya River and her vast pulmonary system of anthropogenic canals. The profession is passed on from generation to generation, from father to son. The drivers mostly live along canals in Thonburi, where they tie their boats at night. "I always knew that I would drive the long-tail", one man said. "I will never leave this line of work." When told about my prior speculations, he said, "All of the drivers are locals—if not people of Bangkok, then people of the central region. None of us come from Isan. Outsiders don't come into this line of work."

Commuter routes persist, but here, on this stretch of the Chao Phraya, not many use the long-tails for day-to-day transportation. The drivers have created a niche in the tourist industry. Bundles of cash are counted on the table at night. This trans-generational trade ties the drivers to place and waterways. However, from another perspective, the drivers are outsiders: Reds in Yellow Bangkok—or if not Yellow, a city widely suspicious of Reds. Many observers have highlighted the rural-urban dynamics of the Red-Yellow conflict. Some point to its class dimensions: though concentrated up-country, in rural Thailand and lesser urban centers, the Red Shirts also include some of Bangkok's urban poor. Red Shirt intellectuals describe it as a conflict between old and new forms of capital (see Sucha n.d.). It is also a conflict over the monarchy, over the king's position in Thai society, a matter tied to dangerous questions of identity. Official institutions repeat over and over that Thai identity is based on three pillars: Nation, Religion, King. Meanwhile we stand at the edge of the river, in the twilight of the Ninth Reign, as "the ideological edifice of Thainess begins to crumble" (Streckfuss 2011: 3). The long-tail boat is unambiguously Thai, a reflection even of a uniquely Thai intelligence. The drivers are regional insiders, and yet the young man waves a dissident red flag, and his older sibling, arms covered in tattoos, declares himself, with a tone of bitterness, a servant in feudal Thailand. People often said, "The Red Shirts love Thaksin rather than the king", a grave reproach, essentially an accusation of treachery. Bangkok had become a city of vehemence, contempt, and fear, a city of anxiety, driven not only by past loss, but also impending loss and an uncertain future, gnawing the edge of a decaying present. Anna Tsing, in her ethnography of an "out-of-the-way place", describes a spatial imaginary in which "potency" is concentrated at the center (1993: 22). Thailand offers a strong parallel. Now, however, not only power but also uncertainty swirls in Bangkok, spreading steadily, inexorably, out into the provinces. Rama IX, the world's longest reigning monarch, receiving end-of-life care on the top floor of a riverside hospital, was known for hydrological wisdom. People knew the Ninth Reign would not last forever. Yet few spoke openly of death or the ensuing transition.

Time, Progress, and Ghosts

Time is unevenly distributed in the landscape. Modernity congeals in hotels, condominiums, shopping complexes, along certain roads that have "progressed". The river is also making progress. Downstream, in a more affluent community, I sat on a veranda overlooking the river, taping an interview with a wheelchair-bound woman. Nearby, an abandoned, ghost-haunted rice mill had recently been demolished to clear space for a resort hotel. "It makes our country more beautiful", she said. But in the alley, the story was different: "Look at those hotels along the river. We don't benefit from that. Just across the water, they're renovating the market. The old buildings are being torn down. An underground train station is under construction. We, the *chao baan* [people of the village or community], gain nothing." Progress, signified by concentrated wealth and such luxuries as air conditioning, sterility, and escalators, had not taken place in the alley.

Nothing changes. Things just deteriorate.

But so-called progress can also be destructive.

For some it means expulsion, a collective loss of place.

The rice mill was demolished, the ghosts evicted. This is part of the story of continuity, change, and loss in the landscape. Ghosts lurk along the waterways. The maternal river evokes a time when women were exalted for their ability to communicate with spirits. Across Southeast Asia, spirits controlled rain, lightning, earthquakes, and floods (Sujit 2016: 36). Buddhism, by contrast, elevated men, but animism was never vanquished. Even today, some spirits will only enter the bodies of women (ibid.: 43). Many informants, natives of the city as well as migrants from up-country, said that ghosts have an even stronger presence in rural Thailand. A woman from a village in the east, near Cambodia, said you can see them at night, dots of light flickering over the fields. Those are *pii krasue* (ผีกระสือ), a kind of female ghost known since ancient times. At close range, she appears as a floating, decapitated human head, with long hair and guts dangling. She eats infants, filth, frogs, and snakes. Another migrant to Bangkok, a man from the far north, explained that the presence of ghosts varies with time and place. Some are region-specific; some are from certain eras. "Ghosts have to exist", he said. "With people come ghosts. But in some places, you know for sure there are no ghosts, like Central World [a large shopping complex]. Ghosts stay in old places, places where people have lived and died."[6]

---

[6] Central World was burned in 2010 during a gigantic Red Shirt protest, which was dispersed by gunfire and ended in a massacre. A number of Red Shirts and others were shot and killed in the vicinity of Central World, but—in Bangkok, at least, if not in the outlying provinces, which remain Red Shirt strongholds—these killings have faded from public memory. The space is inhospitable to ghosts and memory alike.

House on the river at sunset

Places for ghosts are still found along the river. One evening a woman pointed to an abandoned, dilapidated, crumbling house, where she had seen a ghost. She often passed this house, and the ghost had appeared many times and tried to frighten her. Belief in ghosts is ubiquitous in Bangkok. All too often, late at night, a horrific chorus of howling dogs, a sign of unwholesome presence, could be heard in my alley. After a few months in Bangkok, I had nightmares about ghosts, so a friend gave me an amulet to keep in my room. It depicted the guardian figure of Vessavana, protector of Buddhism, while the back depicted the royal swan-headed barge. Others said ghosts do not intend to frighten us—ghosts want us to make merit for them, so they will be released from wandering between worlds. Some women adopt the wandering ghosts of children. Though invisible, the ghosts follow their adoptive mothers. One day an informant was watching a television show about a boy haunted by the ghost of his dead girlfriend, who had a terrible wound across her forehead from a fatal car accident. Many drivers hang flowers from rear-view mirrors, a tradition from the waterways, where Mae Ya Nang, a protective spirit, is honored by adorning the prows of boats with garlands. Bangkok is a city of spirit houses and shrines, where people make offerings to place-bound spirits. Mother Nak is honored and feared along the Canal of Phra Khanong. In the 19th century, she died in childbirth. Her husband was away, having been conscripted by the military. He returned home, not knowing she was dead, then ran away from her ghost. Forlorn and vengeful, she roamed the canal, terrorizing villagers, until a sorcerer (หมอผี) trapped her spirit in a jar and dropped it into the canal. Later, a fisherman unknowingly caught the jar in his net and released her spirit. Again she roamed the waterways. Her corpse was exhumed and a piece of bone cut from the skull. A monk made a belt buckle from the bone fragment, thereby restraining her spirit. But her story is remembered and her power persists. Mother Nak despises the military. Thus young men make offerings at her shrine to avoid conscription.

Anderson describes a shift in recent decades, the re-centering of Bangkok: "As late as 1960, Bangkok could still be described as the 'Venice of the East', a somnolent old-style royal harbour-city dominated by canals, temples, and palaces. Fifteen years later, many of the canals had been filled in to form roads and many of the temples had fallen into decay. The whole center of gravity of the capital had moved eastwards, away from the royal compounds and Chinese ghettos by the Chao Phraya river to a new cosmopolitan zone dominated visually and politically by vast office buildings, banks, hotels, and shopping plazas" (Anderson 1998: 143). The old aquatic artery ties together many old places. Ghosts proliferate there, in part because of accidents and suicides. Spirits, people say, sometimes drag victims into the depths. A man who worked part-time with a rescue unit said he sometimes removed corpses from the river. "The smell is terrible", he said. "But I'm used to it. Most people can't do this work. It's not just the smell—they're terrified of ghosts. But when I handle the bodies, I'm always respectful. I never step over a corpse. I've been doing this for more than 10 years, and not even once has a ghost come to haunt me."

A woman walked out of the next hovel. She had been listening to our conversation. "Do you want to go searching for corpses in the river with uncle?" she asked. "Are you scared?"

Eviction

The community in the alley was being evicted. "I'm not leaving", one man said. "Let them call the police. Let them arrest me, drag me out of my house." The community was built on temple property, a long-standing practice in traditional Siam. Srisak writes, "A temple is the social center of a community, and is necessary for the existence of a community" (2014: 7). The monks passed daily in the early morning through the alley—renunciants, depending on goodwill. The people gave them food, made donations, and received blessings. The abbot, however, would not appear. One day a man in the alley said, "The abbot is chasing us out."

"I've lived here my whole life", he said. "This is my temple. He has no right to chase us away. It was never in the constitution." The latter expression was surprising. Rarely did people in Bangkok talk about constitutional rights. Another man had said, "The constitution is not so important. It's just words, written by people." This resonates with an observation by David Streckfuss, who writes, "Constitutions [in Thailand] are suspect for they are mere words" (2011: 301). But this is arguably an over-generalization. Consider, for example, the October 1973 demonstrations, which opened with demands for a new constitution. Furthermore, when the constitution of 1997, known as "the people's constitution", was "torn up" after the 2006 military coup, it sparked widespread and tenacious outrage. Thai society is deeply divided over questions of power and legitimacy. The revolution of 1932 marked a transition from absolute monarchy toward democracy, but many see this as an incomplete process. In a sense, this is true on both sides of the Red-Yellow divide, with Red Shirts decrying feudalism and dictatorship, while Yellow Shirts argue that many Thais are still unfit for political participation, an argument with pre-1932 roots. Sondhi Limthongkul, a Yellow Shirt spokesman, said, "I do not agree with the Western way of electing representatives. As for people with voting rights, shouldn't they know about politics? And if they should not know, then why have politics? If you're going to be a doctor, you need to know about medicine. If you're going to work in mass media, you need to know various techniques. The matter is simple: some Thais are ready, some are not." Across the divide, Nattawut Saikua, secretary-general of the Red Shirts, emphasized deep continuity: "This is a conflict between two ideologies, which has persisted for a long time, ever since the change of government in 1932.... I am ready to drive the process of turning this country into a democracy, and making everyone accept, equally, the humanity of each person."[7] Many people are embittered by arbitrary power, which could be mitigated by a constitution, but because so many constitutions have been forcefully discarded, any promises of stability and protection are compromised. The constitution of 1997 (number 16) lasted nine years. Siam's second constitution, ratified on December 10, 1932, was the longest lasting: 13 years. Between 2006 and 2017, Thailand had five constitutions. Counting from the revolution, the military coup of September 19, 2006 was the 12th successful coup in Thailand.[8] A pattern can be discerned: power is seized, order overturned, the coup leaders grant themselves amnesty and request recognition from the king; the constitution is "torn up", nullified, and a new one is written.

"The previous abbot was very close to us", he said. "But this abbot, I've never seen anything like this. Even the monks scorn this abbot. He has power, but no moral authority." The man lit a cigarette, then continued, "This community used to be different. Now at the front of the temple it's quiet." I didn't understand. Why is it quiet? "Because there's nowhere to sit! The abbot removed the trees and benches. Listen. I'll give you another example. Look at this building." He pointed to a structure outside the concrete wall along the narrow alley. "Do you know why it's been left to decay? So he [the abbot] can tear it down. Our community used to gather there. We had events, celebrations. Now that door is locked. We haven't gone in there for years."

"This abbot has no vision", he said. "We have a good location, a well-established community. We have the river. Nearby there are two other communities, one Catholic, one Islamic. My daughter married a Muslim. There are three religions here. It's a very good location. You know what we should build? A water market! Then we, the people of the community [*chao baan*], would benefit. Do you see? Let me ask you: Would the people of the community benefit? Right. But this abbot has no vision. He'll demolish our houses and build a parking lot."

---

[7] The above quotes from Sondhi Limthongkul and Nattawut Saikua are from episodes of *Answering Questions* (ตอบโจทย์), which aired around 2011–12 on Thai PBS. At the time of writing, the episodes could easily be found online.

[8] For a summary of coups from the 1932 revolution onward, see Kasian (2007: 41).

He called to one of the children: "Bring me the photographs from last year's festival!" A moment later, the album appears. "Every year we bring the sacred statues out of the temple." The statues are loaded onto pickup trucks and carried through the surrounding streets. The people honor the statues by splashing them with water. "It's similar to New Year [Songkran]—but this is not New Year. This is a local community festival." It was reminiscent of an observation by the scholar Jan Assmann: "Festivals and rituals ensure the communication and continuance of the knowledge that gives the group its identity. Ritual repetition also consolidates the coherence of the group in time and space" (2011: 42). Without such coherence, a unique, place-bound collective memory faces annihilation. The album includes many photographs of three particular statues. One is a Buddha image; the other two are cast in the likenesses of previous abbots. One, he says, was the student of the other, a master of meditation and magical arts (เกจิอาจารย์). "And this is our previous abbot, who we all loved very much. The current abbot will not participate in our festivals. He will not come seeking alms. He thinks he's big. He thinks he's royalty." Pages flip, as a child leans over, intrigued. "We're going very deeply into things now", the man says. There are many photographs of performances, various displays of power. Here is a man with strings of firecrackers around his neck, popping and engulfing him in smoke. I gasp, much to the delight of the man and children. Here is another photograph, a child rolling in broken glass. And here is a picture of the man himself, kneeling, with his palms pressed together. He honors the statues—the Buddha and the previous abbots—and incants. In the next photograph, he takes a large knife in his hand, raises it, and then presses the blade into his tongue. Streams of blood run.

He repeated his observation of the abbot: a man with power, but no moral authority. The festival also entails displays of power, but of a different kind, unlike the power to chase and demolish. It is a power associated with place. In the photo album, the power performances are intermixed with images of the sacred statues. He honors the statues before cutting his tongue. These power-filled objects—living beings of a sort, entities of spirit inhabiting material—cannot be separated from this place. One photograph depicts the three statues side-by-side. Pages stop turning. "These", he says, "are the heart of the people [*chao baan*]." The people, that is, of this riverside community, in these deteriorating houses, on the property of this temple. In the annual festival, the people reassert their bond to the statues. The statues bind the people to this place.

Landscapes of Loss

Rivers are ideal for studies of continuity and change. Rivers flow, suggesting an endless flux, the cycles of birth and death, decay and renewal, and yet, for flesh-bound mortals, rivers seem everlasting. The Chao Phraya also evokes the momentum of industrial time, of profit-driven destruction and development, as skyscrapers rise along the banks, cast in relief by temples, ruins, and ramshackle communities. In *Chao Phraya River: Mother of Siam*, a history of the river as a cultural landscape, the authors, near the end, in a rather melancholic tone, write, "Given our country's direction of change, it appears that life will move further and further away from the river and canals. But no matter what, Thais cannot be separated from waterways. Thai lives are bound to waterways, from birth till death" (Sujit and Puwadon 1999: 131). This is another phrasing of the aforementioned paradox: Thais are becoming disconnected from waterways, and yet Thais are mortally bound to waterways. But note the profound contrast, for although the authors assert that Thais, collectively, nationally, will remain bound to waterways, many small-scale communities along the river are vulnerable, and many have already been destroyed.

Along the Chao Phraya River, loss, including death and a dying way of life, pervades the culture of memory. One could call it the melancholy of the landscape, but we need not assume that melancholia is merely a condition of pathological attachment to a lost object. Memory of the vanished and departed can also be a source of vitality. Rebecca Solnit writes, "Memory itself fades, and so memory is always ultimately about loss, a map of the interior border of a continually eroding territory" (2001: 194). Both map and territory alike are in states of decay. Memories, if pursued, lead us to a limit, a frayed edge beyond which lies the unrecoverable. But the Chao Phraya River, as a poetic landscape, continues to evoke loss—past, present, and impending. It is a haunted landscape, in which a great and perhaps even growing number of ghosts wander the river and canals, dwelling in shadows, depths, and resilient places.

Every landscape has a complex temporality, its own unique mesh of continuity and change. This is not only a matter of material, measurable fact, but also sensibility and recollection. Stories, images, and fragments of a withering way of life, both real and imagined, persist along the waterways as memories. Loss is part of what is remembered—charged with emotion, affect, power and possibility—and thus one might suggest this as a project for ethnographers: to study how loss lives in the collective memories of peoples, and the persistence of loss in landscapes.

The Chao Phraya River is also haunted by impending loss. Not only a turning-away, but forceful evictions. The sword-maker spoke of an abundant past, when society was less corrupt and the river was full of fish. Memory helped make sense of collective life. The story set a stark contrast with the present, in which the community's future was being violated by the abbot of their temple. And yet the collective heart was bound to this place. The people in the alley engaged the landscape, asserting their place within it. The river offered a broader story, a collection of narratives. It offered possibilities, such as the construction of a water market: a traditional mode of commerce could be adapted to the present. But the immediate circumstances were seen as abandonment and betrayal, an especially bitter form of loss. The people expressed commitment to the temple, even though the abbot planned to destroy their houses. These too are memory practices. The past, as a dynamic source, enables claims to place. Connections between place, river, and kingdom were forged through memory. Memory is a tool and building material—without memory, the houses would have collapsed long ago. Some have few other means of collective self-defense. And they know the dangers of both forgetting and being forgotten.

Chapter 3

Erasure

Upstream lies Ayutthaya, which was destroyed by the Burmese. Why did so many people bring this fact to attention? It was seemingly the first thing one should know about the Chao Phraya River. Ayutthaya, an ancient city-kingdom, was defeated in 1767 and is now remembered as "the old city", the former center of the Thai past and the predecessor to Bangkok. Since at least the mid-19th century, with the growth of royal antiquarianism, Siamese rulers have emphasized a connection with Ayutthaya. This story, with Bangkok as rightful successor to a fallen kingdom, is a key aspect of the national imagination. Bangkok, according to Srisak Vallibhotama, is really a "reconstruction" of Ayutthaya (2010: 117). This story of succession, however, is also tragic because the destruction of Ayutthaya—described, dramatized, and drilled, over and over, in a wide variety of media—was carried out by foreign invaders. Burma, an ancient enemy, brought the Age of Ayutthaya to a violent close.[1] Today, this national tragedy is central to the collectively remembered past of the river.

The riverine landscape is tangible and immediate, but also defined by collective memory. A provocative contrast can be drawn between two past events: the destruction of Ayutthaya (by Burma) and the destruction of Vientiane (by Siam). Vientiane, in my usage here, refers primarily to a Lao city-kingdom that was once in a subordinate, colonial relationship with Siam. As described below, it was destroyed by Siamese troops in the early 19th century. What does Vientiane have to do with the Chao Phraya? There is a crucial, often forgotten connection. After

[1] One might question the degree of destruction by Burma. Much of the demolition was actually carried out by the Siamese, who plundered the ruins for building materials (Peleggi 2007: 179; Wyatt 2003: 129).

each invasion of Vientiane, and especially after its ultimate destruction, much of the city-kingdom's population was transferred to and resettled in the basin of the Chao Phraya River. That is to say, this Lao population became part of the riverine landscape of Siam. Lao were among the builders of Bangkok—Lao war captives shoveled earth, constructed the city walls, built fortresses (Sujit 2005: 158), and also participated in the shaping of Bangkok's rural hinterland. But Vientiane's destruction has been mostly forgotten, erased from Thai collective memory, as have the stories of the Lao captives who were forcibly transferred to this same river basin.

In the decades after the fall of Ayutthaya, Vientiane was invaded by Siam at least three times. On each occasion, it was defeated and depopulated. These events precede the emergence of the nation-state of Laos, of which a reconstructed Vientiane is now the capital. In the aftermath of each Siamese victory, people of Vientiane, ethnically Lao, were removed from their homes and resettled south of the Mekong in territory that now belongs to Thailand. The first invasion was ordered by King Taksin, ruler of Thonburi, who is credited by post-revolution official history with re-consolidating the Thai nation after the defeat of Ayutthaya. Vientiane was crushed and "thoroughly looted. Its most sacred images, including the Emerald Buddha, were carried off to Bangkok, along with members of the royal family as hostages" (Stuart-Fox 1997: 14). The removal of the Emerald Buddha, as will be observed, is of great significance. At the end of Taksin's campaign, many of the war captives—"hundreds of Lao families"—were resettled in the basin of the Chao Phraya River (ibid.). Several decades later, during the Bangkok-centered reign of Rama III, Lao discontent rose in response to Siamese practices of tribute collection and labor conscription (Srisak 1990: 268). In accordance with standard Siamese practice, each conscripted body was tattooed (see Jit 1998: 163). King Anuvong of Vientiane invaded the plateau of Korat, now in northeastern Thailand, with intention to repatriate ethnic Lao. The campaign was unsuccessful and Vientiane was punished: in May of 1827, it was sacked, razed, and depopulated—and again, Lao were forcibly transferred to Siam (Stuart-Fox 1997: 15). But King Anuvong survived, fleeing briefly to Vietnam. In 1828 he returned to Vientiane. In retaliation, Siam again invaded. Keyes summarizes the

Statue of King Anuvong in Vientiane

outcome: "When the Lao were finally defeated, Rama III ordered the complete destruction of the city of Vientiane, the deportation of its population to the Central Plains [that is, along the Chao Phraya River], and the public ridiculing of Cao Anu [King Anuvong] and his family in Bangkok" (1967: 11). King Anuvong, subsequently a national hero in Laos, was put in a cage and soon died in captivity. Approximately 100,000 (Ong 2010: 170) to 150,000 (Baker and Pasuk 2009: 29) Lao were transferred to Siam. Vientiane was obliterated. According to the royal Siamese chronicles, the invading troops permitted nothing but "grass, water and the savage beasts to remain" (Ivarsson 2008: 28). Nearly four decades later, in 1867, French explorers, in the course of charting the Mekong, found the city ruined and desolate.

Today there are more Lao in Thailand than in Laos. Many are descended from war captives, but like other "Thais", few remember the destruction of Vientiane. As the historian Charnvit Kasetsiri has said, "Most of us [in Thailand] really don't know. We only know about the loss of Ayutthaya. We don't know about the loss … of Vientiane [among other city-kingdoms attacked and defeated by the Siamese]" (Charnvit 2008a: 84). Across the border, however, in Laos, a different culture of memory has been cultivated. A giant bronze statue of King Anuvong, the most prominent landmark of contemporary Vientiane, now gazes across the Mekong.[2]

Landscape Perspectives

Memory shapes, frames, and pervades landscape. Memory is not merely a record of events; it is part of culture, and the power dynamics of culture impact what is and is not remembered. Memory may include events that one did not experience directly. Memories of this sort often belong to a group; it is not "my" past, but "our" past, the past of a collective. Shared tragedies or triumphs, real or imagined, are an important aspect of collective self-definition. No one alive today witnessed the destruction of Ayutthaya, but Thais are obligated to remember. The story carries a moral message. Children are taught that Ayutthaya was defeated not only because of external aggression, but also internal disharmony. This pattern of memory reflects a pattern of domination in society. It reflects only one of many possible national imaginaries.

Memory is shaped by nation-building, but nation-building is an ongoing process. In recent years, there have been increasing demands in Thailand for a remolded culture of memory. A comparison between these two events, one remembered, one forgotten, suggests that the nation could be imagined in other ways, for the landscape of the Chao Phraya River, the center of Siam and birthplace of the Thai nation, has been shaped by many different peoples.

The royal barge procession in Bangkok is a cyclical event, a royal-state ceremony that maintains, as one mechanism among others, the connection between Bangkok and Ayutthaya. In the pages ahead, I describe two of these events: one practice run, followed by the official procession. However, these events are interpreted through a much broader context,

---

[2] The statue of King Anuvong was unveiled in 2010. For a discussion of its symbolism, see King (2017: 81–2).

including fieldwork during 2012 and 2013. This preceded the seizure of power by the Thai military in May 2014 (a return to dictatorship), as well as the death of Rama IX on October 13, 2016. The barges, sparkling gold, copies of vessels from the Age of Ayutthaya, serve as a reminder of a connection between the present and a particular past. That past belongs—officially, at least—to the entire nation, as well as to the landscape of the Chao Phraya River.

J.B. Jackson writes, "[A] landscape … is simply the by-product of people working and living" (1984: 12). This is a useful point of orientation, but to understand the Chao Phraya, we also need to see the landscape as the product of a hierarchical culture of memory. Furthermore, it is crucial to examine the expressions of the landscape. Keith Basso writes, "Geographical landscapes are never culturally vacant. The ethnographic challenge is to fathom what it is that a particular landscape, filled to brimming with past and present significance, can be called upon to 'say', and what, through saying, it can be called upon to 'do'" (1996: 75). In the royal barge procession, the landscape speaks, but also remains silent. As a landscape event, the procession has a compelling immediacy, dramatizing royal benevolence, national continuity, and military power.

This ethnographic material enables a reconsideration of two, often mutually exclusive, approaches in landscape studies. The first can be called "experience-near"; the second can be called "representation-centered". In an experience-near approach, one describes the landscape from within. One describes movement, perception, emotional and sensory engagement with the landscape (see Basso 1996; Desjarlais 1997; Feld 2005; Jackson 1995; Tilley 2008; Tuan 1977). Some aspects of the cultural life of landscapes can only be captured by an experience-near approach. Tim Ingold, an anthropologist who draws from phenomenology, provides a powerful model for thinking about the experience of landscape, which he calls a "dwelling perspective" (1993, 2000). At the same time, he opposes any interpretive strategy that begins with "an initial separation between human persons, as meaning-makers, and the physical environment as raw material for construction" (Ingold 2000: 55). By contrast, in a representation-centered approach (see Cosgrove 1998; Duncan 1990; Kabir 2009; Mitchell 1994), one focuses on images of landscape. How is landscape depicted? What is included or excluded? Such an approach entails a study of spatial narratives, the storytelling of landscape images. My aim is to build a bridge between these two approaches, combining a descriptive, engaged, experience-near approach with a critical analysis of the power dynamics of remembering and forgetting.

Look at the landscape. Consider not only what appears, but also what can no longer be seen. Robert Desjarlais writes, "Many 'experience-near' approaches are bereft of serious analyses of the political and economic forces that contribute to the apparent reality or nearness of experience. Anthropology is in dire need of theoretical frames that link the phenomenal and political" (1997: 25). The destruction of "our Ayutthaya" (Srisak 2010), is one of those apparent realities. Here both will be considered—the apparent and non-apparent, as well as the ways that relations of power contribute to both nearness and distance. Standing by the river's edge, nearly anyone can tell you: upstream lies Ayutthaya. Few, however, remember Vientiane. This is not because too much time has passed. The defeat of Ayutthaya came first, decades earlier. Nor is it because of the city's physical location. The people of Vientiane, as well as the Emerald Buddha, Thailand's most sacred object, were transferred to this same landscape. But the stories of Vientiane—even those recorded by the scribes of the victors—did not fit within the narrow, state-supported, and evidently expiring national imaginary created in Bangkok.

A poem from the 19th century, said to be written during the Fourth Reign, describes the hardships of war captives in Bangkok. Known as the "Lao Phaen" (ลาวแพน), it is written in Thai interspersed with Lao. The poem opens with an invitation: "Come, I'll tell you a story of Lao, who play sweet melodies on the khaen." The storyteller then describes loss of family and homeland, followed by a life of hard labor and punishment: "Shackled and whipped by Thais, our backs and shoulders are cut and scarred". A life of begging and devastating poverty, "like having fallen into hell". And in one vivid scene, the poem describes hungry captives searching amid rain and darkness in the royal cremation field (ทุ่งพระเมรุ), now a large, manicured park by the river:

By night we take our torches and baskets to the cremation field
mud stained and rotten stench
catching frogs, crabs, and white-bellied mice
taking everything
boiling it and bolting it down with booze[3]

Outsiders Within

The contrast between the two events—one remembered, one forgotten—is especially striking in relation to ethnic composition in contemporary Thailand. Not only are there more Lao in Thailand than in Laos, but Lao may outnumber non-Lao in Thailand itself (Streckfuss 2012: 312). Ethnic categories are a complicated matter, but it is clear that numerous people in Thailand self-identify as Lao and speak a variant of the Lao language. Notably, at the time of the 1932 revolution, the majority of "citizens" (พลเมือง) spoke, not Thai, but rather the language of Isan (Nidhi 2014b: 136). People of Bangkok and the surrounding region, provide a simple way to define Lao as an ethnic group: "Natives of Central Thailand use the word *Lao* to describe anyone who eats sticky rice", the staple food of Thailand's northern and northeastern regions (Ong 2010: 357). Or as an informant from the northeast once said, "Of course I eat sticky rice—I'm Lao."

Vientiane's destruction is a formative moment in a centuries-long pattern of ethnic inequality. Sujit Wongthes, a descendant of Lao war captives, writes, "Lao have long been subordinated for economic and political reasons, but the most important event was the war with King Anuvong ... which gave rise to a contemptuous perspective and the disparagement of Lao" (1987: 3). Today, Lao are among Thailand's "others within" (Thongchai 2000) and Isan remains the poorest region of the country (Kermel-Torrès 2004: 175). In the 19th century, King Mongkut said, "Lao are servants of Thai. Thai have never been servants of Lao" (Sujit 1987: 3). Decades later, during the dictatorship of Field

[3] I have translated from Sujit (2005:170–1) and have also referred to a recording of the same author reading the poem. A friend from northeastern Thailand provided helpful comments on some of the Lao expressions.

Marshal Pibulsongkram, efforts were made to resignify the Lao of the north and northeast, to make them Thai. The government issued to the masses a mandate to stop describing the people of these regions as Lao, to call them Thai instead. A song titled "Land of Isan" (แดนอีสาน) from a government-sponsored drama about the northeast commanded the listener: "Remember, people from Isan are Thai." But if one watches contemporary Thai television dramas, one observes again and again: the character from Isan is the servant. Moreover, the Lao language is mocked on television (on variety shows, for example) and often disdained in Bangkok (Kakizaki 2014: 279).

When migrants from Isan were asked if they considered themselves Thai, the answers were always affirmative. However, in everyday life, people from Isan also make explicit comparisons between Thais and themselves. For instance, one day while sitting in the park with northeastern friends, one of them noted that "the fermented fish [*bpla raa*] that Isan people eat is different from the fermented fish that Thai people eat". Furthermore, many people from Isan still describe themselves as Lao. On that same day in the park, while walking across the grass, one of them said jokingly, "The Lao are migrating!" The word translated here as "migrating" (อพยพ) carries an implication of hardship, more so than the English expression. It implies pulling up roots, migrating under difficult circumstances. A suitable example would be forced transfer from Vientiane. This playful interjection reflects an enduring theme of hardship in the lives of Lao in Thailand.

Some Thais use the word Lao abusively, to "disparage" (เหยียดหยาม), as informants said, people of the north and northeast. Sujit writes, "No matter if one is northern Lao from Lanna or northeastern Lao from Isan—Lao are all similarly disparaged (1987: 3). One evening, while sitting at a restaurant in Silom, a Thai woman from Bangkok suddenly exclaimed, "Don't act like a Lao!" I asked what she meant. She said, "Like stupid people from the countryside."

Two wrecked city-kingdoms—one remembered, one forgotten. This is not altogether a matter of contested memory. In some quarters the memory of Ayutthaya is contested, but in the case of Vientiane, there seems to be little or nothing to contest. It is an absence. Minimal space is available for dispute, though this may be changing. Aleida Assmann, a theorist of memory, provides two useful and appropriate concepts, canon and archive: "I … refer to the actively circulated memory that keeps the past present as the *canon* and the passively stored memory that preserves the past past [*sic*] as the *archive*" (2011: 335). The other side of this metaphor is that which is altogether forgotten and irrecoverable. Total recall is an impossible project. Thus, the canon and archive refer to the marginal mass, so to speak, that has been preserved. The metaphor of the archive is rather problematic. At the risk of generalization, archives have keepers and organizers. Materials are gathered, filed, boxed, indexed, and often kept in climate-controlled conditions. However, much of Thai society's "stored memory", passive or otherwise, is too messy and dispersed to fit this metaphor, and some of it is outdoors, rotting under the tropical sun.[4] But the archival metaphor could be applied within limits, insofar as there are recoverable traces. The erasure is not absolute. Traces persist, though hidden, obscured, or otherwise out of sight.

Canonization implies a conscious process of selection. Collective memory is not always so rigorously shaped, but in Thailand, the fall of Ayutthaya is a powerful example, a past event made present, actively circulated, that has been canonized as national tragedy: a disaster made sacrosanct. Notably, the destruction of Vientiane was recorded—vividly, even celebrated—in the royal chronicles. The national story, by contrast, was arranged later, in a different context. Canonization, implicit or explicit—a political process modulated by power dynamics—is a basic tool of nation-building, and also guides experiences of landscape.

This pattern of memory crosses ethnic lines. Children of all regions are taught about the great city of Ayutthaya and its tragic fall, but this reflects a Thai nation imagined from Bangkok. Nonetheless, it is also clear, and increasingly so, that many among Thailand's Lao-descended population are restless, growing intolerant of Bangkok's scorn and neglect.

Consider again recent socio-political upheavals in Thailand. The Red Shirts, a pro-Thaksin, anti-coup movement, emerged in the run-up to

---

[4] For a discussion of metaphors in the conceptualization of memory, see *Metaphors of Memory* (Draaisma 2000). See also the analysis of archival metaphors in *Forgetting* (Draaisma 2015: 180).

the 2006 military coup.[5] As discussed in the previous chapter, most Red Shirts are from outside Central Thailand, especially from the north and northeast. Migrants to Bangkok, mostly from Isan—still, in most cases, very much connected to their places of origin—often tell the same story: when Thaksin was in power, life in the village improved. It was tangible. New roads. Vehicles. Sturdier houses. Satellite dishes. Change was visible in the landscape. Many said, "Back home, everyone is a Red Shirt." The spatial dimensions of the conflict are widely recognized; the Red Shirts draw membership primarily from an up-country base, including a large number of people from rural communities. But perhaps we should also consider the conflict's ethnic dimensions, especially since most Red Shirts, or so the evidence suggests, are people of Lao descent. The Red shirts refer to themselves as *prai*, a word that previously referred to those subject to annual labor conscription. This word has a strong "feudal" taint, suggesting the field-power system and monarchy. It implies systematic exploitation and the persistence of an antiquated structure of power. The Red Shirts emerged in opposition to the Yellow Shirts, a Bangkok-centered, outspokenly royalist, anti-Thaksin movement that has openly advocated seizures of power by the military. The Yellow Shirts have often spoken in the name of "Thai" or the "Thai nation", a tactic implying that the Red Shirt opposition is non- or anti-national, an intolerable alien element in Thai society.

Glory and Collapse

Bangkok is usually seen as the successor to Ayutthaya, but I avoid describing it as a "reconstruction". The belief that Bangkok is or was such a reconstruction, in conformity with contemporary royal-state myths, is widespread in Thai studies. In the late 18th century, Rama I, initiator of the current age, called his city Krung-Rattana-Kosin-In-Ayodhya, which can be translated as "Ayodhya, the Great City of the Jewel of Indra". The last four words refer to the Emerald Buddha,

[5] Thaksin [ทักษิณ] is the former prime minister, not to be confused with King Taksin [ตากสิน] of Thonburi. The names look similar in Roman characters, but less so in Thai. They are also pronounced differently.

captured from Vientiane by the general who later became Rama I. One can also hear echoes of an ancient city: Ayodhya (อโยธยา), originating in the Dvaravati period (Srisak 2010: 22), was built at the confluence of the Pa Sak and Chao Phraya, then later absorbed into the city-kingdom of Ayutthaya (อยุธยา). The names are closely related, traceable etymologically to the mythic city of Prince Rama. Furthermore, the name Krungthep, as Bangkok is generally known in Thailand, was used centuries ago to refer to Ayutthaya, the original name of which was Krungthep Maha Nakhon Bwon Thawarawadi Si Ayutthaya, the center of the name being Thawarawadi, but commoners preferred to call it Krungthep (Jit 2021: 135). This was an ancient practice: the names of new cities often incorporated older place-names (ibid.: 115). One can easily find a semantic connection between Bangkok and Ayutthaya. This might seem to suggest reconstruction, but one should also consider the numerous deviations. First, unlike Ayutthaya, Bangkok is identified more with Indra than Rama (Chatri 2015: 68–9). Thus Indra, mounted on an elephant, appears on the seal of Bangkok. And although some place-names from Ayutthaya were borrowed in early Bangkok, this point is sometimes overstated.[6] Most place-names, including within the royal compound, were not borrowed from Ayutthaya. Further, although scholars have often emphasized that Rattanakosin Island was a physical reproduction of Ayutthaya, a comparison of same-scale maps shows that the island of Ayutthaya is of a different shape and at least twice as large.[7] And although one could find similarities or emphasize shared principles, the layout and orientation of the Rattanakosin complex was different. There are many reasons to be skeptical of expressions like "reconstruction", "reproduction", and "resurrection".

---

[6] One example is the Maha Nak Canal, most likely named after a canal in Ayutthaya (see Chapter 4).

[7] Michael Herzfeld emphasizes similitude: he writes, "The relationship between the Rattanakosin city plan and that of Ayutthaya materializes as urban space the logic of the *moeang* as an infinitely reproducible moral community" (2016: 83). He also refers to the "reproduction of the walled ground plan of Ayutthaya" (ibid.: 203). Similarly, Claudio Sopranzetti writes of "radical topographic and architectonic interventions to mimic the previous capital" (2017: 39) and refers to the "structure of the city inspired by Ayutthaya" (ibid.: 46).

The builders of these cities were not only driven by cosmic ideologies, they were also sensitive to the immediate topography. Ayutthaya was built at the confluence of three rivers, whereas Bangkok was built along a single river. Moreover, both cities were and are products of gradual, organic development. Also, it is questionable to identify Bangkok of the early Chakri period exclusively with the compound now known as Rattanakosin Island. Sujit Wongthes emphasizes that after the overthrow of King Taksin, a new center was built *not across from* but *within* the fabric of what was previously known as Thonburi. Bangkok, like Thonburi, is a "split-breast city" (เมืองอกแตก). That is, split by the Chao Phraya River. In other words, it is fundamentally the same city, but expanded and re-centered (Sujit 2005: 111). Srisak Vallibhotama writes, "When Rama I ascended the throne, he proceeded with the *expansion of Thonburi* on the eastern bank of the shortcut canal, which had already become the Chao Phraya River" (2017b: 290, my emphasis). In the Age of Thonburi, the primary royal compound was on the west bank; in the Age of Bangkok, it is on the east bank. But in both ages, the rulers oversaw construction and canalization on both sides of the river. Some of the canals incorporated by the Rattanakosin complex were dug in the previous age, under the command of King Taksin, including the canal that, after the king's execution and the re-centering of power, closed the first aquatic ring around the new palace—a canal now called Khlong Ku Muang Doem (Sujit 2005: 78–9). Furthermore, in the early decades of the Chakri dynasty, even after the relocation of the palace, many nobles, servants of the royal state, and others still lived on the west bank of the Chao Phraya.

Chatri Prakitnonthakan, an architectural historian, has also opened this question. At the beginning of his book, he writes, "We have often heard that in the Age of Rattanakosin [or the Age of Bangkok] the primary ideal was to restore or copy the qualities of Ayutthaya" (Chatri 2015: 3). He then dismantles this proposition, page after page, in great detail, examining innovations in architectural form, especially in temples built or renovated during the reign of Rama I. Other decisive deviations from Ayutthaya include the exaltation of the Emerald Buddha and the new king's identification with Indra. According to Chatri, "The collapse of the kingdom of Ayutthaya gave rise to fear among the Siamese ruling class, because it was not only a material loss—it was also the collapse of the state ideology, and the failure of the systems of administration, politics, belief, and values" (ibid.: 88). In other words, it was not desirable to resurrect a failed city-kingdom. Thus the ruling class was compelled to build anew. Moreover, Rama I, formerly a military general, was not royalty by birth. A king like this had never arisen in the Age of Ayutthaya, thus presenting a unique problem for the establishment of royal legitimacy. Chatri's unusual and provocative suggestion is worth serious consideration: "The essence of Rattanakosin was the creation of a new ideal, rather than the replication of the old" (ibid.).

Remembering the Enemy

The past of the Lao, an internal other—the servant of Thai—has been erased, but Burma, the external other and destroyer of the old city, must always be remembered. Once, while sitting in a friend's house, a woman in her mid-twenties, a graduate from Silpakorn, a fine arts university in Bangkok, observed, "Usually when people talk about [Thai] history, they talk about the wars with Burma." These wars, the centerpiece of national history as taught in public schools, culminate in the destruction of Ayutthaya. Burma burns the city and scatters its people, now all-too-often imagined as homogeneously Thai. The story carries a key message: Ayutthaya was lost because Thais fell into internal conflict. At the same time, the call for internal harmony is packaged with contempt for the external enemy. This problem is gaining recognition. A panel in the Museum Siam, for instance, encourages visitors to see the wars as between kings, not peoples. Some university-educated informants expressed concern over this issue. A graduate from Thammasat University complained about a serialized drama currently playing on television about King Naresuan, one of the most revered kings of Ayutthaya. "This is very bad", she said. "When Thai people watch this, they will hate the Burmese." Ayutthaya was defeated by Burma twice, first in 1569 and then in 1767. Following the first loss and period of vassalage, according to semi-legendary accounts, King Naresuan declared Thai independence, drove out the Burmese, and, at the peak of subsequent war, killed the crown prince of Burma in an elephant battle.

The drama aired during a massive state-and-media campaign to prepare Thais for the creation of the ASEAN Economic Community (AEC). The campaign appeared to entail an increasing acknowledgment of Thai prejudice against neighboring countries. Programs aired daily, including documentaries about the cultures of other countries in the Association of Southeast Asian Nations (ASEAN). This, informants said, was new. It will be interesting to observe how the AEC, which officially opened in 2015, will impact perceptions of neighboring countries in the years ahead. Will the AEC, over time, reorient the Thai landscape? How will Thais see themselves and their neighbors as Thailand becomes—or rather, begins to be perceived as—a part of Southeast Asia? During fieldwork, opinions regarding Burmese were overwhelmingly negative. Informants mocked the accents of Burmese migrants and their failure to "speak clearly". Burmese were derided for failure to understand the Thai language. A Thai-born Chinese teacher at an international school in Bangkok said that Burmese students are bullied by Thais. A small-business owner said, "The Burmese are vicious! I would never work with a Burmese." Some said that media coverage made them and others ill-disposed to the Burmese: the Burmese are drug traffickers. Or the Burmese come to work as servants in Thailand, kill their masters, rob them, and return to Burma. The collapse of Ayutthaya, framed as a national tragedy, sets the stage for these prejudices. A man said that, after ravaging the city, the Burmese carted away gold to build temples in their own country. Books for children, as I found in a public library, depicted anger as the natural and proper response of a Thai child who learns about the fall of the old city. As one historian explains, "Thais have been instilled with hatred for the Burmese, who are seen as invaders. When Burma is spoken of, Thais imagine men in sarongs with turbans and swords, chasing and killing Thais" (Sunait 2004: 27).

How does politically charged memory shape perceptions of landscape? Here the connectivity of landscape glows and crackles like a wire, surging with national ideologies. Looking at the Chao Phraya and feeling the wind blowing from the north easily summons memories of enmity, but few recall the Lao war captives who were transplanted to this same river basin.

Royal Barges

In the year prior to my fieldwork, the royal barge procession was canceled during the floods. Under ideal circumstances it would be an annual event. It goes hand-in-hand with the king's annual distribution of robes to Buddhist monasteries, a form of merit-making. It is an expression of generosity, potency, and also a powerful, tangible reinforcement of royal-national history, a stark, theatrical contrast to extractive models of center-periphery relations—the center gives. The vessels are stored and maintained in dry docks at the Royal Barge Museum, a warehouse-like structure near the edge of the Chao Phraya River in Bangkok.[8] To approach on foot in the early afternoon takes one through a dense residential area, a nest of winding alleys, footpaths over canals, and clothes drying on the lines, and then the river and warehouse appear. Over and over, people emphasized, reminded me, that the barges were copied from Ayutthaya-era originals. Each barge features a large, elaborately carved prow in the form of a Brahmanic deity, icons of the ancient court culture of Ayutthaya. In full-scale processions, the king occupies the swan headed barge, the swan being the vehicle of Brahma, deity of creation. Nagas, mythical serpents associated with water, fertility, and protection, are coiled around the prows. The barges are often thought to be based on warships—nowadays they are commanded by soldiers. But according to a detailed study, such vessels were not traditionally used in battle. They are likely descended from sacred vessels, images of which adorn ancient bronze kettle-drums. Such vessels were used ceremonially to chase away floodwater at the end of the rainy season (Sujit 2019).

The words of Rama IX are precise: "Every brick is valuable. Every brick should be preserved. [Because] if we did not have Sukhothai, Ayutthaya, and Bangkok, Thailand [ประเทศไทย] would be meaningless" (Wira 2008: 99).[9] An emphasis on centers, and linkage between centers,

---

8 The museum is at the mouth of Bangkok Noi, a canal that splits off from the Chao Phraya River. Bangkok Noi is a vestige of the river's original course. The river was long ago rerouted by digging a shortcut canal (คลองลัด).

9 On this quote, a former minister of education offers the following commentary, which resonates strongly with Chapter 5 ahead: "When one hears these words, one is deeply moved by royal grace—these words of caution to Thais who care more for material development than the development of the heart-spirit" (Wira 2008: 99).

Path to the Royal Barge Museum

One of the royal barges—the prow depicts Vishnu and Garuda

is found across the lowlands of Southeast Asia (Wolters 1982). Anderson, for instance, observes that "in the historical tradition [of Java] the names of empires and kingdoms are those of the capital cities" (1990: 41). This is also the case today in Thailand, where official history is periodized as a succession of capital cities, and the current age is the Age of Bangkok (*samai krungthep*). Javanese rulers often sought to make connections to the "residues of previous centers" of power (Anderson 1990: 39). A parallel can be found in Bangkok, especially from the mid-19th century, when the Siamese rulers demonstrated an emerging interest in ruined cities. However, in the early Bangkok period, long before discourses of preservation, the Siamese did not preserve Ayutthaya. To the contrary, they dismantled the remains. In the 18th and 19th centuries, construction in Bangkok utilized materials plundered from Ayutthaya, including "thousands of boatloads of bricks" (Wyatt 2003: 129). This seems to reflect a mundane need for building material, rather than a spiritual connection between the cities. In the process of establishing a royal dynasty and consolidating power, Rama I borrowed, or revived, some elements of the court culture of Ayutthaya, thereby initiating a linkage between the cities. Decades later, however, in a new political context, this connection was further emphasized. Contact with powerful outsiders urged a refinement of storytelling: the story of the royal polity, its origins, terrain, and evolution. Siam and the royal rulers needed a biographical account.

The age of Thonburi ended with the execution of King Taksin. The new king, Rama I, formerly the foremost general of King Taksin, organized the construction of a fortified complex of temples and a new palace on the east bank of the river. The city was re-centered and expanded, under protection of the Emerald Buddha, marking the initiation of a new age. According to the royal chronicles of Thonburi, as revised in the Age of Bangkok and printed in Thai by the Christian missionary Dr Bradley, King Taksin had declared himself a Stream Enterer—one who has attained the first stage of enlightenment (Nidhi 1995: 94–130). He thus demanded that a group of monks, including the Supreme Patriarch, prostrate before him. When the monks refused, the king had them whipped. Following this event, the king's ministers issued a series of accusations, calling him a "thorn in the kingdom". The account ends with the decapitation of King Taksin in front of the Vichai Prasit Fortress, a compound by the Chao Phraya River.

King Taksin had allegedly gone insane and ceased to be a righteous king. Nidhi Eoseewong, examining the case in depth, argues that it is extremely difficult to verify, or deny with certainty, the allegations of insanity, but it is clear that the story of Taksin has been used as a political instrument (1995: 98, 115). Note that the manner of execution described above deviates from tradition, whereby fallen kings were honorably dispatched. Traditionally, such a king would be hooded with velvet and struck in the nape with a sandalwood club. Although some scholars claim that the king was executed in the traditional way (Wyatt 2003:128), Nidhi argues it is more likely that King Taksin "was decapitated like a commoner" (1995: 99–101). King Taksin has a complex legacy, as both a savior of the nation, who reunited Thai people after the fall of Ayutthaya, and as a dethroned ruler.[10] Prior to the Siamese Revolution of 1932, his official legacy was rather negative. His more heroic legacy is a product of post-1932 re-evaluations of the national past. The construction of a statue of King Taksin was proposed shortly after the revolution. The statue now towers over Wongwian Yai, a traffic circle west of the river.

The demise of King Taksin marks a rupture, sometimes alluded to evasively. His successor, Rama I, the founder of the Chakri dynasty, was not of royal descent. Some of the Red Shirt long-tail drivers wore amulets with King Taksin's image. One of the drivers said that he especially admired King Taksin. To illustrate the king's cleverness, he told a story of how the king once evaded his enemies by overturning and hiding beneath a boat on the Chao Phraya River. Since King Taksin has been characterized as both a hero and villain, one can praise him openly, but his legacy can also challenge the existing order. Away from the ears of authority, some people question the formal accounts of the king's deviance and madness. When asked about the king's demise, the long-tail driver said, "Well, there are competing stories."

Prior to the official procession of the royal barges, there were many practice runs. Crowds gathered at the banks to observe. A middle-aged

[10] King Taksin's legacy could be much further complicated by not only the 18th-century invasion of Vientiane, but also his role in subjugating the north, bringing Chiang Mai and Lampang under Siamese control (see King 2017: 38).

man from the Thai navy said that when people hear the melody, rolling over the water and banks, that accompanies the barges, their hair stands on end. He added, "They feel at peace, calm and quiet." People are encouraged to visit the river and observe. Two northeastern informants, self-described Lao, wanted to watch the procession, and so I went to meet them. Most observers of this event must find a passage through the city. There is a powerful contrast between the barge procession and ordinary, frenetic city-life.

I wait in a bus shelter in the noise-filled core of Bangkok. The bus arrives and I am fortunate to find a seat. We pass a kaleidoscope of commerce and infrastructure. Cafes, health spas, an Indian grocery. We approach railroad tracks. Clouds gather in the sky. Pools of rainwater rest between the trestles. The bus stops under the shade of a bridge. Traffic lurches forward. Above, on a footpath to our right, people pass. A skytrain station is nearby, drivers stab the horns, a construction site appears. Clouds clear and the sky returns to blue. Sunlight reflects from the glassy surface of a skyscraper. A motorcycle roars and slices through traffic. We approach the Erawan shrine, with its mounds of marigolds and veils of incense smoke. And now, Siam Square, the pinnacle of modern shopping and high-society youth culture. The bus rattles. Its hydraulic doors flap open, then heave shut. The driver cranks the wheel, shade falls away, and the sun begins to bake my arms. Bright light reflects from the page. Noise: everything is loud. A pink and blue three-wheeled vehicle—the *tuk-tuk*, an icon of Bangkok—speeds unwitting tourists to a jewelry shop. Again, a construction site: an embryonic inner-city train station. We turn into Chinatown and are confronted by a massive arch, a monument to the king's completion of six 12-year cycles. Yellow banners hang overhead announcing the vegetarian festival. Shops advertise shark-fin soup, popular among affluent Chinese for its medicinal properties. Pawn shops. Gold. Porcelain. Beckoning cats. Hardware stores. Air-conditioning units, wires, gray concrete, and chipped white paint. Black plastic bags, stuffed to capacity, are strapped to motorcycles with elastic cables. We hear saw blades and jackhammers. White walls rise, enclosing the Grand Palace and the sanctuary of the Emerald Buddha. The man in the next seat removes his hat, presses his hands together and lowers his head, honoring palace and sanctuary.

I exit the bus at a small riverside park. It has a green lawn in the center, some trees, but mostly it is concrete with minimal refuge from the sun. The Temple of Dawn, with its iconic gray spires, lies in view across the river. Others are waiting, but the crowd is not oppressive. This is a practice run; no royal figures will appear. Two informants, now friends, women from the northeast, mother and daughter, ethnic Lao, have already arrived and sit by a tree under a hand-held purple umbrella. We sit together on the concrete bench. The younger one, Fon, is in her late twenties, a university graduate who works as a nurse. Her mother, more at ease speaking Isan, a variant of Lao, rarely says more than a few words in Thai. Their home province lies on the border between Thailand and Laos, along the Mekong. They live in Bangkok, but Isan is home. Fon lives in a building behind the hospital, sharing a room with three other nurses. Her mother lives near a bridge that crosses the Chao Phraya River. Today is a day off, and on such days, mother and daughter are almost always together. As we sit, they exchange words in Lao.

The crowds are thickening. People line both banks of the Chao Phraya. The river is calm, her surface barely disrupted. Usually one sees express boats, waste collectors, long-tails, and lumbering black barges full of sand and soil. Now only a navy patrol boat passes.

Will the king participate next month in the full-scale procession? Rumors circulate. Expression concerning the monarchy has been restrained and directed for decades, so it is not easily discerned what people think about the institution. On the surface, Rama IX was surrounded by a public culture of adoration. The process of creating that elevated, even magical, persona has been described as "redivinization" (Jackson 2010: 32). For the devoted, it would seem, to see the king is highly auspicious. I better understood this after a chance sighting in Thonburi, just a few blocks from the river. I was on foot. A police officer ordered me to sit on the ground.[11] Shortly thereafter, the king's ivory-colored vehicle passed. A small group of elderly men and women waved yellow flags and cried

---

[11] This is among the practices resurrected by Field Marshal Sarit. In the late 19th century, Rama V abolished the tradition requiring those under the monarch's power to kneel or crawl in his presence. In the Fifth Reign, and until the Ninth, subjects stood before the king.

out, "Long live the king!" In the following weeks, I told this story to many people, and was surprised by the story's magnetism—people stared and listened with unusual intensity. It is easy to forget the extent to which the monarchy was curtailed in the decades before 1957, when Field Marshal Sarit seized power in a military coup. Absolute monarchy ended in 1932 (see Nakarin 2010); the royal institution was not dissolved, but dramatically scaled back. Later, under the rule of military strongman Field Marshal Pibulsongkram, the king, Rama VII, was stripped of his assets and the state confiscated all property of the crown (Thamsook 1978: 244). Display of the king's image was forbidden (ibid.), a reality almost unimaginable in contemporary Thailand, where royal images lie in every direction. Rama VII died in exile in London. The monarchy was waning, as portrayed in the exalted royalist novel *Four Reigns*. During the reign of Rama VIII—who later died of a gunshot wound to the head, still a sensitive topic of discussion—Ploy, the main character, visits a friend in the palace compound and finds it in a state of rot: "Every place in the compound spoke of and revealed an absence of life—decay and death. Royal power and magnificence had ended, were no longer to be seen" (Kukrit 2011: 920).

In the late 1950s, the regime of Field Marshal Sarit (notably, a man of the northeast) began to rehabilitate the monarchy. Since the revolution, royalist factions had been restless. Although some distrusted Sarit, they mostly supported him against the aggressively anti-royal reign of Pibul (Nattapol 2020: 248). Sarit and his fellow generals "believed the monarchy would serve as a focus of unity, and a force for stability, while remaining susceptible to … control" (Baker and Pasuk 2009: 175). Meanwhile, many royal rituals were reconstructed, including the royal barge procession. In 1962, for the first time in decades, the barges appeared on the Chao Phraya River, with the king, Rama IX, occupying the throne of the primary vessel (Tambiah 1976: 229). Now past curtailment of the monarchy has widely vanished from collective memory.

Rama IX, the world's longest-reigning monarch, crowned in 1950, was hospitalized for the entire course of my fieldwork. He made occasional brief public appearances, as on that afternoon in Thonburi. The hospital is on the bank of the Chao Phraya. Newspapers frequently reported that the king had cast his "royal eyes" on the river, inspecting her condition.

Sarit's project cultivated an image in which nation and monarchy are inseparable. Furthermore, it is significant that the rowers of the barges are soldiers. As one man put it, "Soldiers are servants of the king." I asked: Are power seizures by the military justified? He replied, "Most of the soldiers are loyal to the king, but there are also some Red Shirts." A curious response, implying that coups are honorable if the soldiers are royalists. Not all, however, share this view. Many, especially in the north and northeast, want the military to depart from politics. I observed the barge procession in the company of faithful royalists. Nonetheless, one does not speak freely about the monarchy. Speech is curtailed by law and a culture of fear (Ivarsson and Isager 2010; Pavin 2012; Streckfuss 2011). In 2012, Worachet Pakeerut, a law professor at Thammasat University, was assaulted after making modest, rational proposals for revision of lese-majesty laws. One day an informant from up-country turned the pages of a magazine, perusing images of royal figures, and said, "We do not have the right to speak. If we speak, our heads will be cut off."

Barge Processions

We hear the procession before we see it. The barges approach from upstream. A slow, repetitive melody emits from a speaker. It is a male voice, soft but powerful. Based in an ancient vocal tradition, the voice amplifies the ceremonial aura—profound, dignified, almost otherworldly.[12] Crowds move closer to the banks. Conversation quiets. Boats begin to appear. The royal barges, with their dramatic gold-painted prows, are escorted by long black canoes. The rowers are soldiers, and each crew is outfitted in one of three colors: brown, pink, or blue. The rhythmic rise and fall of oars shows military discipline. The vessels have different rowing patterns: 1-1-1, 3-3-3, 1-1-3. These cycles, with the oars striking the water, set a textural contrast to the melody. We stand at the edge of the river now, by the rail. Observers take pictures with

[12] Evidence suggests that the melody was composed during the Fifth Reign (Sujit 2019: 14) and based on an old tradition of "boat songs", which had been sung by commoners along the Chao Phraya and Mekong (ibid.: 27).

cellphone cameras. Clouds and sunlight alternate. Fon gives me a cloth to wrap my head. "Can you figure it out?" she asks. Like others, she is waiting for the swan-headed barge, which in full-scale processions carries the king. An orderly series of vessels, black and gold, now fill this expanse of the Chao Phraya. The melody repeats over and over, pausing between cycles. The rhythmic clacking of oars proceeds. Near the center of each vessel are the pole-bearers. In intervals, the men lift the poles, pause briefly, then strike the planks. The resonant impact signals the beginning of a new rowing cycle. Horns emerge and retreat. People on the banks speak little. The melange—voice, poles, oars, horns—is punctuated with brief moments of semi-silence.

The procession ends at the Temple of Dawn. The melody stops and bodies pull away from the banks. Fon then talked about their recent visit to the Emerald Buddha, the shrine of which was very close, within walking distance. Visiting sacred objects (สิ่งศักดิ์สิทธิ์) is extremely important to many people in Thailand.[13] Most of my meetings with Fon and her family centered on visits to riverside temples to ritually honor sacred objects. After making merit together for the first time, Fon said, "This means we'll meet in the next life." One evening we walked to Wat Saket, also known as the Golden Mountain, formerly the tallest building in Bangkok. The gates were locked, but we could see the golden spire glowing against the night sky. We returned a few weeks later with her mother and sister. We honored the Buddha images inside the temple, then climbed the stairs to the roof and looked out at the city, which was submerged in gray smog. We joined a group carrying a red cloth in circles around the spire. Another cloth was spread, and on it we wrote our wishes. It was then tied around the spire. On another day, we traveled by train to visit Wat Sothon, a temple in a neighboring province. The sanctuary was crowded, frenetic, and noisy. Gongs resonated. Numerous scraps of paper littered the floor. After applying gold leaf paper to the Buddha images, Fon told the story of how three statues, one of which was brought to the temple, were found floating on the Bang Pakong River. I asked an absurd question: What were they

---

[13] For a discussion of Thailand's Buddhist landscapes and the tradition of visiting sacred sites and objects, see *Monastery, Monument, Museum*, especially the chapters on "Sacred Geographies" (Peleggi 2017).

doing in the river? And who put them there? These, she explained, are "sacred objects". Buddha statues are known to float magically on waterways.[14] Such objects are mysterious and powerful, and thus people seek contact with them. She had once made merit here before taking a difficult exam, which she passed, a demonstration of the objects' power. At another temple we saw a collection of gem-like fragments of bone, relics of great monks. The bones of monks, after many years of practice, she said, become "like crystal, not like the bones of ordinary people".

Of all sacred objects in Thailand, the Emerald Buddha is the most exalted. It is "patron and guardian" of both the country and the ruling dynasty (Tambiah 1984: 214). Carved from lustrous green stone, it is less than a meter tall, a figure seated in the lotus position with a pointed gold crown. The fortified compound on the east bank was named for the object: Rattana-Kosin, meaning the Jewel of Indra. It was installed facing east to watch the "ghost gate" (ประตูผี), by which non-royal corpses were removed—a vulnerable point in the compound walls, through which malevolent spirits would be tempted to invade (Sujit 2011: 140–2). Few Thais remember, however, that the Emerald Buddha was among the war spoils from Vientiane. For over 200 years it was the Lao kingdom's most revered Buddha image. Contrary to what many believe, it is likely a product of Lao craftsmanship (Sujit 2011: 16; Sujane 2012: 63–5). In the 19th century, Rama IV observed: "It appears to be the work of an ancient northern Lao craftsman, from somewhere around Chiang Saen [that is, around the ancient Lao kingdom of Lanna]. It closely resembles the craftsmanship of those lands.... It is truly the work of a master craftsman" (Sujane 2012: 65). Today, however, this has been obfuscated by a myth that the Emerald Buddha was created in Sri Lanka, a myth that serves the royal-national story of Thailand as inheritor, center, and protector of Theravada Buddhism—a myth that severs the Lao roots of the object.[15]

---

[14] Consider also the origin story of Phnom Penh, capital of Cambodia, where Lady Penh, in search of firewood, is said to have pulled from the river a drifting tree, in which she found four Buddha statues and a statue of Vishnu. She thus built a shrine for the statues on a hill—thenceforth known as Phnom Penh (Osborne 2000: 36–7).

[15] See also *Monastery, Monument, Museum* (Peleggi 2017), especially the second chapter, "Itinerant Icons of the Theravada Ecumene", which offers a detailed

The Emerald Buddha is memorialized in Vientiane. Along with it, as described earlier, came the captives: the royal family and tens of thousands of Lao, most of whom were transferred to the riverine landscape of central Siam. Some captives, those not transferred to the basin of the Chao Phraya, were resettled closer to the Mekong (Ong 2010: 170)—right around the place that Fon and her family call home. But it seems that, for these sojourners in Bangkok, as for many people in Thailand, the memories of Vientiane have faded away.

One month later came the full procession. As the day approached, people again emphasized that the royal barges are hundreds of years old, based on originals from Ayutthaya, a city destroyed by the Burmese. One boasted that the swan-headed barge is even more beautiful than the royal vessel of Queen Elizabeth. "Everybody in the world loves our king", she said. People described the barges as *boran* (ancient or very old), a word that suggests the dignity of age. People expressed feelings of reverence, and also well-being, feeling at peace (สงบ) in the presence of the barges.

Traffic is heavy, the bus is slow, police are swarming. A rumor circulates that police are looking for Burmese illegals, especially in Chinatown. During an interview, a Chinese woman (a native of Thailand) in a warehouse by a large riverside market had said, "We used to hire the Lao. But now they want to be big. These days the merchants in Chinatown [เยาวราช] are from Isan [that is, Lao from the northeast]. They don't want to be workers; they want to be the boss. So we hire Burmese and Cambodians." Whistles blow, vehicles are stopped, papers checked.

Vendors surround the park, selling royal-yellow flags as well as tricolor national flags with the words "Long Live the King!" added to the middle stripe. A woman hollers, "Flags to receive the royal visit!" People warned that there would be a large crowd, with many visitors from up-country. A man with thick hands and sun-baked skin, a farm laborer, sits next to a water-filled concrete basin, waiting. The barges will come in the mid-afternoon. People arrive in the morning and wait for hours. Many carry open umbrellas to guard against the sun. A few people sit on the grass, forming circles. Knowledge spreads through the crowd. There are 52

---

examination of narratives concerning the origins, travels, and power of the Emerald Buddha, and also points to the object's probable Lao origins.

vessels, mostly escorts. The rowers are carefully selected and must train for eight months. The king will not appear. His son, the crown prince, will take his place. Facing the river stands a large royal photograph, framed in gold—it shows the king aboard the swan-headed barge.

Umbrellas and flags accumulate as the crowd grows. The surface of the river is calm. Patrol vehicles pass. Dark clouds are encroaching. A man passes, his cellphone pressed to his ear, encouraging a reluctant other to come to the park. He describes the auspicious circumstances: "It's not raining, nor is the sun shining." Or rather, not shining too intensely. Across the river, we see a large, rectangular building, draped with royal yellow and the national flag. Thunder cracks and a roar of excitement spreads across the crowd. But no rain falls. A girl with a red toy monkey throws a tantrum. People continue chattering while fidgeting with phones and cameras. One woman, speaking to Dutch tourists, notes that the king completed the seventh cycle (turned 84) last year, but the royal barge procession was not held. She says the king was sick, then corrects herself, "No, it was because of the flood." The crowd shifts as the sound of the procession draws near. The melody returns, punctuated by oar cycles and the strike of poles. With the appearance of the first vessel, arms and phones rise into the air, obscuring much of the view. A woman says she already watched the procession upstream, then came here by motorcycle to watch it again. Observers wait eagerly for the swan-headed barge, which now carries the crown prince.

Landscape and Erasure

The Chao Phraya River is a landscape of presence, absence, and power—it both reveals and dissimulates.[16] The barge procession dramatizes a benign, paternal king, royal-national history, and also the Thai military, with soldiers positioned as guardians of the old order, as protectors of royalty, and thereby (ostensibly) above politics. The landscape becomes

[16] Henri Lefebre writes, "Dissimulation is necessarily part of any message from power. Thus space indeed 'speaks'—but it does not tell all" (1991: 142). A fitting point, but power is arguably more variegated. Abundant examples exist of unconcealed, brutal expressions of domination, as well as more subtle, deceitful, and entrapping forms.

vivid and the river becomes an aquatic stage for the promotion of a power-infused culture of memory.

Ingold writes, "To perceive the landscape is … to carry out an act of remembrance, and remembering is not so much a matter of calling up an internal image, stored in the mind, as of engaging perceptually with an environment that is itself pregnant with the past" (1993: 152–3). Such an approach challenges conventional divisions, emphasizing instead the enmeshment of flesh, mind, and world. But landscapes also conceal. The perceived world is also a realm of absences, of pasts that cannot be seen or remembered. The royal barge procession was resurrected under dictatorship, a project of consolidating military power and reimagining the nation, including efforts to remold collective memory. When one perceives the landscape, the past does not present itself whole. Some of the past has faded, or even been erased, while other aspects have been promoted, elevated, and made obvious. People have learned to see and to remember. Jan Assmann writes, "Remembering the past is not the result of instinct, of some innate interest, but of a duty that is part of culture's impact on man" (2011: 233). Indeed, perceptions of landscape are oriented by obligations to remember, but sensory worlds are also shaped by erasure—injunctions to forget. Thus, invoking a violent, obscure past, such as the destruction of Vientiane, creates dissonance in an experience-near account of landscape.

Cosgrove describes landscape as "a way of seeing the world" (1998: 13), arguing that perception is shaped by historical conditions and power relations. Landscape, he writes, is "a controlling composition of the land" (ibid.: 270). He examines works of representation that describe the landscape from a distance, such as landscape painting. On reflection, however, we might see representation at work in the landscape itself. Experience-near accounts can provide a sense of place and bring readers closer to cultural life, but such accounts also need sensitivity to the control of the landscape, including the forces, institutions, and relations that shape collective memory. Otherwise one risks writing a politically sanitized account. Along the waterways, one would be trapped within the limits of the royal-national narrative of the landscape.

Cosgrove, in a criticism of his own book, writes, "The viewers of landscape [in the book] appear and communicate to us as *eyes*, largely disconnected from any other corporeal or sensual aspects of their being" (1998: xviii). In other words, they are disembodied outsiders, working in the realm of representation, always at a remove from the landscape. Ingold, by contrast, guides us from an outside view to a view from inside. In one essay, for example, he leads us into a 16th-century painting by Bruegel. First, we are merely looking at the painting, then suddenly we are inside, embodied, with a sense of expanse and direction, on paths, under trees, among fields, among the harvesters and their bundles of freshly cut wheat (Ingold 1993: 164–71).

Landscape means shaped earth—shoveled, molded, and built upon. Landscapes are also shaped by memory, all the more so if we relinquish strict, ontological divisions between earth and beings. Canonization, based in an architectural metaphor—a building implement, a pole used for leveling stones (Assmann, J. 2011: 95)—is also a process of shaping and construction. The sensory world, with all its intimate entanglements, is a political form, especially when enclosed as territory. Seeing the river, feeling the cool wind, hearing the melody of the barge procession, can summon and reinforce official royal-national narratives. W.J.T. Mitchell writes, "Landscape ... is an instrument of cultural power" (1994: 1–2). One of the modalities of power is to control the flow of recollection, closing the canon, enforcing the line between visible and invisible. The barge procession is a kind of storytelling, a tangible account of the riverine past and present, emerging through a political architecture of memory—a force directing the experience of landscape.

Memories in Quarantine

Siam was renamed in 1939, thereby becoming the land of Thai.[17] It was a curious moment, shaped by a forward-looking spirit of fascist nationalism, the refinement of new ethnic myths, and a struggle to cast off the heritage of royal Siam. An ethnic designation was grafted to the land, with long-term consequences. This was the official end of old Siam. It created an ethno-

[17] The name changed back to Siam in 1945. Field Marshall Pibulsongkram (who had changed the name in 1939) seized power again in 1948, and thenceforth the country has been known as Thailand.

national ranking, according to which only some are True Thai, only some have full access to national belonging. Today, the concepts of nation and ethnicity are frequently confused in Thailand. This is an artifact of top-down nation-building, especially the attempt to fuse nation and ethnicity in a complex, heterogeneous land. Charnvit Kasetsiri has long argued for a return to Siam, changing the name of the country, or rather for the creation of a new Siam, and a more inclusive national concept: "Given the historical evidence, academic principles, and given the importance of identity, we really should separate that which concerns peoples from the name of the country.... There is a great diversity of peoples in Siam—and they can come together. When we solve this problem, we will understand many things" (Charnvit 2008b: 40).

Thais are said to be river dwellers, clever in every aspect of life with water. Looking at a topographical map, one sees a density of waterways in the central region, the heartland of Siam, flowing north to south, down from the highlands of Lanna, and excluding most of the northeast. Central Thailand, or the region now known as such, has been integrated by water for countless centuries, with the Chao Phraya River as its main artery. The river is navigable in all seasons from gulf to the confluence at Nakhon Sawan. Modern, reliable roads came late, beginning in Bangkok in the latter half of the 19th century, and many decades passed before such roads stretched into the northeast. Mountains line the edges of the Korat Plateau and no river flows from the depths of the northeast to Bangkok. The Pa Sak River, which joins the Chao Phraya, originates in Loei, a province at the edge of Isan, adjacent to the central region. But the vast bulk of Isan is east of this waterway, access to which is limited by mountains. The Mun River and Chi River, the primary waterways of Isan, flow east toward the Mekong. This lack of aquatic connection slowed the integration of the northeast into the Bangkok dominated nation-state. The first rail reached Korat in 1900. Even then, the journey from village to railhead could take weeks—an arduous, overland trip, traveling by foot, carrying provisions on one's back, as depicted in *Child of Isan*, an ethnographic novel written by a native of the northeast (Kampoon 1993: 3).

Regional identity as the "Northeast" (Isan) developed slowly. Northeast, that is, in relation to Bangkok. In the late 1960s, Keyes observed the emergence of this identity, adding, "It must be stressed that this sense of

Isan identity is of very recent origin" (1967: 3). Isan's linkage to Bangkok was facilitated by the Friendship Highway, a smooth, reliable road from the Mekong to Korat, a project that began in 1955 as a supply route for US military bases. Lao arrived in Bangkok in large numbers after World War II when migration from abroad—especially the steady, massive influx from China—was cut off by the central government. Many took jobs driving three-wheel bicycle cabs. An American ethnographer, with the help of Thai students, conducted research with some of these drivers in the 1950s. The drivers self-identified as Lao, and residents of Bangkok hated them. The Lao migrant, having newly arrived in the city, "soon develops a fear—not without some justification—that the Bangkokians are looking down on him as a rustic bumpkin who cannot even speak 'proper' Thai" (Textor 1961: 17). Social interactions were often tense: "Rough fights break out with fair frequency because a Northeasterner senses an ethnic insult from a Bangkokian, or a Bangkokian perceives a Northeasterner as an economic throat-cutter" (ibid.: 19). But the capital city was becoming a center in the world of the newly dubbed Northeasterner. Meanwhile, the memories of Vientiane's destruction have mostly remained across the Mekong, restrained by the Thai borderline, quarantined in Laos.

Traces of earlier connections do persist. The Mekong River was not always a borderline. On the day that Fon received her nursing degree in Bangkok, we were sitting on a bamboo mat on a knoll of grass near the Rama V equestrian statue. After a round of photographs, Fon went into the auditorium to receive her degree, a tightly managed event. Her sister Fa began talking about their village near the Mekong. "People used to cross the river all the time", she said. "People could go in the morning, return in the afternoon, just go back and forth." People still cross the river, of course, but officials will ask for passports. "It's not the same", she said. "Now if we cross the Mekong, we'll be foreigners." A striking statement because, once upon a time, before "Thailand", and prior to French colonization, the riverbanks were intimately bound to one another. Fa was born in a world of borders and border police. In the old days, Bangkok was far away. On that day, however, we were all sitting in Bangkok, and her older sister was receiving a degree from the royal hand of a figure from the Chakri dynasty—another tradition from the Sarit dictatorship.

A few weeks after the royal barge procession, I invited Fon and Fa to visit the Museum Siam, which is within walking distance from the Chao Phraya River. The express boat stopped at the pier and we met again in the park. The Museum Siam is an impressive project, with beautiful displays and arrangement, all designed to push back against narrow definitions of Thai. The message of ethnic variety and mixture is emphasized in every room. I wondered what my friends from the northeast would think. The layout is temporal and follows the progression-of-centers narrative—Sukhothai, Ayutthaya, Thonburi, Bangkok—but attacks it from inside, making each center a point of confluence. One panel asks: "Who built Bangkok?" Among the ethnic groups identified are Malays, Cambodians, Russians, Chinese Muslims, Indians, Burmese, Dutch, and Lao from Vientiane. Fon and Fa were not interested in these panels, but they enjoyed the visit. Later that afternoon, after we had separated, they sent a text message in Thai: "Today we had much happiness." One of the highlights of the museum is a panel of five buttons that provides a glimpse into the linguistic diversity of Siam. Each button offers a greeting in a different language, including Mon, Hmong, Karen, Semang, and Lao. Push a button, hear the greeting. Little groups hover over this display, clicking and giggling. Fon and Fa were no different, clicking the button that says "Lao" five or six times before turning away.

Lao informants never suggested separation from Thailand, but the old order and its national imaginary are under pressure, and the loudest demands for reform and inclusion come from the north and northeast. Upstream lies Ayutthaya, but someday one will see the "Central Thai" landscape, including the Chao Phraya River, in a new way. During fieldwork, a book by a brilliant young scholar was published in Thai. The author, Sujane Kanparit, writes about Vientiane's destruction, the transfer of its population to Central Thailand, and the erasure of these events from collective memory. The book is full of startling observations. Near the end, with a Thai audience in mind, he writes, "In the current age, we find many ethnically Lao people in Bangkok. Even you, the reader, may not know yourself. If you could go back into the past, you might find that your bloodline includes Lao—people who were driven, herded [into Siam] during the wars with Chao Anu [of Vientiane]" (Sujane 2012: 169). Such work is among the emerging forces gradually prying open collective memory—reopening the canonized landscape.

Chapter 4
Belonging

Water splashes and sprays as fares are collected. A boy climbs along the edge of the boat, his nose and mouth covered with a skull-face cloth. We are packed tightly on the planks. Faces are moist with sweat. Graffiti is scrawled along the concrete rim of the canal. We pass under the shadow of a bridge, then emerge. Slums proliferate against a backdrop of skyscrapers. Ropes are pulled and the blue tarp rises. Gears engage, the engine growls, and the tarp flaps in the wind.

Saen Saeb, the Canal of a Hundred Thousand Stings, branches off from the Chao Phraya River, cuts through Bangkok, and goes east toward Cambodia. Dug in the early 19th century, under orders from Rama III, it is an extension of Maha Nak, a canal dug during the First Reign. Saen Saeb was originally used to move troops and military equipment (Sangkhit 2011: 105–7). Siam's neighbors had not yet been conquered by Britain and France. Siam was in conflict with Vietnam over control of the Mekong. The canal was also used to transport agricultural products, such as rice and sugar (Walailak 2017: 89). Furthermore, it formed new terrain for the settlement of immigrants and war captives, including Muslims from the east and south (Srisak 2017a: 27). Today the canal has an insalubrious reputation as a realm of sewage, rot, and poverty. The stench is notorious. In addition to associations with low society, the canal is seen as a magnet for foreigners: labor migrants and refugees from Cambodia, Burma, and Bangladesh, merchants from India and Pakistan. Outsiders refer to the filth with derision and amusement. Once, while crossing a bridge over the canal, an informant said, "If you fall into Saen Saeb, you will die for sure, even if you can swim." In a popular Thai comedy skit, Note Udom uses Saen Saeb to describe the Ganges River in India: as wide as the Chao Phraya, as filthy as Saen Saeb. This is what happens when water is abandoned. It turns black. Garbage floats on the surface.

But from another perspective, Saen Saeb is intensely alive. Passenger boats ply the canal, contributing to its polluted state. Pollution, though one deplores it, is a sign of life. The boats, engines screaming, pass the hovels in intervals, rattling the doors. As a passenger, one's senses are pummeled with heat and heaviness. Most seem resigned to the noise, though nearly everything is drowned out by the engine's roar. People fill the boats during peak hours. As bodies squeeze together on wooden benches, the vessel dips deeper into the canal. We pull the ropes, raising the blue tarps on both sides to avoid being splashed by the poisonous, foul-smelling water. Packed together on planks, almost no one talks. One merely names a destination for the fare collectors. Coins are exchanged for soft paper tickets. The fare collectors, referred to in Thai as "bags", cover their faces with masks and make rounds on the edges, supported by ropes, moving hand over hand, stepping carefully to avoid falling into the canal. Saen Saeb is not only dirty, but also dangerous. People tell stories of passengers who have slipped and drowned. An old couple from up-country said, "Sometimes the boats catch fire. People are burned to death."

The landscape of canal-hugging hovels is set against a background of high-rises. When the tarp goes up, our surroundings are partly concealed, drawing us inward, away from the concrete, plaster, scraps, and passing forms of life. One is partially isolated, unable to speak to one's neighbor. Some passengers bring a cloth to cover their mouths and noses, attempting to protect themselves from the noxious fumes. Once, having fallen sick, an informant said, "It's surely because of Saen Saeb." The passing landscape, even when not concealed by the tarp, is for most not something to look at or contemplate. Ramshackle houses. Caged heaps of waste. A woman from southern Thailand, who used the canal for her daily commute, had seen foreigners on the boat taking pictures. She found this strange and confusing: "What are they taking pictures of?" But occasionally a space opens, some breach in the stitching, and a temple appears in the distance, golden spires against a gray sky. Looking carefully, one might notice green domes, golden crescents, or a sign in Arabic—or perhaps hear a resonating call to prayer.

The mosque of Maha Nak is built next to a canal of the same name, a polluted trench continuous with the hopelessly reviled Saen Saeb. Islam is usually associated with the far south, the provinces and borderlands just north of Malaysia, but here we find Islam at the center, a community of Muslims in Bangkok. Thailand is both a "Buddhist kingdom" and a "modern nation-state" (Keyes 1987). Muslims born in Thailand, sometimes called Thai Muslims, are thus in a curious position, both socially and spatially. We will explore the geography of belonging and how belonging takes place. The mosque is a powerful, sustaining center, pulling the community inward; at the same time, the community is situated in broader geographies—a multiplicity of landscapes, a distinctive mesh, an extensive patchwork of collective memories.

Muslims in the Center

Most studies of Islamic communities in Thailand have focused on the south (see Chaiwat 2005; Gilquin 2005; Wanni 2010). Such communities are concentrated in that region, especially in the three southernmost provinces, where, according to one study, "Muslim Thais

Path along the Maha Nak Canal

of Malaysian origin make up almost 80% of the population" (Kermel-Torrès 2004: 38). During fieldwork, the south was in conflict, as it had been for years. Over the decades, thousands have died. Non-Muslims in Bangkok sometimes described the situation in the south as a "political game". Some said, "They [the Muslims in the south] want to be big." Others raised the specter of foreign colonial designs, suggesting that Malaysia was secretly fomenting the conflict, arming the separatists. Malaysia, they said, is colony-hunting, aiming for the southernmost provinces of Thailand. Yi-Fu Tuan points out that "countries have their factual and their mythical geographies. It is not always easy to tell them apart, nor even to say which is more important, because the way people act depends on their comprehension of reality, and that comprehension, since it can never be complete, is necessarily imbued with myths" (1977: 98). From Bangkok, the southern region, and especially the far south, which borders Malaysia, appears dangerous, untamed. If not shootings, then drug traffickers. If not drug traffickers, then some terrible accident, some unsuspecting person attacked and disfigured by a tiger. Children are kidnapped, sold, and enslaved. It is also the land of rubber plantations, but above all, the land of Islam and car bombs. Headlines appeared frequently in Bangkok, announcing to readers and passers-by that another bomb had exploded. The media coverage, both print and television, was mostly void of narrative, strangely empty. Bomb. Exclamation point. Conflict. The three southernmost provinces. One learned the details of when and where, the names of the victims, the names of the arriving police officers. One saw photographs of the wreckage. One was reminded of the conflict and where it takes place, but there was little discussion, background, or analysis. There was no sense of why, no context. In Bangkok, this void was filled with fear of the south and Muslims were imagined as violent.

What does Thailand look like from the perspectives of Thai-born Muslims? Near the Saen Saeb canal, there was a Lebanese restaurant, where the guests were mostly Arabic-speaking foreigners, many of them Muslims and long-term residents of Bangkok from the Middle East or North Africa. Along the Chao Phraya River, roti vendors from Bangladesh set up their carts, often decorated with Islamic designs. Near my apartment in Bang Rak, a short walk from the river, there was a dilapidated mosque. A descriptive panel, posted outside, explained that the mosque had once been the center of a community of Javanese. My curiosity about the mosque was met with confusion, and also worry, in the largely Thai-Chinese neighborhood. People expressed ignorance, saying they were not aware the mosque existed. It was merely across the street, a short walk down the alley. One woman said dismissively, "This only interests you because you are a foreigner." A man from southern Thailand, Thai-Chinese, who recycled metal, said, "You should not be concerned with the Muslims. You are in Thailand, so you should study the Thais." I asked about Thais who practice Islam. "Thais", he said, "do not practice Islam. Thais are Buddhists." But what if a Thai person had a change of faith? What if a Thai person converts to Islam? "Thais are Buddhists", he said. "Muslims are not Thai."

In contemporary Thailand, according to Keyes, "Malay-speaking Muslims in Pattani in southern Thailand, upland-dwelling Karen in northern Thailand, not to mention the Lao of northeastern Thailand and the Luk Cin [ethnic Chinese born in Thailand], are as much Thai as are the Siamese of Central Thailand" (2002: 1193). This is a very new idea, as he also observes, and older, contrary views persist (ibid.). Even those who accept the first position—that everyone born in Thailand, regardless of ethnicity, faith, region, or native language, is Thai, with no gradations of being more or less so—may still hold contradictory views. It is true that a we-are-all-equally-Thai view is sometimes promoted by the state. One can certainly find examples. But messages from the state do not necessarily form a coherent whole. Some are contradictory, and the notion that everyone born in Thailand is equally Thai is drowned out by other notions, popular and also state-promoted, that establish standards of ethno-national authenticity and narrowly circumscribe the possibilities of being Thai. As Ong Bunjoon points out, Thailand's up-country cultures, even those that are Buddhist, are marked as "not up to Thai standards [ไม่ได้มาตรฐานไทย]" (2009: n.p.). This reflects the concentration of power in Bangkok, including Thailand's Bangkok-centered, Bangkok-directed national culture. But Bangkok itself, in part because of its power and extreme urban primacy (London 1980; Rigg 1991: 138), is also multiple, full of varieties and mixtures (see Ong 2010). Many "non-standard" peoples live in the city, but as the metal-recycler's words illustrate, Muslims, even if they are born in

Bangkok, loyal to the king, and speak Thai as their only language, are not necessarily regarded as Thai.

Muslims in Thailand are seen as an ethnic or racial group, as indicated by the term *cheua chat islam*, which literally means ethnically or racially Islamic. A similar phenomenon has been observed in colonial census-taking in Southeast Asia, beginning in the 19th century, efforts to define communities of shared faith as ethnic groups (Anderson 2006: 170). Muslims in Thailand are commonly referred to as *khaek*, which literally means guest. The term implies foreignness; a guest is not a member of one's house or country. Moreover, these so-called guests are not always welcome or hospitably received. *Khaek* is also a culturally specific racial designation—a category unique to a Thai imaginary of the world and human types—which lumps together Malays, North Africans, Indonesians, Arabs, and Indians (usually but not always including Hindus), among others. A basic anthropological insight worth keeping in mind is that the categories people use to divide the human species are not universal, nor do they simply emerge from nature. Such categories should be questioned and denaturalized. Thai informants said, and even insisted, that *khaek*, such as Javanese and North Africans, have a shared facial structure, distinct from other races. This perception of otherness, in the way that it packages (biologically) ethnicity and religion, says much more about the ethno-national cultural imaginary of Thailand than it does about North Africans. Such reifications create problems for those who write about Thailand. Penny Van Esterik observes that so-called Thai culture "is easily objectified by outside analysts because it is so completely objectified by insiders and delivered, thinglike, prepackaged with shiny surfaces that attract for both theoretical and aesthetic reasons" (2000: 239). One evening, in a working-class karaoke bar on Rama IV Road, a woman was singing "Sayam Muang Yim", a classic song: "Thai people love their nation and religion." Images of golden temples passed on the screen. Could those words be accompanied by an image of Mecca?

I attempted to meet people by the old Javanese mosque. One evening, I asked a small group of people living next to the mosque if there were still any Javanese in the community. "No, there are no Javanese", they said, "only we Thai Muslims." The term Thai Muslim is worth closer examination. From the perspective of the metal recycler, it is self-contradictory—one cannot be both. Self-application, on the other hand, calling oneself a Thai Muslim, might be a counter-claim. The matter is complicated. The ethnic associations of "Thai" have not dissolved. Charnvit Kasetsiri (2008b), in a thin volume titled *Siam or Thai*, makes the case for changing the name of Thailand back to Siam. Near the end of the book, he turns to the southern conflict. What one sees in the south, he suggests, is happening all over the country, only at lower intensity. It is a crisis of identity and belonging. The expression "Thai Muslim", he argues, is an imposition, especially in the south: "Most of the people of the three southernmost provinces are 'Malay', not 'Thai Muslims' as we have branded them" (ibid.: 40). The expression "Thai Muslim" sounds inclusive, but is also exclusionary, for it denies other forms of ethnic identification. One question is: Are the people of the far south Thai? But perhaps the question should be: Is there a place in the nation for those who see themselves not as Thai or Buddhist, but as Malay and Muslim?

The matter of Islam in Thailand shows that a fissure remains. There is, on the one hand, "Thai" as an ethnic designation; on the other hand, there is "Thai" as a national designation. But the latter is encrusted with ethnic and religious associations. It is true that meaning has shifted. After the change of the country's name from Siam to Thailand in 1939, the state ran aggressive campaigns to change the identities of non-Thai peoples within the borders (Barmé 1993). Many people started, for the first time, to call themselves Thai. Since that time, many previously non-Thai ethnic groups have recognized themselves as Thai and attained some (though not total) recognition by others as such. Although the term Thai Muslim has been criticized and rejected, Muslims in Bangkok often self-identify as Thai. This does not obviate the issue of imposed labels. Such imposition is evident. Yet it remains problematic to say they are not really Thai, but rather Muslims of another ethnic group. Being non-Thai is problematic in Thailand, which might be the only country to which one can belong.

To clarify, there are basically five positions. According to the first, exemplified by the metal recycler, Muslims are not Thai, cannot be, and Thailand is not their country. This position is strictly exclusionary. It is the position of the Buddhist who sees Muslims as non-national outsiders. It is promoted both directly and indirectly by the state. The second position is that some Thais are in fact Muslims, and a special term is needed in order to include them in the nation: Thai Muslims. This view is also state promoted. The third position is that the label Thai Muslim is an artifact of an exclusionary national concept. Rather than let people self-identify, rather than open conceptual terrain for multiple ethnic groups, the state has imposed this label on Thailand's Islamic population. The fourth position is that of Muslims who see themselves as non-Thai and encircled by a hostile, Buddhist nation-state. This is the position of the southern separatist. The fifth position is that of those who self-apply the term Thai Muslim. In their view, one who is born in Thailand is Thai, regardless of faith or ethnic background.

Water and Faith

The metal recycler called to his wife: "Bring one of the prayer books." They had made donations at an up-country temple so that these books could be printed. She brought out the book. It was thin, held together by staples at the spine. The prayers, or chants, were in Pali, rendered in Thai script. Thai Buddhists are likely to recognize some of the chants, the syllables and rhythm, but Pali is mostly unintelligible to the laity, as well as monks. He flipped pages, turned to where their names were printed, recognition in ink of their merit-earning donation. "Study this", he said. "Read it little by little. You need to learn about Thai culture—not just the Muslims."

He sometimes emphasized his Chinese heritage. He was only a single generation removed from China, but securely identified with Thailand. He and his wife spoke Chinese at home. Sitting together on wooden stools on the sidewalk, he narrated his memories of life on a southern rubber plantation. During the dry season, he said, one works very hard, but the region receives an abundance of rain, during which one cannot collect rubber. The plantation, which had belonged to his Chinese father, was lost. He found his way to Bangkok. "The Chinese are not like the Muslims", he said. "The Chinese can go anywhere, work anywhere. The

Chinese create no problems. But wherever the Muslims go, there is a problem. They are very violent people."

Saen Saeb, the Canal of a Hundred Thousand Stings, which joins Maha Nak, is used for day-to-day travel. One day, while passing through on a passenger boat, an Islamic call to prayer resonated over the canal, so I decided to find the mosque. There is a large market at the edge of the water, a sprawling collection of stalls and covered pathways. The boat tilted as passengers rose from the planks, moved toward the edge, and stepped up onto the pier. Without care, one's foot could easily slip into the water. Racks and mounds of cloth overflowed the market. The mosque was on the opposite bank. The community was small, comprised of several hundred families, living mostly in single-story wooden houses along a network of concrete paths.[1] Vendors in the alleys were talkative. People in the community, they said, are Bangkok natives, not people from the south. During subsequent visits, people were always generous. It was even surprising, the warmth with which a stranger was received. Kru Kati, a teacher at the Islamic school, said, "Allah has sent you. Muslims believe one must assist travelers."

Although Saen Saeb was said to be an abandoned waterway, derided as an open sewer, the people of Maha Nak were very much aware of the canal, its presence, condition, and reputation. It was a defining feature of the place and the immediate urban landscape.

The mosque of Maha Nak, named after the adjacent canal, was the community's tangible center. Saen Saeb began across the nearest bridge. Maha Nak is older, but the two canals are one, sharing the same water and foul reputation. The mosque is almost precisely where the canals meet. Maha Nak means Great Naga, a serpent king and king of serpents. According to Buddhist folklore, as Siddhartha sat in meditation—after countless failures, at last approaching enlightenment—a giant poly-headed serpent emerged, curling into a canopy, to protect him from

[1] A school teacher later provided me with photocopies of two documents containing information about the community. The authors are not named. One of the documents is from Suan Dusit University, dated 2011. It enumerates the community's total population as 1,384 people. The other document is undated, apparently extracted from a master's thesis. One of the footnotes cites a lecture from Ramkhamhaeng University.

At a bridge over the canal

storms. Thus the Great Naga is revered as a protector of Buddhism. The name binds the mosque to the canal, and marks it as a place in a Buddhist city and kingdom, a landscape replete with Buddhist names. Nagas are a synthesis of traditions, a blend of Indic myth and the animism of Southeast Asia. The word *nak*, one of countless imports carried by the monsoon winds, comes from the subcontinent, but serpents have been exalted since primeval ages (Sujit 2016: 66–8). In Lao tradition, nagas are creators of rivers, and the Mekong River is the dwelling place of a giant serpent, which throws streams of fire into the night sky. Downstream, the king of Angkor ascended a golden tower in the darkness to mate with a nine-headed serpent, thereby preserving order in the kingdom (Fernández-Armesto 2002: 165–6). In Thailand, the Great Naga is a force of the underworld, a symbol of water and fertility—a protector, but potentially wrathful.[2]

[2] Michael Wright, a British scholar who settled in Thailand and wrote mostly in Thai, once said, "If you ask me where Thai people came from, I will say they came from water—they are nagas that became human" (1998: 87).

People said the canal was once clean. Some who lived and worked near the mosque remembered the canal's better days. Old people had memories of swimming in the canal. Vendors used to paddle through in canoes, calling out the names of their goods, drawing residents to the canal's edge. Until the Sixth Reign (1910–25), there had been a nearby water market, which subsequently went ashore. Until well into the Ninth Reign (1946–2016), fruit vendors entered the canal system from the river, but later the canals were closed. The cries of the vendors had faded from the landscape, persisting only as memories. Such canoes, if they still plied the canal, would be capsized by the rough wake of the engine-equipped passenger boats. The vendors, prominent in the recollections of the elderly, brought vitality to the canal. All landscapes change over time, being composed of both durable and transitory elements. The coming and going of the vendors was rhythmic, part of daily life. Their final disappearance reflected the canal's ruin. Also gone were the fish and fishermen. Although there is much life along the canal, not much life (aside from microorganisms) remains in the water, which used to be—amazingly, considering its present state—full of fish. The bookshop by the mosque used to sell fishing nets.

A community on the bank of Saen Saeb is a slum by definition. Negative perceptions of the canal went hand-in-hand with negative perceptions of its people. Anand Pandian describes how outsiders see the harsh, arid terrain of southern India expressed in the harsh, arid dispositions of the Kallars (2009: 205). This raises a broader question: How do perceptions of landscape relate to how those who live in the landscape are perceived? At another site, near a church on the other bank of the river, a woman said, "We Christians will not tolerate uncleanliness." It was an expression of pride in her community and religious commitments, but also suggested a linkage between terrain and morality. She thought the canal's poor condition reflected the inferior ethical standards of its people. Suzuki Shunryu, a Zen teacher, once said, "In Buddhist scripture there is a famous passage that explains that water is not just water. For human beings water is water, but for celestial beings it is a jewel. For fish it is their home, and for people in hell or hungry ghosts it is blood, or maybe fire. If they want to drink it, water changes into fire, and they cannot drink it. The same water looks very different to various beings" (2003: 95). Water also looks different depending on one's position in the landscape.

Slum Community

Friday. In the alley, across from the mosque. A boy is on the bench. He prays, rocks back and forth. Green cap. His lips are moving. Kids are climbing on the bench. One of them pushes open a small gate. A woman scoops him up like a sack of potatoes. A motorcycle rumbles through the narrow lane. Electric saws, somewhere out of sight, cut and scrape. Beggars sit on the ground, just across from the entrance to the mosque. They are always here on Fridays. Each woman has a small bowl. Kids run out of the school. Bits of chicken are roasting. The vendor sits, barely moves. A metal bowl of lettuce by her side. Smoke rises from the grill. Men on benches smoke cigarettes. Checkered sarongs and knit caps. Legs bounce and swing. Seen through the upstairs window of the mosque, overhead fans spin. Near the entrance, men shake hands and tap their hearts. Speakers are set up overhead. A male voice resonates through the alley, spreads over the canal and into the market. The voice slows down, stops. He clears his throat. The voice returns. A teenager rides by on a black bicycle with a pink shirt, a gold watch, and a knit cap. A man stoops to talk to a boy with Down syndrome: "Hello! Peace be upon you!" At the school, the buzzer goes, the door opens, a loud, thick droning sound pours out into the alley, followed by the footsteps of children. Two girls in white headscarves run out of the school, feet clopping, then disappear into the back of the alley. A man in a collared shirt, a resident merchant from Pakistan, approaches the mosque, checks his watch, then sits to chat with others on the bench. The imam arrives. He stops briefly, greets people, keeps his momentum. Bells approach, a delicate tinkle: the ice-cream vendor. Meanwhile, a fruit merchant sits on the concrete steps. He is not a Muslim. It is past noon now, prayer time approaches, the collection of bodies thickens. Clean, well-groomed and well-dressed. More and more people enter the mosque. Some still sit in front, chatting. Others pick up their feet and hurry inside. A man limps through the alley, but his movement is brisk and powerful. He commands attention, speaks to a few people in passing, then vanishes into the mosque. Men on the bench take their last cigarette drags.

The community was strong. It was tangible, immediately present in words, gestures, in the environment, in the ways bodies gathered and separated. But long-term residents, including several community leaders, said it was stronger in the past. The owner of the bookstore, for instance, described his memories of the old days:

> In the past, the community was stronger, even stronger than now. This system that we see—a community of Muslims, the mosque, an imam looking after the community—this is normal. The community has had this system for a long time. But in the past it was stronger because people in the community had closer relations to one another. Because people weren't so burdened with making a living and raising a family, with commerce; people weren't squeezed and constrained like they are nowadays. So people would walk by, greet one another, chat; they'd meet each other daily. Relations were better. Nowadays everyone has to go work, raise a family, take care of themselves—it's led to a lack of good relations. Everyone has to leave the house, and when they come back in the evening, they're tired, and they don't have time. In the old days, when I was young, the front of the mosque was like a center. Around 6 o'clock in the evening, which is prayer time, and also around 8 o'clock, people would sit in that area, they'd sit together and chat. Relations were better. Nowadays around that time it's very quiet. Everyone goes into their houses. No one comes to sit, socialize, talk to one another—that's vanished. When I was young, right here [he points out the window], there would be children running and playing. The scene has changed. In the old days it was more organized. Nowadays people are pursuing commerce, seeking profit, without thinking of the image of the community, or the impact on others.

Teachers at the Islamic school described the community as a "slum". Many people used this expression, but it was a slum of a particular kind. Congested, but orderly, with recent campaigns to improve standards of cleanliness. Most of the land is owned by the Treasury Department and the Crown Property Bureau. No one spoke of poverty. One was not confronted with scenes of deprivation, but that is not to say poverty was entirely non-existent. One of the teachers emphasized that "people here have money". The word *slum*, a transliteration from English, seemed to indicate a combination of factors: congestion, conditions of land ownership, proximity to the polluted canal, as well as certain social problems, such as the prevalence of narcotics and addiction.[3] In Bangkok, narcotics are often front-page news. Traffickers, if caught, are transformed into media spectacles. The format is standardized: young men (and sometimes women) sit at a table, side-by-side, with the drugs neatly packaged and arranged before them in still-life. Officers in uniforms, self-satisfied, stand in an arc, forming the backdrop and flanks of the scene. The officers pass around a microphone and narrate the case. The captives sit motionless, heads lowered—meek, resigned, shamed. In the city, one often saw signs, especially at sites of employment, but also on the glass door to my apartment building, that read: "Work gives life. Narcotics destroy the nation." Narcotics circulated in the canal-side community, but among non-users there was no effort to conceal this problem. To the contrary, the matter was open. One day, a man walked into the school and said, "Are you doing research on narcotics? We have a big problem with narcotics." This was an important feature of the community: its members' recognition of internal challenges, coupled with collective effort to improve conditions.

Local leaders and local police were carrying out an anti-narcotics campaign. One day, anticipating an event, I arrived early to meet Kru Kati. She was a native of the community, living in a small, wooden house at the canal's edge. A few years previously, she traveled to Saudi Arabia and completed the Haj, the pilgrimage to Mecca. After her pilgrimage, she became more strict in the arrangement of her headscarf, carefully covering her hair. We set out on foot. She stopped to inquire about the merchant's children. Soon we arrived at the graveyard (กุโบร์), where an old man rested on a bench. She asked about his pain-afflicted leg, reminding him to take care of it. We hear roosters. Grave markers include names as well as the year of pilgrimage. This is a Buddhist-majority country, in which the king is an upholder of Buddhism, and most bodies are burned, not buried. This place of death and remembrance symbolizes a cohesion of community. It marks time, showing the people have been here for generations. But if one could observe the

[3] In *The Making of the English Landscape*, W.G. Hoskins discusses slums in early industrial cities: "The word *slum*, first used in the 1820s, has its origin in the old provincial word *slump*, meaning 'wet mire' … and that roughly described the dreadful state of the streets and courtyards on these undrained sites" (2013: 206).

national terrain of Thailand from above, and yet still see the landscapes of small-scale communities, this Islamic imprint, an enclosure of earth and graves, would appear rather peculiar. It indicates the spatial and temporal integrity of place and people, but also difference. We soon leave the graveyard, entering paved backstreets, where arrangements are underway: tents for shade, with rows of folding metal chairs. Children in matching colors are herded into groups. A man from the government will appear, along with local police, teachers, and the imam.

The theme is simple. Addicts are encouraged to report themselves, in return for which they will receive treatment. Cameras take numerous photographs. Several men handle the microphone, all repeating the same line: "We will not press charges." But the promise needs a demonstration; onlookers are shown a voluntary, exemplary addict, a man with disheveled hair dressed in oversized clothing. With his awkward smile, creased face, and lurching gait, the audience knows immediately why he is present. There is no need for him to speak. The police officer announces, "Many have registered already. Let me remind you, we will not press charges." Pamphlets, which summarize the campaign, are distributed to the audience, including an illustrated guide to identifying addicts. We sit shaded under the tent. Volunteers distribute water and iced coffee. Cameras snap and roll, creating a record of the event, but also creating the event itself, contributing to the official atmosphere, showing that it is worth recording. Leaders line up for photographs. The event is built around an hour-long announcement. As it comes to an end, children are recruited, lined up, and sent back into the alley. They pass the graveyard, then pass under the eaves of the houses, chanting all along: "Don't mess with narcotics!"

People of the Place

Residents belonged to this place. Committed, highly visible leaders cultivated a sense of community. Kru Kati was proud of her long-term role as a leader. She spoke frequently of the previous imam, whose passing became a turning point in her life. One day she said, "Our new imam is still, unfortunately, a youth [วัยรุ่น]." He was nearly 50 years old. She often repeated this observation. "He's no match for the old imam", she would say. During our meetings, she shared photographs of the old imam, mostly from events in which he had received awards. “In Islam”, she said, “a man must be a leader.” She emphasized that he supported her, enabling her to develop a prominent role in the community. One day I arrived early, while she was out on errands. People always knew what she was doing. It was an unhurried day by the mosque, as passenger boats buzzed through the canal, waves of green-black water sloshed against the banks, and men worked under the bridge with welding torches. Then she appeared, crossing the bridge on foot, waving her hand, and we met by a concrete staircase. She stopped several times, talking briefly to people in the alley, then we entered the school, and she said, “A leader must be like this. I talk to many people. I need to know what’s going on in the community.”

It was a deeply rooted place, but starkly distinctive, encircled by a Buddhist society—as if transplanted, compelling a question of geographical origins. What were the characteristics of the originating landscape? Men wore checkered sarongs, an Islamic form of dress more commonly seen in Malaysia. One could reasonably guess it was a community of southerners, ethnic Malays, but the people emphasized local identity, calling themselves “people of the place” (คนพื้นที่), for which an informant offered the following definition: “It means one was born in a place and knows it well. One knows every alley and corner. One knows everyone, and one knows everything that happens.” Such a definition implies limitations of scale; one cannot know every corner of a city. The word *place* approximates the term *peun-ti* (พื้นที่). *Peun* means ground or surface; it refers to earth or pavement, surfaces on which people walk, build, sit, reside, or prostrate. *Ti* means location or site. This place congealed around the mosque, the enduring center, its temporality far exceeding the human life cycle. Leaders live and perish, but the mosque endures. In Mediterranean antiquity, philosophers saw place as a container: a place began at its outer boundary (Casey 1997). Similarly, J.B. Jackson underlines the power of boundaries in landscapes: boundaries bind, creating and maintaining collectives (1980: 115). Here, however, place began at its center. The outer boundary was sustained by the mosque, which pulled the community inwards, like a star holding planets in orbit. Conversations ended at prayer times, as people excused themselves and entered the mosque.

Being a person of the place depends on a place's stability and cohesion. Not everyone has such a place. One woman, decades previously, had left her childhood home, which was on the bank of Saen Saeb. She recalled a vibrant canal culture and a landscape of orchards. But the orchards, like the itinerant canoe-paddling merchants, had vanished. "I would not be able to find that place", she said. "Now everything has changed." The canal remained, but the community of her birth had dissolved and dispersed, persisting only in memory. Two Chinese sisters, both born in Bangkok, asked about my research and then surprised me, saying, "That is very good to have the mosque as center of the community. We go to the *saan jao* [Chinese shrine], but we are outsiders. We don't know the other people at the shrine. We are surrounded by strangers."

The site's first Muslims built a small mosque. Later, a larger mosque was built, said to have been completed sometime before 1851. In 1929, that mosque was destroyed by fire. According to one story, a leaking gas tank had ignited. The wooden mosque and nearby houses quickly burned. Sympathetic Muslims from other districts came to visit and helped build a new mosque. In subsequent years, as the community grew, the mosque became increasingly crowded, thus it was expanded in 1968. During my fieldwork, few of the living had witnessed the fire, but it was a central story in the collective memory, passed on from generation to generation, and often repeated, suggesting the scale of devastation, a collective trauma. It was also an enduring feature of the mosque's biography: the new mosque had always been a replacement for the old. To be people of the place, to belong, is to remember—to share collective, place-bound memories.

Intersections

The mosque was a powerful, sustaining center, but the community had also formed within broader geographies. As a place, Maha Nak wove together, and emerged within, a patchwork of landscapes, near and far—a geographically extended mesh of collective memory, both within and beyond national boundaries. Belonging took place within this patchwork, the key elements of which included the canal, Bangkok, ancient Ayutthaya, the broader national terrain, the Malay Peninsula, and the transnational expanse of Islam centered on the Arabian Peninsula.

Saen Saeb was inevitably woven into the story. As Ingold writes, "Life is lived ... along paths, not just in places" (2007: 2). The canal was a vital path of urban infrastructure, connecting this place to others. Unlike many other old canals, Saen Saeb was never transformed into a street. It had survived, albeit in a corrupt form. The canal was laden with meaning, including decay, abandonment, poverty, crime, and foreignness. Its unwholesome reputation was part of an "imaginative geography" (Said 1978: 54), a broad, imprecise picture of the world, partly imposed from outside, within which day-to-day life unfolded at Maha Nak. The people of the place knew the canal's reputation, that outsiders viewed it with apprehension and disdain, but also made their own associations. Even negative aspects looked different through their eyes. Although stigmatized as a drug-flooded slum community, they made collective efforts to grapple with narcotics, showing that the community was strong, organized, and fortified by faith.

Memories are sometimes marked by place-names.[4] The mosque was named after the immediate waterway, which is continuous with Saen Saeb. Practically speaking, the waterways are one—the same trench, filled with the same filth, trash, and black water. Every utterance of the mosque's name potentially evokes the adjacent canal. Maha Nak is a protector of the Buddha, thereby invoking the Buddhist kingdom; it is also the name of an ancient canal from Ayutthaya, said to have been dug for defense. The name Saen Saeb is similarly evocative. The word *saen* means a hundred thousand, and is also used as an intensifier, meaning exceedingly. *Saeb* means sting or burn. Thus Saen Saeb could be translated as "exceedingly stinging", or "a hundred thousand stings". People said that, in the old days, the canal and its environs were terribly

[4] One of the most outstanding ethnographic studies of place-names is Basso's (1996) *Wisdom Sits in Places*. See also Carter's *The Road to Botany Bay*: "By the act of place-naming, space is transformed symbolically into a place, that is, a space with a history. And, by the same token, the namer inscribes his passage permanently on the world, making a metaphorical word-place which others may one day inhabit and by which, in the meantime, he asserts his own place in history" (1987: xxiv). Place-names can also express or conceal domination.

infested with mosquitoes. Thus the name invoked an earlier phase of urbanization, for such giant swarms of insects have long been driven out of Bangkok—unlike rural areas, where mosquito nets remain a necessity of life. Another story, though rarely heard: the name might come from the old watery terrain, consisting of marshes and lakes. According to this story, *saeb* (แสบ) comes from *sap* (สาบ), meaning lake or large swamp. Others said the name alluded to the suffering of the captive laborers who dug the canal. A street vendor said, "In those days, they had few tools, so the diggers had to dig with their bare hands. They were digging and crying at the same time." This resonates with other memories that have persisted more widely in Bangkok: memories of coerced labor and violent punishments, such as whipping and decapitation, said to be common practices in the not-so-distant Thai past. Such grim images are parallel to national-scale visions of a golden age. The community of Maha Nak, emerging at the intersection of scales and landscapes, was embedded in multiple, overlapping bodies of collective memory.

The people generally spoke in terms of shared origin. Most claimed local origin, grappling no further. Some claimed southern origin—in peninsular Thailand, or even Malaysia—but others firmly denied it. Some expressed uncertainty; although seeing themselves as people of the place, they were unsure of the origin of the community. Was it, after all, the south, or even the Malay Peninsula? Malay-Thai dictionaries were for sale at the local Islamic bookstore, and some people expressed interest in learning Malay. But why learn Malay? Some said it might be useful for the study of Islam, thus it was not necessarily about origins, but rather about gaining access to a world of spiritual, cultural, and historical knowledge. Everyone was aware of the concentration of Islam in the south, as well as the southern conflict. They knew these realities had an impact on their community. Many noted the prejudiced view, common in Bangkok, that Muslims are people with "violent heads". Some tried to explain the causes of these prejudices, citing ignorance, absence of knowledge of Islam, lack of relations with Muslims, and also the ongoing violence in the south. Some said that in recent years the conflict had grown more violent, and thereby amplified negative perceptions of Muslims, including their own community. This may have motivated disconnection from the south. Although some spoke movingly about the suffering inflicted on the faraway Palestinians, rarely did anyone discuss injustices inflicted on Muslims in southern Thailand. This is surprising, given the extremes of brutality. Thaksin, the former prime minister, was notoriously heavy-handed with the southerners. An especially painful collective wound was inflicted in 2004, when over a thousand protesters in Tak Bai were rounded up by the military and crammed into trucks—"like pigs", as described by one informant, a man from outside Maha Nak. Reports say 78 died of "suffocation" (Baker and Pasuk 2009: 230). However, the people of Maha Nak emphasized that they had no conflicts with Buddhism or Buddhists. People frequently said, "We can enter one another", which is to say: get along, speak peacefully to one another, and live in harmony. A school teacher said, "We can live together [with Buddhists]. We can mix together. There's no problem. There are no arguments or fights."

Prior to my departure from the field, Kru Kati gave me a souvenir. "So that you will remember me", she said. It was a T-shirt with the state-promoted slogan "Long Live the King" (ทรงพระเจริญ), an expression, perhaps, of her own loyalty to both the king and Thailand. The people of Maha Nak described themselves as Thai Muslims, a label unacceptable to southern separatists. But although they emphasized local identity, the ongoing conflict in the south was still part of a broader set of conditions and coordinates that defined their position in both space and society. Belonging took place locally, but was not strictly local. It was within a geographical mesh, at a place of intersections, that belonging was negotiated, established, felt, and threatened.

Stories of origin were conflicted. Some people expressed uncertainty, saying, "One must talk to the big people", meaning older, higher status members of the community. This reflected an uneven distribution of knowledge, a value system in which "big people" had greater power to know, interpret, and communicate. One of the most prominent figures, the imam, said, "We don't have any immigrants from the southern region in our community." He offered a rather unusual origin story, claiming the community had roots in the ancient city of Ayutthaya.[5] This story had a

---

[5] According to the aforementioned document from Suan Dusit University, the community had origins in the southern sultanate of Pattani. A sultan (รายา) from Pattani was captured in 1779 and taken to Bangkok. Other Muslims are said to have

curious resonance, both harmonious and discordant, with the dominant narrative of the Thai nation. After the destruction of Ayutthaya, the center of power moved downstream. Many of the people of Ayutthaya had been captured and transferred to Burma, never to return. During my fieldwork, however, far more emphasis was given to the destruction of the city, and the reconsolidation downstream of the Thai nation. The imam's story placed Islam and the people of Maha Nak at the center of Thailand's royal-national past, binding the community to the riverine topography of Central Thailand, including the downstream migration of Thais after the old city's collapse. Ayutthaya was among the biggest and "most cosmopolitan" cities of Southeast Asia (Baker and Pasuk 2009: 13). Indeed, it was a city of many peoples and faiths. The imam's story reflected an often-forgotten history of Islam at the center of Siam, thereby offering a basis of belonging to the people of Maha Nak. The story highlighted spiritual multiplicity and diverged from tendencies to imagine Islam as a faith mostly confined to Thailand's violent southern fringe.

However, others said the community had roots in the Malay Peninsula, that the people were originally, ethnically and culturally, Malay. For example, a school teacher discussed the founders of the community, saying, "They came from Malaysia. They came to live in Thailand, and dug canals—like Saen Saeb [Kru Kati interjected, 'Maha Nak']. And they dug and dug, until the canal arrived here. The canals are connected; it's basically the same canal. My father told this story. He was from the old generation. He said they dug the canal, and when they'd finished digging, the king gave them this land. And so they had land, and came to live together as a big community. Previously there was a wooden *surau* [a Malay-style mosque]. And then there was a fire [which destroyed it]. After that, they built this big mosque [*surau*]." Later in the interview, she said, "We are Thai people, one hundred percent, because we were born here and grew up here, so we are Thai, but we believe in Islam."

"followed" him, but the conditions are ambiguous. The document says the migrants first settled in Bang Lamphu, then the king gave them land by Maha Nak (c. 1802–07). Later, Muslims from other parts of Siam, including Ayutthaya, entered the community. Siamese invasions are not mentioned.

A local businessman offered another narrative of southern origins. He was in his 50s, well-read, well-established, and respected in the community. "I think we came from the south", he said. "In the south there used to be an independent kingdom [or sultanate] called Pattani. The people were Muslims, Malays. Then came the age of colony-hunting. Siam took Pattani as a colony. It was just like the French and British imperialists. Siam wanted to be a civilized country—Siam wanted colonies of its own. So they invaded Pattani, and the people were captured and driven [or herded] to Bangkok." Rarely did informants describe Siam as a predatory state. Pattani, a center of Islamic culture, was situated on the Malay Peninsula, in terrain that roughly coincides with (what is now) northern Malaysia and the southernmost provinces of Thailand. Siam invaded Pattani in 1786, during the reign of Rama I. The sultanate was defeated, sacked, and subordinated, and part of its population was captured and transplanted to Bangkok. Among the spoils was the Phaya Tani cannon, now installed in front of the Ministry of Defense, across from the Grand Palace. But in day-to-day life, in the recollections of most Thais, at least in Bangkok, a much different pattern of memory prevails, in which Thailand is seen as both victim and escapee. As the story goes, Thailand was squeezed and dismembered by the imperialists, but ultimately evaded colonization. The British and French, they say, took territories from Thailand, and these territories were inherited by neighboring post-colonial nations. Rama V is remembered as the king who, as one man explained, "sacrificed the arms and legs of the nation in order to save the body". This story submerges Siam's past as a colonial power. The violent incorporation of the southern states has no place in this story of an already-bounded national body.

A trace of Siam's colonial past persisted at Maha Nak, but it was merely a faded scar, not an open wound. It did not, so far as one could discern, stir emotions. Such memories had been subordinated or neutralized by other collective memories, and also perhaps by the imperative to claim place. The people of Maha Nak knew where they belonged: in Bangkok, by the canal and the mosque. True or false, verifiable or otherwise, all of the stories were suggestive, offering insights into the coordinates, topographies, and intersections of collective memory. Within the community itself, it was most often ties of faith and shared borders, rather than shared origins, that bound Maha Nak to the peninsular landscape. The people of Maha Nak did not fight to establish an independent Islamic state, nor have aims of doing so, but rather continued, steadfast, making their place by the canal as a community of Thai Muslims in Bangkok.

Lastly, examining the geography of belonging, we behold the transnational terrain of Islam, which extends around the earth, and is centered on the parched Arabian Peninsula. In keeping with Islamic tradition, many of the people of Maha Nak had made the pilgrimage to Mecca. These journeys were turning points in life. In the graveyard, a short walk from the mosque, one could see the years of pilgrimage marked on gravestones. Here there is a profound contrast with Buddhism, Thailand's state-enshrined religion. Buddhism in Thailand has been, to a great extent, nationalized. In spite of origins on the subcontinent, well beyond Thai borders, Buddhism now appears to be almost indigenous. Prapas Cholsaranont, a Thai columnist, writes, "Strange, isn't it? Many things in our world were born in one place, but grew up [เติบโต] in another place.... Theravada Buddhism has grown up in our country—so much so that, today, Thailand is the center of Buddhism. But don't forget, the founder of our faith was an Indian" (Prapas 2011: 50). One might question the word "Indian", considering Siddhartha's birth as prince of the Shakyas in a time long before nation-states, but for the present discussion, the broader point is the tendency to forget the externality of origins, and even if one remembers, Thailand is already imagined as the world's contemporary center of Buddhism. Buddhist practice in Thailand does not usually connect Thais to Buddhists who exist beyond national frontiers.

By contrast, the people at Maha Nak had a powerful sense of belonging within a transnational community of believers. It was November, just before Loi Kratong, when banana-leaf boats are set afloat on the waterways. No such tradition existed at Maha Nak. We were outdoors, gazing at the canal, standing in the sticky heat of Bangkok, a tropical metropolis. A man steadied himself at the rail. When asked about Loi Kratong, he said, "Our faith was not born in this environment." Indeed, as the essayist Richard Rodriguez observes, "It was within the ecology of the Middle Eastern desert that the mystery of monotheism blazed"

(2013: 36). At prayer times Thai Muslims face the Arabian Peninsula. The mosque is one of millions. In distant cities and villages, places far beyond the national horizon, the same call to prayer resonates.

Chapter 5
Trajectories

We were sitting on crates next to a wall in the alley. Uncle took the brush in his thick, calloused hand and spread red paint along a wooden sword. We were talking about changes in the way of life along the Chao Phraya River and the consequent transformations of the landscape. The wooden ferries had been replaced by iron vessels. Factories had proliferated upstream, while downstream a shopping complex had recently opened and its "warehouses" as well as statues of Chinese laborers invoked an antiquated river-scene. Near the mouth of the alley, there was a pier where people waited for the iron ferry. Just across the river was a sparkling new cafe where one could enjoy espresso or a slice of cake, if only one had the cash or credit. Indeed, as he observed, tangible signs of development had spread along the river. Then he turned his tired face toward me and said, "We've developed materially, but not in terms of heart-spirit."

This curious expression was not unique to the sword-maker. It emerged so frequently in conversation that I began to ask people about it during interviews. Everyone knew the expression. It was so familiar that when I began the quotation, most informants completed the sentence. The foregoing themes—origins, loss, erasure, and belonging—all entail connections across time and space. This brings us to another kind of connection, one with momentum, a line pointing into the future. How do people imagine collective movement through time? Although recollections are assumed to pertain to the past, future-oriented trajectories are a crucial aspect of collective memory. "What would we be without memory?" asks the German novelist W.G. Sebald. "We would not be capable of ordering even the simplest thoughts, the most sensitive heart would lose the ability to show affection, our existence would be a mere never-ending chain of meaningless moments, and there would not be the faintest trace of a past" (1998: 255). Memory enables the formation of meaningful chains, lines, and trajectories. It enables us to integrate past and present, and also to imagine the future. People in Bangkok, observing life along the waterways, talked not only about how society had changed, but where it was going, as if there were a line, and they could see themselves and others moving collectively along that line.[1]

Earth carried downstream

Bronislaw Malinowski, attempting to build a firm, empirical basis for anthropological fieldwork, once described culture in a three-part scheme consisting of skeleton, flesh and blood, and spirit. According to Malinowski, to examine the spirit, which includes the "views" and "opinions" that characterize a culture, one needs to collect "ethnographic statements, characteristic narratives, typical utterances" (1922: 22–3).

[1] Such an imagination is by no means universal. Clifford Geertz, for example, describing the Balinese, writes, "Their life, as they arrange it and perceive it, is less a flow, a directional movement out of the past, through the present, toward the future than an on-off pulsation of meaning and vacuity" (1973: 445).

Is this lament about the backwardness of heart-spirit an instance of the spirit's self-expression? Reifying society or culture as an organic being is problematic, but the expression above, this pervasive habit of contrasting material and heart-spirit, offers an intriguing comment on the trajectory—real, imagined, or desired—of society.[2] One might recall the Thai *suphasit*, proverbs of antiquity, knowledge of which is valued, but some *suphasit* speak more than others to contemporary society. Consider, for example: "In the water there are fish, in the paddy there is rice." Children learn that this proverb comes from Sukhothai. The engraved words celebrate the reign of King Ramkhamhaeng; on school field trips, children see the inscribed stone at the National Museum. The condition of abundance, as declared by the inscription, is generalized to present-day Thailand: a land that is plentiful. The expression is elevated, both officially and in everyday life. It is a shining image of "Amazing Thailand".[3] By contrast, the sword-maker's lament will not be taught in schools. It lives in non-official circuits, and yet is remarkably standardized. There are variations, but the basic structure is consistent: a contrast between two kinds of development, material (วัตถุ) and heart-spirit (จิตใจ). I asked dozens of informants, from a wide variety of occupations, and they all recognized the expression—often well enough to finish the sentence.

Michael Herzfeld has written about "rueful self-recognition" (1997: 6), which emerges from the tensions between the presentation of the individual self and official notions of national character (ibid.: x), which could manifest as a discordance between image and reality, where the individual falls short of national pretenses. Here, however, we find a distinct variation, as the target or culprit becomes the national self. What is ruefully recognized is a trajectory of the Thai nation.

The expression "heart-spirit" is my translation of the compound *jit-jai*. The word *jai* (heart or mind), one of the most common Thai words, is often paired with other words to describe emotional states and personal dispositions. The word *jit* is similar in that it also relates to the

---

[2] An example from email correspondence (original in Thai): "A lot has changed [in Thailand], probably because there's been so much material progress, but it's at cross-purposes [สวนทาง] with the progress of heart-spirit. People have become more selfish. They're willing to do bad things, and they even see this as normal."

[3] "Amazing Thailand" is a slogan from the tourist industry.

human interior. A mentally ill person, for instance, is *rok jit*, a person with a sick spirit. I translate *jit* as "spirit", in part because it is said to persist beyond death. Buddhadasa, one of Thailand's most prominent Buddhist teachers, has said, "When one's spirit [*jit*] is at last freed from attachment, then it will be unbound. It will cease to be a slave of this world and the cycle of birth, death, and rebirth" (n.d.: 54). Heart-spirit also connects the individual to the collective. Consider, for instance, the first public announcement by the generals following the military coup in 2014. The last line reads: "The National Council for Peace and Order [i.e., the coup leaders] will maintain loyalty, protect, uphold, and preserve the monarchy, the center that unites the heart-spirit of the Thai people, and which is above all conflicts" (*Thai Rath* 2014).

Culture, Nation, and Linearity

Clyde Kluckhohn once noted that "the most interesting claims people make are those they make about themselves" (Basso 1996: 37). This brings us to a question of scale: Is the claim about a singular being, a family, a village, a nation? Society is not an organism, but collective claims and senses of collectivity are living realities. Laments of the heart-spirit speak to a national scale. Drawing from memories, people imagine a nation in motion. The question of material and heart-spirit brings the nation down to an immediate, personal level, where people make sense of the present, criticize the collective, and also express views of the future.

Culture and nation are not easily separated in Thailand. The Thai approximation of the word *culture* did not exist prior to the self-conscious process of nation-building. Barmé observes that "the word *wathanatham* (culture) was a recent addition to the Thai lexicon, having been coined some time in the early 1930s" (1993: 160). Culture, or *wathanatham*, usually has a positive meaning in Bangkok—people take pride in their inheritance of culture. Some informants emphasized that culture consists only of "good things" passed on through the generations. The word "good" (ดี) often has hierarchical connotations—good belongs to and graciously descends from higher realms. But people also disagree on what constitutes good, and not all would insist on this good-only notion of culture. Corruption, at least for some, could also be culture. Police bribes, for example, as one woman explained: "We keep bills aside for encounters with the police, and this can alleviate many small problems. Some people attach the bill to their driver's license. We call it tea money [ค่าน้ำร้อนน้ำชา]. It's corruption, but everyone does it. It's culture."

Linear models of cultural evolution have long been under attack in anthropology, the most despised being universal, unilinear models, according to which all societies advance along a single path and can be assigned ranks. In American anthropology, the effort, especially by Franz Boas, to obliterate those models is remembered as a foundational struggle. A similar unilinear, evolutionist logic can be found in dominant models of economic development. In response, some have proposed alternative or multiple modernities, but according to the anthropologist James Ferguson, these latter formulations, good intentions notwithstanding, fail to attend to a global hierarchy of status. The unilinear model of development, in spite of its flaws, provides a timeline of hope—people can aspire to move upwards. The problem is not only theoretical. Ferguson emphasizes that many have lost faith in development, including the possibility of attaining higher status. He writes, "As people lose faith in developmental time, the global status hierarchy comes to be understood in new and disturbing ways" (2006: 189). With the unilinear model shattered, there may be no visible escape route from a low position in the global hierarchy.

Along what lines do people live? Ingold observes that anthropologists remain suspicious of linearity: "Alterity, we are told, is non-linear" (2007: 2). But perhaps this arises from a limited imagination, neglecting the complex possibilities of lines, which need be neither straight nor universal. This can be refigured as an ethnographic question. For example, one informant thought the sword-maker's lament about the heart-spirit was universal. Thus it is not a matter of whether or not to apply a linear model, but rather that a study of trajectories can illuminate how people perceive their position—in time, space, society, and the world.

This is related to a long-standing issue in Thai and Southeast Asian Studies, and also in Thailand's internal politics. Thailand is often said to be an exception among Southeast Asian nations, and most of the so-called Third World, because it escaped colonization. This idea is deeply ingrained in everyday life in Thailand. Children are taught to be proud

Express boat waiting to depart

that the country was not colonized, and above all, to be ever-grateful for the goodwill, wisdom, and foresight of the Chakri monarchs, said to have saved Thailand from subordination. This is a key part of the culture and politics of memory. It shapes notions of time, momentum, and possibility. Given the absence of a colonial experience, one might wonder, is Thailand's trajectory altogether unlike, and incomparable to, that of its neighbors? Benda (1969) raised the question of continuity and change at a time of anti-colonial struggles in Southeast Asia. The myth of Thailand as exception, though prevalent in day-to-day life in Bangkok, has been heavily criticized by scholars, who have argued that Thailand is better understood as a semi-colonial (Anderson 1978; Jackson 2007) or "crypto-colonial" case (Herzfeld 2002). Much of the argument hinges on the degree of subordination to the French and British imperialists. But it should be observed that Siam's rulers drew inspiration from the colonial regimes and tried to create comparable institutions in Siam. If anything, what makes Thailand an exception among Southeast Asian nations is the absence of a *de-colonization* experience. Thailand has no independence day. The end of absolute monarchy and establishment of Siam's first constitution, carried out by force in 1932 by a circle of civilian and military conspirators, is now widely remembered—in a rather clouded conception of the past—as a gift to the people from the king (Peleggi 2007: 134; Barmé 1993: 73).

If Siam was a semi-colonial case, when did it end? The experience of decolonization was profound in other parts of the region. The closest parallel in Siam would be the fissure beginning in 1932, which now appears as the opening move of a long, ongoing conflict. The revolution was compromised by dependence on the old royal-state bureaucracy (Nidhi 2014b: 134). Other vital structures also remained intact, such as the military formed under absolute monarchy (Nidhi 2021: 86). The collective mood of that era is still being explored. The still living, dynamic character of that moment, at least in some circles, is certainly of significance, but the transition has been restrained by internal opposition, cycles of military rule, and the erosion of memory.

Power and Illusion

I wanted to see the remains of the cannibal.[4] The corpse is in a museum in Siriraj, a riverside hospital complex on the Thonburi side of the river in Bangkok. A woman in the alley downstream had talked about the corpse with great excitement. The exhibit also includes, as she noted enthusiastically, children preserved in jars (เด็กดอง). An express boat stopped at the pier by the hospital. A busy market was there; one could buy magazines, clothes, or strawberries. An informant was working in the market, a coffee vendor, his stall within sight of the dock. This time it was a Tuesday in December. A soft wind blew in from the river. "It comes down from the north", he said. "It's cold in the morning. The cold season arrives in the north first, then gradually makes its way into Bangkok." Boats of many descriptions passed. Tugboats were dragging massive, sand-filled barges. Uniformed students crossed the river,

[4] The cadaver is known as Si Ouey (ซีอุย). A sign on the case says "cannibal" (มนุษย์กินคน).

shuttling to and from the universities. Groups disembarked from iron ferries. Others boarded.

The coffee vendor, around 60 years old, with his eyeglasses, a body shaped by iron, and with seemingly endless reserves of energy, commands this space. When asked about the museum, he explains exactly where to go. "Listen", he says. "I want to tell you a story. Our country wasn't always like this." His hand sweeps the built-up skyline of the river. "It was forested, dark at night, especially up-country. Even in Bangkok, we didn't have all these artificial lights. The city had many obscure and frightening places. I was a child when I heard about the Chinese cannibal. He came up from the south. He killed people, ate their liver! I was terrified, afraid even to leave the house. That man had a sickness of the spirit [*rok jit*]—just like a *farang*!"[5]

The exhibit was perfectly horrible. It included deformed fetuses, cancerous limbs, gruesome photographs. The place had a distinctive, musty smell. Two schoolgirls hovered near a wood-and-glass case, in which the cannibal's black, withered corpse was displayed upright. A newspaper article in Thai, attached to the case, explained that he had deserted the Chinese military and entered Thailand through the south. His execution was carried out by the authoritarian government of Field Marshal Sarit, a military dictator still prominent in collective memory. Known for his drinking, brutality, and commitment to public order, Sarit, who died in 1963, is still admired today by many Thais. Thak Chaloemtiarana's observation in the late 1970s has remained current: "It is still common … to hear remarks that political uncertainty in Thailand could be stabilized by a leader like Sarit" (1978: 410). Nidhi Eoseewong refers to it as "a yearning for Sarit". It has, he adds, "afflicted a large number of people—in part, because they believe that under a dictatorship, in which there is

[5] *Farang* is a word of Persian origin, translation of which is problematic. Usage in Thailand is not entirely consistent. Thai dictionaries commonly say that it means Westerner, but that is a vague and mutable category. Considering the range of usage, one finds that these categories overlap, but do not necessarily have the same boundaries. The word is also used for various imported crops and goods. Notably, in a novel by Noi Inthanon (2010), set in the former terrain of the Inca Empire, the protagonists encounter a gigantic "*farang* snake" (งูฝรั่งมังค่า). In short, the word is part of a distinctive way of imagining the world, types, and otherness.

only one absolute power-holder, no matter whether it be a military officer or the king, politics will not be political" (Nidhi 2010: 130).

I noted the otherness of the cannibal's spirit disease. It was distinctly non-Thai. Such sickness was to be found in Europe, Africa, the Americas, but should not occur in Thailand. He came up from the south. By Sarit's hand the disorder of spirit was restrained. A nostalgia for power above politics is not difficult to find in Bangkok, nor is it confined to the right wing (Nidhi 2010: 128–32). This nostalgia is based on an imaginary past, a time not so long ago, widespread in collective memory—and in some quarters bitterly contested. A past that has been preserved and circulated, according to which politics is only a recent development in Thai society. Some yearn for a time before politics, for the return of a latent power that could transcend and contain the divisions and conflicts of the present, a power that could put Thailand on the right path. According to Kukrit Pramoj, a staunch royalist, politics had never existed in Siam until the overthrow of absolute monarchy in 1932 (Nidhi 2010: 128; Kukrit 2011: 671–3). Images of a collective past are crucial elements of present life. Such images can also be deployed in efforts to create the future. So often one heard the same diagnosis of Thailand's problem: an absence of stillness. Such was the opinion of the coffee vendor. "The political situation fails to stabilize", he said. "We argue with one another. It's disgraceful. We could sell our faces." The cannibal was executed in 1959, several months after Sarit seized power as prime minister. Parliament was dissolved and the constitution nullified. Sarit's power was formalized by the "temporary" charter of 1959, which was issued as a command in the royal gazette. The charter closes with Sarit's title and full name, and his description as "recipient of the royal command". Article 17 gave Sarit absolute power over life and death: "... in order to stop or suppress actions that undermine the security of the kingdom or throne, or actions that undermine, disturb, or threaten peace". The charter enabled the elimination of disorderly otherness, both cannibal and communist. Others bring turmoil, crisis, dangerous waves of ideology, threatening the viability of collective life.

Dictatorship creates stillness.

The black cadaver stands motionless in the case.

Late in the afternoons, the vendor and I sometimes sat by the pier. He had previously run a retail business at the airport, and in those days, he was far more affluent. Now he was nostalgic. He once had an upscale riverside condominium with a panoramic view of Bangkok and the Chao Phraya River. The Asian Financial Crisis of 1997 took that away. The shop closed and he lost his house. The years following "Tamil May", the 1992 massacre in Bangkok, were a time of exuberant growth, with the battlefields remade into markets. Capital was confident. But the crisis, referred to in Thai as "*Tom Yum Gung*" (a kind of shrimp soup), left Bangkok with a grim skyline of half-finished skyscrapers. This man recreated himself as a coffee vendor. When business was slow, he would read the newspaper, staying up-to-date with the economy.

He watched the river. He could see the poor condition of the heart-spirit. Without the cultivation of heart-spirit, material progress is fragile. It will be crippled and vulnerable to breakdown, crisis, large-scale disasters. He provided an example: "Thai people have a flaw, namely poor waste-water management. They dump garbage into the water. They use the river as a toilet. It's disgusting. They throw their deceased pets into the canals. The entire family loved that animal, but when it dies they just toss it into the water." This is an old and persistent problem. As early as the mid-19th century, Rama IV condemned such practices and issued an order according to which anyone caught throwing a dead animal into the river would be arrested and publicly humiliated. The king stated in his proclamation:

> Henceforth it is absolutely forbidden for anyone to throw a dead dog, dead cat, or any other sort of animal corpse into the river or any canal, big or small.... If one's dwelling is on the bank of the river or canal, if one cannot go to the charnel grounds, then bury the corpse in the earth, out of sight. Don't let it float, bobbing up and down, hither and thither, along the waterway. Consider carefully that tossing animal corpses into the water is despised by all who use and depend on the waterways. When people come to Bangkok, such as people from up-country, or such as monks and apprentices from the Lao regions and small towns of the north, they are resentful and say in contempt that one becomes sick in Bangkok due to unclean water. Such criticism is also voiced by foreigners from abroad: *farang*, English, Chinese, and *khaek*, who come to Bangkok to do business (Sombat 2010: 142).

At the time of the above proclamation, all of Siam's neighbors were under colonial domination. The king had likely considered how foreigners, especially those with steamships, cannons, and imperial intentions, would perceive his ability to manage the kingdom. Such concerns were amplified in the subsequent reign, especially during the French blockade of the Chao Phraya River in 1893, said to have plunged Rama V into deep sadness. In the aftermath of the blockade, territories across the Mekong became French possessions. During his reign, Rama V visited Dutch Java as well as British Burma and India, investigating colonial administration and infrastructure (Peleggi 2007: 14). Subsequent reforms in Siam, initiated by the monarchy, were based on these colonial models. In the late 19th century, Rama V attempted, very successfully, though not without resistance, to disempower up-country rulers. He enacted a new, far more centralized system of territorial and administrative divisions, whereby the country was divided into provinces, districts, townships, and villages, all tightly bound to Bangkok, a pattern of rule that has been described as "internal colonization" (Srisak 2017b: 4).[6] In recent decades, concern with foreign perceptions has persisted, but the dangers have changed. The old variety of colony-hunters no longer threaten the Thai throne. In the 1960s and 1970s, the most feared and despised form of otherness was communism. Thailand's military, royalty, and certainly many ordinary people, watched with trepidation as an insurgency grew in the northern forests, as armed uprisings advanced in neighboring lands, undeterred by the assaults of the US military, and then as the hammer and sickle ascended in war-torn Laos and Cambodia. Still today, a sense of collective vulnerability persists. Negative perceptions are dangerous. In 1997 foreign investors lost faith in Thailand and attacked its currency. The Thai Baht was set afloat, surrendered to the market, and then sank, plunging the country into a steaming soup of economic meltdown. During fieldwork, people sometimes expressed concerns about how Thailand would be represented in my writing. A housekeeper balked when she heard the line about material and heart-spirit. "It sounds pessimistic", she

[6] Srisak uses the expression การสร้างอาณานิคมภายใน, then offers the straightforward translation "internal colonization". However, a haunting question lingers: What is meant by *internal*? Consider, for example, territories forcefully annexed to the Bangkok-centered state. When does a process of colonization become internal?

said. Then she described a documentary made by Korean filmmakers in which "everything [about Thailand] was negative". On another occasion, a stranger brought me sweets from the market, and said, "Now you won't say anything bad about Thailand." As she climbed into a taxi, she yelled, "Say only good things about Thailand!"

The coffee vendor began describing the riverside house of his childhood, but turned the conversation to the military-ousted former prime minister, a high-ranking police officer who had morphed into a telecommunications tycoon before entering politics. He said:

> I don't think foreigners know much about this. I'm saying that the worst prime minister was Thaksin. He's a very bad person. He was the worst prime minister, and he committed the most crimes [ทำบาป] against Thailand. He likes to claim that people of other countries, no matter whether Europe or America, don't accept ministers that come from the overthrow of a government [by a military coup]. And it's true, it's true. He uses this as his primary pretext to call for democracy. But don't forget that he did many things that were illegal. And he was condemned by the court. He was unwilling to go to prison, so he ran away, and he doesn't have the courage to come back [to Thailand].

Later he talked about Thaksin's populism, saying, "Populism can't be sustained. Don't you agree? We can't feed greed and laziness." It was widely believed on both sides of the Red-Yellow divide that Thaksin, in exile in Dubai, continued to run Thailand by video conference. He was like a ghost hovering over society. His sister, Yingluck, elected in 2011, was said to be a "medium" (ร่างทรง), channeling his voice. Many in Bangkok said Thaksin "ate the country", using his position for profit, at the expense of the population. Many also believed he posed a threat to the monarchy, the super-electrified third rail of Thai politics. For the coffee vendor, populism went hand-in-hand with Thaksin's abuse of power. Populism was a form of deception, a vast illusion. In his view, Thaksin deployed such illusions to expand his own power and profit.

I asked the coffee vendor about the expression: We've developed materially, but not in terms of heart-spirit. "Oh!" he said, "I definitely agree. That's exactly right. Look at our railways and the central station. When these were built, we were at the leading edge of this region. But we're using the same old trains. Everything is decayed." He said Thailand had the potential to lead the region: "We could be the top." Notably, his interpretation was not anti-materialist, rather material progress was restrained by the backwardness of heart-spirit. Thaksin, he argued, was an apt example, because material progress under Thaksin's rule was hollow and short-sighted. Populism appeases the myopic. They saw roads, satellite dishes, credit, and for them this meant progress, but the coffee vendor was a disbeliever: "Soon a new governor will be elected. What Thaksin wants is the governor of Bangkok. Everyone thinks that up-country people elected the prime minister, and then the people of Bangkok chased the prime minister away. And it's true! Because people in Bangkok are knowledgeable; they see through his schemes—they know what he's up to" (รู้ทันเขา). Thaksin and the Red Shirts, he said, are "clever image-makers" (เขาสร้างภาพเก่ง). These illusions, and the greed and blindness of those persuaded, had left the country backward. Furthermore, they had created turmoil, conditions bad for investment. Only cultivation of the heart-spirit would bring long-term material progress.

The heart-spirit was within sight, but one needed the right kind of eyes. We were sitting on a concrete bench and the embankment was under construction and I could feel the heat of the welding torch on my neck. "Look at those yellow boats", he said. "You want to know about government incompetence? They scoop trash and water hyacinth out of the river with fishing nets. Those are for fishing! These people are idiots, mentally impaired. We should use machines and start upstream. The water hyacinth floats down from the north, but they don't go to the source. This is all just for looks. It only appears that the government is doing something."

Songs for Life

The art of each age proceeds according to the condition of the heart-spirit, or the way of thinking, of that age.
Jit Phumisak, *Art for Life* (2009 [1957]: 204)

Upstream in Thonburi lived an artist, a graduate from Bangkok's University of Fine Arts. He was a painter, originally from a rice-growing village in Phayao, in the far north. That place, he once said, was the inspiration for all his work. I asked him about the sword-maker's lament: "We've developed materially, but not in terms of heart-spirit." He said, "People say this often, and I agree. Nowadays people do not build material things—material things build people."

He had rented a house near the river. We had many conversations there. It became a sanctuary. The front doors were usually open. Pedestrians, mostly neighbors, often passed. People stopped by throughout the day to relax, read, have coffee, or talk. Some visitors brought sketchpads, pens, and pencils, seeking advice. Guitars came out in the evenings. The walls were decorated with old black-and-white photographs of Native Americans. Here we once watched a Thai-dubbed version of *Soldier Blue*, a film about the massacre of the Cheyenne at Sand Creek. One day we were listening to a rare live recording of Caravan, a band formed in Bangkok around the time of the October 1973 protests against dictatorship. Caravan's early music, with rhythms and melodies reminiscent of the countryside, was performed with acoustic guitar, flute, harmonica, and percussion, as well as regional instruments, such as *pin* (พิณ), a northeastern lute, and *so* (ซอ), a stringed instrument played with a bow. The songs were driven by the voice of Surachai Jantimathawn, a democracy activist who came to be known as Nga Caravan. Still today, "uncle Nga"—with his wild gray hair and broad smile—remains an iconic figure. The lyrics covered subjects from rice cultivation to the bombing of Vietnam. One song celebrates the memory of Jit Phumisak, who was killed in 1966. Jit had joined the communist insurgency in the forests of the northeast. Accounts of his death vary; some say the assailants were villagers, others say soldiers or paramilitaries. The song describes his descent from the mountains "under the shadow of the eagle"—suggesting the presence of the US military—and then his murder "at the edge of the forest". The words evoke a landscape. A man's corpse beside a wagon. Blood on the soil. The song demonstrates the power of art to preserve and transmit memory. Jit's books were banned before the uprising of October 1973, but were widely circulated during the next three years. He had developed a concept of "art for life", emphasizing the context of class conflict and social evolution. It was also a call to arms: "Use your art as a spear and a lamp" (Jit 2009: 92). This led to the emergence of a musical genre: songs for life.

As we sat in the house, the old recording continued. The music was interspersed with documentary-style commentary. Nga Caravan began to sing, a gentle applause swelled, then the music faded and the narrator spoke:

> Art has always been connected to people's lives. Long ago, people began to develop words and melodies; these reflected feelings that arose in different situations. Folk songs or *luk tung* [child of the fields] are songs that reflect the life, the state of being, of people in society. These are the roots of songs for life. These songs are 'for life' because they aim for the betterment of life—the life of the people. They draw from the problems of the people: problems of economics, politics, society, and culture. And they encourage people to rise up, struggle, and call for justice in society.

The artist in Thonburi spent part of his childhood in a temple. When he heard about the alley, where the residents were being driven out by the abbot, his face became tense. "That lizard!" he said. He was quiet for a moment and took a drag from a cigarette. "I don't like monks", he said. "Some are good, but a monk like that abbot is worse than an ordinary person." One of the characteristics of Thai people, it is often said, is that they *wai pra*, which means to honor monks and Buddha images with the *wai*, a gesture made with hands and head. Thus his comment went against the grain of common sense in Bangkok, according to which monks are above ordinary people. This view persists in spite of monastic corruption, a widely known and remarked phenomenon, featured often in the newspapers. Many have heard: monks played cards, took amphetamines, drank booze. Discontent ensued in Bangkok when a monk was filmed tattooing a blond woman. But this situation was much worse. He said, "Ask why is the temple there? Why is the community there? The temple is supposed to be the center of the community." This betrayal exposed the poor condition of the heart-spirit, the deterioration of society.

"It's like those people across the bridge", he said, referring to a place near the Temple of Dawn. "All those houses behind the temple. It's the same situation. They've been trying to drive those people out. Our country is like this. Thailand only." The latter expression was popularized by a skit from the Thai comedian Note Udom, in which he talks about various aspects of everyday culture in Thailand, such as American fried rice, *khaek* bananas, and so on, all of which are perceived as being of foreign origin. But one cannot find *khaek* bananas in India, and Americans have never heard of American fried rice. Thailand only. In my friend's usage, it depicted Thailand as a negative exception, an aberration, a nation outside the world-current.

"This is culture that walks and breathes", he said. "Culture isn't just what is seen in the museum." He thereby drew a contrast between, on the one hand, the formal display of curated, idyllic images of Thai culture, and on the other, the neglect and destruction of living communities. This was also related to the basic idea of songs for life—or, more generally, art for life: art should have a primary relationship with the day-to-day existence and struggles of ordinary people. I asked about the word "culture" (วัฒนธรรม). What do you mean by that? He replied, "I don't think about that word. I don't want to fall victim to that word." He was well educated, with a university degree, and also a large book collection, including Thai translations of García Márquez, Tolstoy, Nietzsche, even a collection of essays by the anthropologist Colin Turnbull. "Culture", he warned, is a "discourse" (วาทกรรม). He was a non-conformist from the periphery, born in a village in a border province, where people speak the "northern" language. If they speak Thai, and some do not, many speak with strong provincial accents, especially the older generations. Bangkok, as he once said, was "another matter altogether". He was committed to creating an alternative path, his own trajectory. "I can't just go work for some company", he said. "I've never even submitted an application. I know I can't do it." Instead, he taught children how to draw. He made and sold handicrafts. And he turned his house into an art studio.

"People must be educated", he said. "That's the way to develop the heart-spirit. I think it's the only way." And then he added, "We also have to erase the old system." The expression "old system" implied antiquated relations of power, as formalized in institutions. At first, his comment seemed to resonate with Red Shirt outcries against feudalism. Red Shirts often said that the old system, or the old hierarchy, no longer works. But he distanced himself from shirts of all colors. He admired an older generation, especially the early days of the songs for life movement. One of the key moments was October 14, 1973, when a popular uprising triumphed over dictatorship. Students had been restless since April, when soldiers, hunting rifles, and gaur meat were found aboard a helicopter that crashed in Nakhon Pathom. An investigation revealed a large hunting expedition in Thung Yai Naresuan, a wildlife sanctuary. The expedition included officers and officials with close ties to the military regime of Thanom Kittikachorn. The prime minister claimed—in spite of evidence to the contrary—that the helicopter's crew were not involved in poaching. After decades of military rule, this scandal built up to an enormous protest, including demands for a new constitution. The uprising ended with an intervention of the king and Thanom's departure from Thailand. It was the generation of Caravan. The artist said, "In those days, people *knew* that society needed to change." In his view, the shirts, Red and Yellow alike, were mostly mere followers, mobs arising from incitement rather than consciousness. By contrast, the Caravan generation was aware and committed, ready to take up arms and go into the forest in the aftermath of the October 6, 1976 massacre at Thammasat University, an event followed by a return to military rule and threats of further violence against the population.

For him, the Caravan generation still represented a promising trajectory. The line may be faded, but it is still visible and remains a source of identity and hope. In a collection of interviews about democracy in Thailand, Thamrongsak Petchlertanan, a Thai political scientist, states, "The memory and experience of October 14 makes the people [ประชาชน] believe that power [อำนาจ] belongs to them" (2014: 83). On October 14, 1973 began a brief period, three years or so, of openness and optimism, and also a sustained flood of creativity. Flood is an emic metaphor. A book dealer, who had been a university student during those years, described it that way: a flood of creativity. It was unprecedented. Benedict Anderson, who had been barred from Suharto's Indonesia and was then recreating himself as a Thai specialist, writes, "In 1974 and most of 1975, Siam was an extraordinarily free and exhilarating place, full of student demonstrations, workers' strikes, peasant mobilizations, and the sharpest political debates. In the spring of 1975 the country's first-ever genuinely free election took place, and for the first—and last—time a substantial number of left-wing people were elected to parliament" (1998: 22).

This period of freedom came to a horrifying close on October 6, 1976, when students were massacred at Thammasat University, a campus at the edge of the Chao Phraya River. A protest had gathered after Thanom

Kittikachorn, the dictator ousted in 1973, had returned to Thailand as a novice monk. He was escorted to Wat Bowonniwet, a temple under royal patronage (วัดหลวง), where kings had previously ordained. It is also an internment site of royal ashes. As protests gained momentum, a paramilitary organization known as the Red Gaurs protected the temple (Matichon 2021). A counter-protest encircled the students, who were derided as communists, anti-royal, and anti-Thai. Soon began the assault. Alan Klima writes, "Both girls and boys were made to strip to the waist and lie still while police rained down rifle-butts or boot heels on their heads and backs" (2002: 79). Enthusiastic mobs watched, "cheering wildly, waving national flags, and singing their ghoulish killing songs" (ibid.). Dozens were murdered. Some were hanged, others burned alive. Corpses were mutilated. Seksan Prasertkul, who witnessed the massacre, writes, "On October 6, in the Buddhist year 2519, the student movement that emerged at Thammasat University ... was crushed. Then and there, the peacefully protesting students were assaulted and brutally killed by state officers and right-wing masses, until the campus was full of dead bodies soaked in pools of blood, the bodies of youth dreaming of something better for their home country" (2016: 11–12). An informant drew a stark comparison between 1973 and 1976, emphasizing the role of ordinary people, saying that on October 14 the *chao baan* supported the students, but on October 6 they were against them. A well-known photograph depicts a boy's bloody corpse hanging from a tree. A man is swinging a metal chair at the body, while a crowd of onlookers watch gleefully, many of them smiling. Reportedly, some of the wounded were received by boat, then intercepted. Some students jumped into the river. Red Gaurs and police shot people attempting to swim away (*Matichon* 2021). The military promptly took control of the country, dissolved democracy, and began incarcerating enemies. Thailand's current lese-majesty laws—including section 112, which forbids any criticism or disdainful expression concerning the king, queen, heir to the throne, or the regent—can be traced to military rule in the aftermath of the October 6 massacre. Section 112, with sentences of 3 to 15 years for a single conviction, constitutes a powerful tool for enforcing silence and obedience. Meanwhile, none of the perpetrators of the massacre were prosecuted. Studies find "indubitable historical evidence" of coordinated efforts to erase October 6 from collective memory, to cast it into "oblivion" (Tanabe and Keyes 2002: 24). Thus emerges a struggle of recollection, to preserve or eliminate a political consciousness of the massacre, a struggle seen, for example, in the documentary film *The Two Brothers* (*สองพี่น้อง*), which opens with contemporary footage of a rusty gate, also depicted in an October 1976 photograph, where two young electricians were hanged. The film thereby brings the half-forgotten, other-worldly horror into the mundane landscape of the present.

October 14, 1973 is also in danger of being forgotten. During fieldwork, on the day of the anniversary, it went unmentioned on the front page of *Siam Rath*, a daily newspaper. The main headline reported National Police Day next to a photograph of uniformed officers in formation. On the evening news there was no mention of the event: an enormous student-led uprising against a widely despised dictatorship. Nothing. No one I encountered that morning recognized the date. The newspaper vendor said, "Today? No, today is not important. Tomorrow! Tomorrow is a Buddhist holy day [วันพระ]." I inquired further. She was bewildered, saying only, "That has nothing to do with me." Some university graduates, who were asked later, recognized the date, but did not hold it in special regard. One said, "It's only important to people in that circle, people of that generation. It's not so important really—they didn't even make it into a holiday."

That morning I took a boat along the Canal of a Hundred Thousand Stings, en route to the Democracy Monument, the center of the October 14, 1973 demonstrations. The boat stopped at the pier. There was a gathering of Red Shirts around the monument. Many had set up vending booths. It was a substantial gathering, but not a heavily crowded or aggressive demonstration. Signs were posted denouncing feudalism, monopoly, and dictatorship. A man stood on a platform in front of the monument, speaking into a microphone. Some of those present were listening intently. All were dressed in red. The faces of Thaksin and Yingluck were printed on numerous posters and shirts. Yingluck, the younger sister of Thaksin, was elected prime minister in 2011, mostly with the support of pro-Thaksin up-country voters in the north and northeast. It was a major Red Shirt victory. Many of the goods for sale at the booths incorporated the memorable slogan "Thaksin thinks, Yingluck does." I went around the traffic circle, taking photographs, notes, and talking to some of the vendors. The organizers certainly recognized the date's symbolism. While speaking to a vendor, I noted the significance of October 14, anticipating recognition. She replied, "It has nothing to do with that. This is just to say that we are free."

Months before, I met the artist for the first time. He was reserved, smoking a cigarette by the door, as someone else talked about the recent floods. Some parts of Bangkok were still inundated or under reconstruction. Deforestation upstream along the Chao Phraya and her tributaries had increased the threat of devastation by water. Perhaps, I suggested, the recent disaster would increase awareness. He interrupted, saying, "Thai people think only for a moment, and then forget." It was the first thing he ever said to me—an observation, lament, and warning.

Songs for life are also songs of another trajectory. A certain past, a certain future, a time of possibility. Caravan's songs for life have kept that past alive. In songs for life, the promise and optimism of another age still walks and breathes. Astrid Erll writes, "Due to its capacity to relate past, present, and future—envisioning alternative trajectories through a recourse to the past, activating forgotten knowledge in the present, making sense of the new by comparing it to the old—memory is the very apparatus that enables change" (2011: 174). Futures can take shape through creative relations to the past; the forgotten can be revived, and thereby nurture a new trajectory. A very optimistic perspective, and one certainly needs optimism, but change is also a matter of scale, and some futures will exist only in certain places, in small, temporary pockets.

Sunset in Thonburi. On the west bank of the Chao Phraya River. Among friends from the northern provinces. A young artist checks the time, then brings more ice and pours me another glass of beer. The last express boat has departed. No hurry. One can always catch a taxi.

"Caravan", he said, "is close to my heart." One day he observed that Nga Caravan, the band's frontman, "hasn't changed". It was an admiring observation, but some people would bitterly disagree. The Red-Yellow conflict has deeply divided the songs for life circle. Nga has performed onstage at Yellow Shirt rallies. He has also been denounced by many leftists for his open support of the 2006 military coup against Thaksin. In self-defense, Nga has explained that he supported the coup because Thailand appeared to be approaching a violent catastrophe. In an interview on Thai PBS, he said, "The purpose [of the coup] was not to suppress the people, but to prevent violence."[7] Many still see this as a betrayal. In a collection of short biographical essays, Nga has written about his involvement with the Yellow Shirts, as well as the days when he—as a young idealist, armed with a rifle—lived in the forest with the communists. The collection is titled *Tang Sen Gao* (Surachai 2010), which can be translated as "the old path" or "the old way". The title suggests reminiscence, a journey, motion in time, and persistence. My friend never mentioned Nga's involvement with the Yellow Shirts. Perhaps he could see more deeply. The music of Caravan endures, keeping alive a certain period in time when youth in Thailand—students, artists, and others—wanted to create a better world.

Temples

Pain, hardship, and suffering are of benefit—not only to the body, but also to the heart-spirit. Pain, hardship, and suffering will teach us patience and give rise to wisdom.
Phra Paisal Visalo (2011: 21)

An informant invited me to the temple. Upon setting out, rain began to pour. Surprisingly, a generous street vendor offered an umbrella. Wat Pathum is a curious sanctuary, a quiet place along a major road, tucked between two shopping malls. During the Red Shirt demonstrations of 2010, soldiers from the royal Thai military shot and killed six unarmed people, including a volunteer nurse, within the grounds of this temple. A concrete wall extends along the road, and just outside the temple grounds one finds the central hub of the city's skytrain system.

She was waiting in the temple's parking lot. We exchanged greetings, then walked along a paved path lined with trees. The air grew cooler and the rain softened to a light patter. She often came here to practice meditation. She was Bangkok-born, of Chinese descent, thirty-something, a teacher, and was studying part-time for a master's degree. She lived with

---

[7] Nga Caravan appeared (circa 2012) on *Answering Questions* (ตอบโจทย์).

her mother, on the other side of the river, in a narrow, multistory house in Thonburi. She said her family was poor, and some people viewed her as "low society". Others, however, thought she was well-established, even affluent, because she owned a car, laptop, and a smartphone.

We removed our shoes and sat in the meditation hall. A few others were sitting on the vast red carpet. The hall included large, imposing images of the king and queen. Such images are ubiquitous in Thai temples, material reminders of the official triad, the ever-repeated inseparability of Nation, Religion, and King. A monk, slightly elevated on a platform, spoke quietly, droning into a microphone. She warned that the monks, with their deep, monotonous voices, are sometimes difficult to understand. The sound of automobile traffic had receded, but the rain returned, striking the ground heavily around the pavilion. This was an opportunity, said the monk, to practice awareness, a chance to calm our hearts. He said, "The rain seems like an inconvenience, but encourages us to slow down. And this is good, because our minds, like urban life, are constantly in motion, rarely settling, running here and there." We sat for an uncertain amount of time. Cycles of chanting in Pali alternated with the sound of rain. She brought laminated pages, each with lines of Pali written in Thai characters, so we could follow the chants. A few more bodies arrived and sat. We had left the crowds and noisy streets of Bangkok.

She suffered from stress and depression. Once she said that she often thought of killing herself, but would not explain why. Our interactions were sometimes tense. She lived with her mother and spoke elusively about troubles at home. From the patchwork of stories, one could surmise that her father had abandoned them, and probably for another woman. She shared a bed with her mother, who she described as pitiable (น่าสงสาร). Once, during a casual conversation, we talked about the figure of the of *jao chu* (เจ้าชู้) in Thai culture. A *jao chu* is a charismatic man or woman with many partners. The *jao chu*—usually but not always male—is celebrated in songs, television dramas, and everyday life. A good example is the story, said to be true, of Chalawan. Everyone in Phichit, a province north of Bangkok, knows the story. Chalawan, lord of crocodiles, lived with his human wives in a cave in the depths of the Nan River. When Chalawan entered the cave he became a beautiful man, attended by his devoted wives, but upon leaving, he became a crocodile, which terrorized villagers along the waterways. One day Chalawan saw a young female bathing in the river. Taken by her beauty, he captured her and carried her to his cave. In the end, Chalwan was killed by Kraitong, a dashing crocodile-hunter armed with a magical spear. As a reward, Kraitong received three wives: a rich man's daughters and one of the wives of Chalawan. High-status, affluent men especially are assumed to be *jao chu*, as if this reflected the natural order. Rama V, for example, an icon of power and virility, had dozens of female companions and fathered 97 children. Some Thais noted, very casually, that their fathers had "minor wives". She was irritated by this observation, and especially the suggestion that it was part of Thai culture. "It's not Thai culture", she said. "It's the culture of men." She was an avid reader of Buddhist literature, especially the popular variety found in shops throughout Bangkok. Many turn to this literature to reduce suffering in day-to-day life. "But some people", she said, "will look at you funny if you read these books. They'll think something is wrong with you."

Months later, we traveled to Amphawa, a district famous for waterways. The town is southwest of Bangkok, centered on the slithering coils of the Mae Klong River.[8] We met next to Rama IV Road, a notoriously congested strip of pavement, which originated as a bi-product of canalization. It once followed, and was named after, the Hua Lamphong Canal, dug in 1856—indeed, the road was originally built from earth excavated from the trench (Walailak 2017: 91). Later, in order to expand the road, the canal was filled. It was a fine starting point for our journey: a microcosm of Thai urbanization. She drove. We went along the perimeter of Klong Toey, an enormous mass of informal dwellings. We crossed railroad tracks, and soon we were crossing the Chao Phraya. I looked down and observed a stream splitting off from the river. She was amused, saying, "You are like a child, looking and pointing at everything." We continued beyond the edge of Bangkok, through an unbroken urban terrain. She was frustrated by a shortage of road signs. After two hours of driving and several stops for directions, we arrived and parked at the Gulf of Thailand, where streets were lined

[8] A network of canals integrate the Mae Klong with the Chao Phraya. Both drain into the Gulf of Thailand.

with vendors selling fresh fish. We sat on a stone wall eating noodles, and could see small boats in the expanse of water and sky.

Then we drove the remaining distance to Amphawa. We stopped at a national park, built in honor of King Rama II. We bought bags of pellets and fed the fish in a canal. The park contained an air-conditioned exhibit in a large, wooden stilt-house that described local traditional life, especially the importance of waterways. In the center of the room was a topographic model: land surrounded, crisscrossed, and held together by water. Panels celebrated artists of nationwide reputation born in Amphawa, thereby linking locality and nation, amplifying the national stature of the town. Panels described the fate of floating houses, which began to disappear, here and elsewhere, in the era of Field Marshal Pibulsongkram. According to official pretense, the materials were needed for land-based structures. But it probably had more to do with changing the face of Thailand. It was the time of the Cultural Mandates, a series of top-down measures imposed to civilize the population: coercing people to wear hats, change habits of speech, and self-identify as Thai. What makes this place appealing to Thai visitors is a sense that the old way of life has been preserved. Visitors from Bangkok can glimpse the past of the metropolis, a way of life fading from the Chao Phraya River. At the same time, the scene reminds visitors that memory is delicate and vulnerable. Memory needs care, otherwise it withers and departs, passing with generations. On the way to the canal-side market, we saw an outdoor exhibit, featuring dozens of small, wooden boat replicas. Line drawings of the vessels were stacked on a table, along with boxes of crayons. Two children were coloring furiously. A panel explained the purpose of the exhibit: so people will remember a way of life that is vanishing.

We entered the market by the canal. She suggested a boat trip, so we could see the waterways and visit five temples. Strangely, the driver told us the trip would last only an hour. We paid the driver, scrambled aboard, together with a few strangers, and soon were in the middle of an idyllic, water-filled landscape. The river was wide, with few other boats. We entered a canal and passed extravagant houses with manicured lawns. A woman was washing a noodle pot at the edge of the canal. Passengers were at ease, unaffected by the crushing volume of the engine.

It was a short trip out of Bangkok, a mixture of merit-making, sightseeing, and visualizing the Thai past. We applied gold leaf paper to the Buddha statues at the temples, all of which contained royal images and national flags. But each temple was unique, with its own charm and gimmicks. We drew fortune sticks. We fed cows. A monk gave blessings and sprinkled us with water. We took turns hitting a large metal gong, which was hanging next to a sign: "The louder the sound, the richer you'll be." One temple had a camel and a six-legged turtle. She said, "Sometimes the strange is auspicious." It indicated a powerful place. We entered a shrine and found a replica of one of the Buddha's teeth, copied, the panel said, from an original in Sri Lanka. One of the temples was concrete, overgrown with tree roots. Another complex contained statues arranged in hand-to-hand combat, some with hands broken off and wires sticking out of the stumps.

We returned to the market by boat, and already the sun was sinking into the horizon. She asked, "Do you prefer sunset or sunrise?" She preferred sunset: "The day is over, things good and bad have passed. Tomorrow is a new day."

Months later, during an interview, she described her perspective on material and heart-spirit. She said,

> Look, it's always been like this, and not just for Thailand. In many countries, I think, or maybe the whole world, they say: day by day, we're developing materially, but the heart-spirit is developing less. Right? People say that, but I don't agree. Material must be developed. Who isn't going to build more roads? That's material! The BTS is also material. And now they're going to build a high-speed train. So ask: Are we going to stop building? In my view, we have to separate the two. Material is material. Heart-spirit is heart-spirit. Are we going to stop building material? Then how are we going to travel quickly to Korat? [she laughed] Material can't be stopped. But actually the heart-spirit is developing. For many of the Thai people that I know, the heart-spirit of each person is developing. Each person is different. But I want to separate this from material. Don't say that if material develops, then the heart-spirit will be low. Material has to be high! There's no relationship. They're separate. Build the BTS, and then come sit and meditate. Isn't that development? If we're meditating then we're meditating! [she laughed again] I think now the heart-spirit of Thai people is developing. A lot of people are turning around, coming back to Buddhist teachings (ธรรมะ), more than when I was a child. I feel like that—I look

> around me. Buddhism has been with Thailand for a long time. It can help Thai people develop the heart-spirit. These days, it hasn't gone down, it's increased. More people are interested in Buddhism. But at the same time, there are more people in society, and people are increasingly complex. It's more difficult to understand people. It's more difficult to live. Everything is more difficult. So people try to come back to their true selves, and that's the heart-spirit. What can we do to develop the heart-spirit? It depends on the person. Some people sit and meditate at home, some people go to the temple. It depends. If one develops the heart-spirit, what's developing? If you develop the heart-spirit, what do you do? Do you have to go to the temple? Well, no. It's more about changing one's thought. We might not have time to go to the temple, but we can learn forgiveness. It depends. Another person goes to the temple everyday just to buy lottery tickets. So we have to ask: If the heart-spirit develops, what's really developing? Because each person develops differently. But I feel that people are giving more importance to the heart-spirit. It might be because life in society is more difficult, more than when I was a child. I don't know if I'll agree or disagree that the heart-spirit is low. The heart-spirit might be low because there are more people. In the past, suppose there were 100 people, and there was one person who was not good. Now there are 1,000 people, so there are 10 people who are not good. It's the same percentage. I've never inspected the official crime statistics, but I think it's because there are more people.

It was a rather unusual response. Most informants, when asked the same question, quickly agreed. By contrast, she expressed confidence in the heart-spirit, but also noted changes in society: more people, more complexity, more difficulty. In her view, with the exception of a small percentage of people who are "not good", most Thai people were developing the heart-spirit, progressing, as individuals, in a positive direction. However, although her response was distinctive, this pattern of dividing the population into good and not good is deeply embedded in the political culture of Thailand. The expression "good" (ดี) has not only moral connotations, but is also associated with manners, education, class, lineage, and nobility. The word has a complex relationship to the discourse of democracy. Notably, in another conversation, she had described the almost total corruption of elected politicians. Along a gradient, from people preferring a more limited democracy to those altogether opposed to it, there is a pattern of a wish to circumscribe sovereignty with some, not always defined, form of good. Before the military coup of 2014—following a proposed amnesty bill that would allow Thaksin, the military-ousted former prime minister, to return to Thailand—a storm of violent emotion flooded the streets of Bangkok. The leaders of the People's Democratic Reform Committee (PDRC), a short-lived group that included many Yellow Shirts, but also had a wider appeal, called on the military to seize power, demanded "reform before elections", and proposed that a new prime minister—a "good person"—be appointed by the king. All to the delight of crowds armed with whistles and national flags.

Buddhist monks often appeared on stage with the PDRC. Suthep Thaugsuban, an aggressive politician and the leader of the PDRC, positioned the movement as upholders of Nation, Religion, and King, and he spoke over and over in the name of "good people". Following the 2014 military coup, Suthep ordained as a Buddhist monk. Prior to the coup, when elections were scheduled, the PDRC called a boycott, aware that supporters of Prime Minister Yingluck would be the majority at the polls. The protesters claimed the result would be distorted by rampant buying and selling of votes. In their eyes, the process was overshadowed by the manipulative power of Thaksin—the embodiment of "vile capital"—and the voters were essentially ignorant, selfish, and corrupt. Polling places were surrounded, sometimes entirely blocked. Many of those brave enough to vote in Bangkok were subjected to outpourings of contempt and abuse, such as, "Go home and eat grass! Let's hear you sing the national anthem!"

The PDRC is a stark example of a political mass mobilized under the slogan "Nation, Religion, King". During the interview, it was not surprising that she emphasized Buddhism as the vehicle to develop the heart-spirit. In the aftermath of the military coup, a collection of powerful and unsettling essays were written by Vichak Panich—a practicing Buddhist, teacher of meditation, and critical observer of Thai society. In the book, he reflects at length on the relationship between Buddhism and politics in Thailand. He writes, "These days, in our country, we are very interested in Buddhist practice [การปฏิบัติธรรม], to the point that some people believe that if 'the entire country engaged in Buddhist practice', it would be the most effective way to resolve the problem of political conflict. But as far as I can see, the fact that more people are engaged in such practice hasn't improved society. Furthermore, all too often, practicing Buddhists still approve, still see it as good and beautiful, if the country is ruled by weapons and tanks, still approve when their fellow nationals' right of freedom is violated. Some even approve of political killings, seeing such killings as good and beautiful" (Vichak 2015: 309–10). Reading this book in Bangkok, while living under dictatorship, it evoked a familiar, commonplace, but also very frightening, image of Thai society—something ever-present, but usually unspoken.

One evening, about two years after the military coup, a taxi driver in Bangkok responded to a question about the next election—for the military had promised elections, but repeatedly pushed them back into an indefinite future. "That doesn't concern me", he said. "I walk the middle path. If we have an election, things will be the way they were before: Red Shirts and Yellow Shirts will fight again. Both sides are stupid. I'm not stupid, so I walk the middle path." He went on to praise General Prayuth Chan-ocha, the leader of the 2014 coup, calling him "clever". The middle path is a Buddhist concept related to the teaching of moderation. Siddhartha had abandoned the techniques of harsh asceticism, instead advocating a practice neither too severe, nor too indulgent. The conversation reflected nothing extraordinary. In Thailand, to follow the middle path can entail submission to and support of military control.

River of Kings

We sat in front of a yellow church, the center of a small community, in the Samray district of Bangkok, on the western bank of the Chao Phraya River. It was morning, and everyone was waiting for the Sunday service to begin. The others, all Thais, waited as believers. Every Sunday, after the service, church-goers gathered for lunch at benches in the shade of an open, riverside shelter. On previous visits, I had interviewed some of the older members of the community. As we waited, some people asked about my research. It was a project about waterways. One of the men, a singer and guitar player in the church band, nodded and smiled, and said, "Our great king has allowed Mon, Muslims, and Christians to live along the river."

The interior of the church was austere, with wooden pews, white walls, a few chandeliers, and with purple curtains along the back behind the podiums. It was a place seemingly transplanted from the American Midwest to Bangkok, and yet firmly rooted. The community traced its origins to Presbyterian missionaries who had arrived in Siam during the Third Reign, in the first half of the 19th century. During the service there were numerous songs. Singers stood at microphones, often smiling, accompanied by guitar and piano. The man next to me was determined to introduce me to God. He brought out his bible, which was—curiously, it might seem—bound in blue denim. He placed his hand on my arm.

The pastor sat quietly on a platform. He was always calm, generous, and dignified. He was held in great esteem by the community. People described him as "down to earth".

Another man, a guest, spoke before the congregation, describing the hardship of missionary work. He told a story about a Christian missionary in Africa. The story did not delve into the specifics of geography or culture, but the rate of conversion was slow. It was very difficult, he said. One needs patience. He illustrated the missionary's resolve. Faced with native resistance to the word of God, the missionary said to himself, "If not today, then tomorrow. If not in this age, then in the next age." It was a patience based on certainty, on events sure to come, a trajectory defined by faith. But one must be reminded. One must remind oneself. And now, here, at a church in Bangkok, on the bank of the Chao Phraya River, the congregation was told about missionaries in Fiji and Borneo. "Can you imagine it?" he asked. "The natives were cannibals!" He then read from Hebrews 11, a passage about persecution, and added this commentary: "Now, here in Thailand—now they say we have freedom, but who knows about the future?" There was a curious and profound movement in the discourse, from missionaries to persecution, and then from the persecution of the ancient Hebrews to a specter of persecution, an undesirable place in the Thai future, arrived at by movement in the wrong direction, a dangerous trajectory.

The pastor came to the podium. He spoke not of persecution, but of North Korea and nuclear weapons. Perhaps he had been troubled by an article in the morning newspaper. "Let us pray", he said, "that God will instill the North Korean leader with wisdom, and that peace will prevail."

When the service ended, we filed out through the doorway, which faces the Chao Phraya River. The water-mother glimmered in the late morning sunshine.

The pastor was in his mid-seventies and referred to himself as a lifelong servant of God. He had been a teacher of religion for most of his life. Four or five years prior to our meeting, he had been established as a pastor. He was not a native of Bangkok. He was born in the north, in a place where waterways were a vital part of day-to-day life. As a child, he lived in a floating house—a "raft house"—on the Nan River, one of the four primary streams that flow into the Chao Phraya.

He recalled Bangkok's waterways, as seen decades ago: "When I first came to Bangkok, there were still many canals. We would row through the canals. We'd go fishing, and we could eat the fish. The water was clean. The water used to be clear. Even 30 years ago, it wasn't this bad. After that, many new buildings were built, and so there are pipes that drain into the canals. The water has been spoiled, corrupted (น้ำก็เน่า). Now, it's very murky. The river is no longer a river." He then panned out, painting a bigger picture: "This started during the Fifth Reign [late

Tires and chains on a dock

19th century]. Up till then, let's say one wanted to go to Chachoengsao [a province east of Bangkok]. Well, they dug a canal, and they'd row. Better to take a boat than walk. Then people didn't want to row anymore, and so the canals were filled and became roads. But our country never made plans."

One might wonder how it happened. How, in this Buddhist-majority country, did he become a Christian? His father was a convert. His father had ordained as a Buddhist monk when he was 15 years old. In Thailand, it is, or at least used to be, standard practice for young males to enter monastic life, usually on a temporary basis, for one season of rain. One who does so earns merit for his parents, and also makes a lifelong transition from "raw" to "cooked". The pastor said that his father, whom he referred to with the ultra-respectful pronoun *tan*, ordained a second time at age 21, and remained a monk until the age of 38. He then decided to get married and start a family. It was only after his father left the monastery that he developed a faith in God. The pastor emphasized that his father had studied Buddhism. His father was, after all, a monk for many years. He tried to explain:

> Put simply, Buddhism teaches: do good, receive good; do evil, receive evil.[9] That is, if one does good, one goes to heaven. If one does evil, one goes to hell. But it's temporary. So, if one does good, one might go to heaven for 10 years. But then, say, one does evil—one goes to hell for 10 years. It's not permanent. It's called the application of karma, or paying for one's misdeeds. Let's say you kill a cow. Well, you'll be reborn as a cow. And so my father began to feel disconcerted, and he began to wonder: Is there another religion, a religion in which one—if one has done good—will not have to go to hell? And he found it.
>
> But, at first, my father didn't accept it. He met an American missionary. I still remember—his name was Stewart. When my father left the Buddhist monastery, he was out of work. Then he got a job driving a private motorboat for the missionary on the Nan River. They called it a '*tok* boat' (เรือต๊อก) because of the sound of the engine: *Tok! Tok! Tok!* They'd go along the waterways, from house to house, and the missionary would distribute pamphlets and bibles. He would also read the scripture for people. You see, in those days, very few people could read. It was mainly just the monks who could read. So

[9] ทำดีได้ดี ทำชั่วได้ชั่ว: "Do good, receive good. Do evil, receive evil." This is among the most prominent *suphasit* (ancient proverbs) in Thailand.

> this American missionary was teaching Thai people how to read Thai. But my father could read because he had studied in the monastery. [Later,] my father let his first daughter, my older sister, live with the missionary, and the missionary taught her about Christianity. My father realized: this is the right way. He began taking his wife and children to the church. Ever since then, I've been a servant of God.

Some would say that Christianity is not Thai culture. Thailand, many would agree, is a Buddhist country. I asked him about this. He replied:

> You see, Thai people love the king and the Chakri royal family very much. Christians also love the king and the royal family. And Christians also follow the biblical teaching that one must be loyal to the rulers [or 'guardians' (ผู้ปกครอง)] of one's country. Every Sunday we pray for the king and royal family. As Thai Christians love the king, Thai Christians also respect [นับถือ] Buddhism. Some people, however, think that if one is not a Buddhist, then one is not loyal to the king. I might get into an argument with someone. And so I ask them: You're loyal to the king, right? And, of course, they say yes. And so I ask: Do you do anything to put the king's heart at ease? Anger, envy, all this grabbing, snatching, and fighting—is this how you show your love for the king? Ah, decide for yourself. But I hold that I'm under the protection of the king, and so I need to conduct my life properly. I need to help develop the country, take care of my family, look after society. This is how we show our loyalty to the king. The important thing is this: God created the sky, heaven, and earth—that, at least, is what I believe. And so religion must be separated from loyalty to the king. I am loyal to the king. I am also a Christian, and so I try to conduct myself properly, and thereby show loyalty to the king.
>
> We don't say that Buddhism or any other religion is bad. One has to study first. If people come here to study with me, I'll teach them. But what if I go teach somewhere else? Some people might not like it, and they might say that it's defamation. If someone accuses you of defamation, you can be sent to prison. So we have to show our faith to God, and also serve society. Still, many people hold that since the king is Buddhist, they must also be Buddhist. And so if one knocks on a door, with the intention to distribute bibles, one can be accused of defamation. One can distribute bibles along the street. If they accept, OK. If not, we don't say anything—we can't coerce them. But we can't knock on doors. It's difficult. It's more difficult [here in Thailand] than in Laos, Cambodia, Burma, or China. There are some things I cannot say, not because they are defamatory, but because it is not appropriate to say them to others. Some things cannot be said.

I began to ask about the imbalance of material and heart-spirit. He knew what I was going to say. Before I had finished the sentence, he pointed to his heart. "That's right", he said.

> Heart-spirit is of the utmost importance. It is the most important thing of all. The schools set up by the government neglect the heart-spirit. Let me give you an example, a very simple example. People throw garbage into the river. People don't have discipline. Don't throw trash into the river—take it to the basket. But it's easier to throw it into the river. And, if one isn't taught from a young age, when one grows up one can't be taught anymore. To this day, people buy snacks in plastic bags, then throw the bags into the water. It has become a habit. They've been saying for tens of years that they'll put this in the school curriculum. But it's still not in the curriculum. This habit, it's what Thai people call freedom, or democracy, *Thai style*. Thai style means not like the rest of the world (สากล). The rest of the world does it right, but Thai people say, 'We don't want it. We want it Thai style.' So we haven't progressed as much as other nations.
>
> Thai style is like this: I'm in my group, and so I want to administer matters this way. Others aren't involved. If you go up-country, you'll see that the houses have no fences. One can just go from house to house. Now in the up-country rural areas they can develop more easily than in Bangkok. Progress has gone up-country. They've got wide roads. But in Bangkok, the roads are narrow. It's because of all these big buildings. This is Thai-style. People say, I don't want this or that. How can progress come into the country? The government wanted to build a dam, so it wouldn't flood, and so there would be enough water for agriculture in the dry season. But the people said, 'We don't want it!' And then what? They went out in a big protest and obstructed the project. The government couldn't build it. And now? We have a flood because there's no dam. This is Thai-style democracy, and so we don't progress. What we need is international-style democracy. Here's how it works in Thailand: if one isn't satisfied with the government, one tells the military, 'Please carry out a coup.' And then the soldiers bring their guns. If you don't like it, you get shot. I don't have a gun, so I have to accept it. And so the military takes control. Now we're trying to keep the military under the law. But they can still declare martial law. And when that happens, they'll control the country. Why do the people have to accept it? Because the military has tanks and every variety of weapon. This is the difficulty.

Thai style is identified with Bangkok, a metropolis with the power to set cultural standards. Here, however, we find a curious turn. Progress has gone up-country because people outside the capital conduct their affairs in a different way, not Thai style. Thai style is associated with fences and borders, a divided, bounded landscape. Fences are a tangible presence, reflecting the character of community and society. An absence of fences is a condition of development, implying a less exclusionary mindset. His narrative moved quickly from fences to "people say, I don't want this or that". The themes are linked: obstruction and refusal. One builds a fence in order to exclude, and this could mean the exclusion of development, or progress. Thai style—above all, the style of Bangkok—means exclusion, a collective mentality that isolates. Thai style means exceptionalism. Not only fences, but borders. Thai style, he said, "Means not like the rest of the world." But his narrative invoked an alternate trajectory, a broader, more fruitful path.

Exceptionalism is a key feature of Thai politics. Unlike its neighbors, Thailand was not officially colonized, nor did Thais experience the socio-temporal break implied by decolonization. Although encircled and absorbed by a colonial economic system, and restructured in the manner of neighboring colonies, a myth has grown that Thailand is an exception. This myth, although a point of pride, and even national arrogance, is also a powerful political weapon. I interviewed the pastor in 2013. One year later, crowds mobilized in Bangkok to condemn and chase out the democratically elected government, to oppose—by force and fear-tactics—new elections, and to replace the elected body with an appointed one. Suthep Thaugsuban, the primary mobilizer of the PDRC, reminded audiences to be proud and thankful that Thailand had never been colonized. Tanks drove through Bangkok's streets in May 2014, Thai style, and the military again took control of the country.

Redirecting the River

The 2014 military coup arrested Thailand's trajectory, yet the long-term significance of this arrangement is an open question. Society cannot be unilaterally controlled. The authorities have been unable to enforce a serene stillness, but the coup has certainly entailed a change of motion. Some sectors have supported the military. On the other side, one finds a mixture of restraint and discontent, bold protests, and a sense that the age has changed. This moment will remain worthy of reflection. In the year following the coup, Nidhi Eoseewong wrote, "I must confess, this coup has brought my mind to an impasse. I cannot see a peaceful political way out, a way without bloodshed" (2015: 12). The new constitution was drafted under military command. It passed a public referendum in 2016, and then was ratified in 2017. Article 257 states the following objective for the "reform" of the country: "The nation-state will be peaceful and orderly, will be in harmony, will develop sustainably in accordance with the principles of the sufficiency economy, and will have a balance between material development and development of the heart-spirit" (Sathaporn 2017: 257). Under dictatorship, it was dangerous to offer critical views of the draft constitution prior to the referendum. In addition to explicit control and prohibition, the military created an atmosphere of uncertainty and fear. In accordance with the 2017 constitution, the upper portion of the Thai parliament will be appointed rather than elected. The appointment of 250 senators was arranged by the military junta, known as the National Council for Peace and Order (NCPO)—thereby deepening the trench. The NCPO was formally dissolved after the elections of March 2019. However, the council's enduring power was evident when parliament convened in June: 249 (all but one) of the appointed senators—together with pro-military factions in the lower house—voted in support of the coup leader, General Prayuth, who continued as prime minister until August 2023. Even with a formal end of military control, the conditions of power and conflict in Thai society will not easily dissipate.

Rather than conclude, let us consider a metaphor of modest hope: the slow, strenuous, collective labor of canalization. The following is a translated excerpt from a monologue by Phra Paisal Visalo, a former student activist, who was briefly incarcerated after the October 6 massacre (Phra Paisal 2018: 115). He is now the abbot of an up-country Buddhist temple.[10]

> The path of our heart, sometimes it changes like a river. The river, or the course of the river—if it goes one way, then that stream becomes wider and deeper. In the beginning, the big rivers that we see were merely little creeks.

[10] I translated this from an audio clip acquired years ago. The file has minimal identifying information. However, Phra Paisal's voice is easily recognizable and the quality sounds much like the numerous recordings from his long-time temple of residence in Chaiyaphum, northeastern Thailand.

After water passes and passes and passes, after a long time, it becomes a river, wider and deeper. But we can change the course of the river. Just like we change the path of our heart.... We can change the course of the river by gradually digging canals, or by creating a new waterway. At first, it will be a small waterway; not much water will flow through it. The water will continue to flow through the original waterway. But if we do not surrender, if we do not retreat, if we try to dig and expand the waterway, the water will gradually begin to flow along the new way. And once it has flowed this way often, this new waterway will grow larger and deeper. One day, the water will flow in this new direction, along this new path, and it won't flow much along the old way. The old waterway will become narrower, and the new waterway will become wider. With our heart, it is the same way. Our habits and dispositions are the same.... It's with practice, with our development of mindfulness. This is the creation of a new path for the heart, so that it may proceed in a wholesome direction, a direction that leads to non-suffering. And the original stream will grow narrow, until it has silted up and become impassable. Or at least it will be smaller than before. Just like the Chao Phraya, where it flows past Thamasaat University [in Bangkok]. Some people might not know: in the past, it was merely a canal, just a little canal. Originally, the Chao Phraya turned at Bangkok Noi, but that was a winding waterway. In the Age of Ayutthaya, King Chairacha [r. 1534–47], ordered the digging of a new canal, a shortcut. So a canal was dug, and it became a shortcut. But as time went by, it ceased to be a canal, and it became a river, a big river, the Chao Phraya. As for the original stream, it became a canal, which we call the Bangkok Noi Canal [Little Bangkok Canal]. But really that's the original stream, the original course of the Chao Phraya River. Our heart is like that—we can create a path for it, a path of compassion, self-awareness, and mindfulness.... It simply depends on our practice, on our choices, on which way we will let our hearts go.

Epilogue

I left Bangkok in 2013, gathered my field notes, and began writing. I returned to Southeast Asia in 2016 and remained in the region for seven months. After returning to Bangkok, I revisited many sites, including the canal-side mosque. The bookstore owner talked about his journey to Palestine and his observations of the occupation, and he said his son was in Egypt studying Arabic and Islam. It was sometimes strange to see familiar places in new forms. The market by Siriraj Hospital was under construction. The coffee vendor was gone and could not be found. In another case, a woman was in her shop, exactly where she had been before. We had spoken dozens of times, but she had aged, and after three years, only barely seemed to recognize me. The artist in Thonburi had closed his studio and moved. It was saddening to see the doors padlocked in the afternoon, but later I found him and we met for coffee. He had purchased a motorcycle and his arms had been tattooed. He shared his leather-bound sketchbook full of ink drawings of authors' faces, and he noticed a book by Seksan Prasertkul in my bag. He talked excitedly about the author: a student leader from the October 14, 1973 generation who had later escaped into the forest, a writer known to blend landscape description with profound meditation. We had a lively conversation about books, writing, life, about the most recent exhibition of his paintings, and his plan to open his own cafe and bookshop. He had already chosen a location and he shared his hand-drawn diagrams of the imagined layout. He was energetic and optimistic, and his presence was rejuvenating, like a gale of freedom in a grim city, for Bangkok was again dominated by the military. He envisioned the creation of a place where people could gather, read, talk, draw, or write—a new sanctuary, a place that would always be, as he said, "in motion".

I also intended to return to the alley described in Chapter 2. The express boat approached the dock from upstream, stopping alongside the Memorial Bridge, which had opened in 1932, just before the overthrow of absolute monarchy, a bridge dedicated to the founder of the Chakri Dynasty, and I made my way along the concrete path, where men go fishing, drink beer, and play checkers with scraps of cardboard and bottle caps. The row of hovels had been destroyed. There was no alley anymore. The concrete wall, the whole enclosing structure, had been demolished. Scraps and rubble were in piles, and one could still see on the ground the outlines of the hovels. A ripped couch was in one of the squares, lined up, as if against the wall, an eerie invocation of a place that no longer existed. A decaying shrine—adorned with national flags, Buddha statues, and a portrait of the king—also stood amidst the ruins. From the concrete path, there was a clear view of the temple, which had been the center of the community. A man passed through, and he said, "It was about a year ago. They were chased out." A group of people sitting in front of a nearby house said the same. I asked, where did the people go? "Somewhere across the river", one said. Later, a friend from the University of Fine Arts said that, in the final days of the eviction, the residents gathered in an aggressive demonstration, holding signs saying: We don't want this abbot! "It was scary", she said. "The people were so furious, almost violent. They had an agreement with the old abbot, but the new abbot didn't recognize it."

After nearly two months in Thailand, I was preparing to travel to Indonesia. A few days prior to the flight, an event was held at Thammasat University to mark 40 years since the October 6, 1976 massacre. In the evening, seats were full in the auditorium, where Thongchai Winichakul gave a speech, followed by a performance by the band Caravan. The stage was decorated with red and yellow cloth knotted together, suggesting a unity beyond recent conflicts. Thongchai was part of the protests that preceded the massacre. In 1976, he was speaking on stage as men began to fire into the campus. One of the speakers at the commemoration recalled Thongchai speaking calmly into the microphone, saying, "Please stop shooting." Thongchai read the names of the victims, but some names remain unknown. Following the massacre, the military promptly seized power and he was imprisoned. The living horror of October 6, 1976 is not merely the toll of injury and death—students beaten, burned alive, bodies desecrated, the deep, unhealed wounds in the hearts of the survivors. It is also the mind-boggling dehumanization of the victims, and the terror of ordinary Thais—righteous patriots, devout Buddhists, loyal subjects of the king—swept up into an unstoppable storm of hatred. During his speech, Thongchai said he still thought of the massacre every day, and he remembered the laughter of the killers, torturers, and onlookers.

After the commemoration, the following morning, an apartment manager offered a comment, noting, in a stark reversal, that students of Thammasat, as well as the University of Fine Arts, are notorious for violent politics. Then she smiled and said, "Events like that [the October 1976 massacre] don't happen anymore. Now we have democracy." The statement was somehow not out of place in Bangkok, as we continued to live under military control, with no signs that the rulers intended to release their grip on power. The city's most recent large-scale street massacre was in 2010, only a few years previous. Subsequently, the democratically elected government headed by Yingluck had been overthrown. General Prayuth, who had played a leading role in crushing the Red Shirt protests, had seized power and become prime minister.

Clouds over Bangkok—one month before the death of the king

The long-reigning king died in Bangkok on October 13, 2016. Rama IX had been hospitalized for years, and everyone knew he was in his final days. I went to a book festival in the morning, then returned to my room to pack for a flight to Jakarta. The news appeared online in the evening, and I turned on the television just in time to hear the announcement from the prime minister. General Prayuth asked Thais to wear mourning for one year, to refrain from entertainment or festivities for one month, and he said, "Don't listen to rumors." Looking out from the balcony, one saw nothing unusual in the alley. Out by the main road, the scene was ordinary, the usual circulation of Bangkok. People were driving and the convenience store was open. No one was weeping and there were no gunshots. Early the next morning, free newspapers were distributed by the steps of the BTS station with the headline "Tears Flow Throughout the Kingdom". It was quiet on the skytrain; they had shut off the barrage of advertisements. Many women were, as the general had asked—but realistically speaking, commanded—dressed in black. People fidgeted with phones, checking social media, playing video games. Still, contrary to headlines and expectations, no one present was weeping.

It was a relief to arrive in Jakarta, as if the air was easier to breathe. There were too many soldiers on the streets of Bangkok. Camps had sprouted at intersections, with armed men in boots sitting at metal tables. Vendors were chased from sidewalks. One night I saw soldiers screaming at a man driving a pickup truck, who was attempting to sell fruit. Meanwhile General Prayuth received generous amounts of television airtime to talk about harmony and public order. An informant observed that Thai people tend to trust military governments. It was evident that, in contrast to a few years previous, ordinary people were more cautious in speech. Up-country migrants in Bangkok sometimes muttered criticism, calling the rulers bullies, incompetent, incapable of administering, and "power crazy". One said, "If we talk too much or resist, we'll eat rice for free [in prison]." Even before the seizure of power by the military in 2014, freedom of expression was severely limited. Cases of defamation multiplied dramatically after the 2006 coup against Thaksin (Streckfuss 2011). A few years later, Pavin Chachavalpongpun wrote, "We see that the situation, in terms of protecting human rights in Thailand, has reached the lowest point.... The lese-majesty law has been used increasingly as a political weapon" (Pavin

2012: 16). Following the coup in 2014, the situation quickly grew worse. The military compiled a list of names, demanding that people appear for review. The list included politicians, academics, and other troublemakers, some of whom fled the country rather than submit to the rifle-carrying authorities. Shortly after the coup, an informant who worked at a printing factory in Bangkok sent a letter describing how armed soldiers had raided the factory looking for subversive materials. In 2018, two Thai dissidents who had fled to Laos turned up as dead bodies in the Mekong, bearing signs of torture and murder. In the same case, a third body is believed to have "disappeared": that of the elderly dissident Surachai Saedan, a Red Shirt spokesman, former political prisoner, and a close comrade of the other victims.[1] Surachai had escaped in 2014 to Laos, where he produced a low-budget political talk show called *Revolutionize Thailand*. An informant observed, "Sadly, Thailand is still savage [ป่าเถื่อน] in terms of the use of subterranean power [อิทธิพล]. People who get involved in politics or take sides openly are often killed, including people who apply for candidacy for political positions." Surachai's comrades had been disemboweled, and their faces had been crushed.

Later I found, among my hand-written notes, a striking quotation from the Indonesian journalist and novelist Mochtar Lubis: "Since Indonesia attained freedom [from Dutch colonialism], I have considered myself to be a free human being. Free to think, free to say what I think. If not, then we are still colonized."[2] Mochtar was born in the colonial period. He experienced the anti-colonial struggle, and then became a fierce antagonist of the post-colonial governments. He was a prolific writer and a sensitive observer of Indonesian society—a critic of corruption, Javanese feudalism, and above all, the abuse of power. He ran afoul of Sukarno and suffered nine years in prison without trial. Later, and again without trial, he was confined under the military

---

[1] The case was discussed in October 2019 by *The 101 World*, a young multimedia outlet from Thailand. At the time of writing, the recording could be found online: 101 in focus EP.13 (ผู้ลี้ภัยมาจากไหน).

[2] Mochtar Lubis: "Sejak Indonesia merdeka, saya menganggap diri saya manusia merdeka kok. Merdeka berpikir, merdeka menyatakan pikiran. Kalau tidak begitu kita masih terjajah dong." The translation is my own. An excellent overview of his life and thought can be found in his book *Mochtar Lubis Bicara Lurus* (1995).

regime of Suharto (Lubis 2008). On finding the above quotation, I was compelled to reflect again on Thailand—as a Southeast Asian country without such memories of decolonization. Siam was deeply integrated into the regional colonial economy. Beginning in the late 19th century, the monarchy was fortified, taking an absolutist form, and the military was modernized. Borders were drawn, territory was mapped, and the rulers reshaped Siam to more closely resemble nearby colonial systems, asserting control over Siam's peripheries. Much of the deep, persistent conflict in Thailand centers on structures that congealed during that time. The myth that Thailand, by the grace of the monarchs, escaped colonialism, has become one of the ideological bastions of the old system—and the Thai military is one of the institutions most invested in that system. In 2014, as the long reign of Rama IX was approaching dusk, the military seized power in the name of the monarchy. That is, in the name of the institution said to have saved Thailand from servitude, the military has overturned democracy, stolen sovereignty, and choked free expression, for such expression threatens to "divide the nation". The military itself, under pretenses of protecting the throne, has become a colonial institution, defended by rifles, prisons, and deception, asserting itself over Thai society, suppressing the emergence of free human beings.

In these troubled times, the Chao Phraya River, mother of Siam, opens many perspectives. Ailing and yet fertile, she connects times and places. As the culture of memory boils, she persists—both tangible and transcendent, a maternal presence in modern Bangkok, evocative of the cyclical dramas of conflict and cohesion, life and death. As rain falls, bringing fresh water to this body of earth, she is a symbol of the confluences that created Thailand, reminding us—all who care for the country—of temporal depth and the potential of renewal. However complex the national terrain, water, as a source of life, has a universal significance. This book is written in hope that the river will not be forgotten. As the cult of power is confronted by the disintegration of official myths, the river opens colorful vistas, encouraging us to consider the mixture of peoples, continuity and change, and the long tradition of canalization. The study of memory and landscape reveals both stark repetition and certainties of growth, as well as the reality of illusions, both their power and fragility. Recent years in Thailand suggest that much is not as it appears. This is one of the lessons of ethnography. Setting out for fieldwork, one never arrives formless. Ethnographers always arrive with questions. One might have read many books, and one always has ideas, be they strange or conventional. But in the course of ethnographic research, one stumbles. Given ideas are subjected to friction and conflict. In Bangkok, one gets caught in the rain. Perhaps a stranger lends you an umbrella. The world is a realm of the unexpected, malleable, but also delightfully and disturbingly intractable. Thus, as a river flows to the sea, but does not end, one awaits the replenishing rain of tomorrow.

Bibliography

Abbey, Edward. 1991. *Down the River*. New York: Penguin Books.

Akin Rabibhadana. 2017. *พระมหากษัตริย์-ขุนนาง: นาย-ไพร่ ในโครงสร้างสังคมไทยยุคต้นกรุงรัตนโกสินทร์* [King and Nobility, Masters and Servants in Thai Society in the Early Rattanakosin Period]. Krungthep: Munnithi phuea Kansueksa Prachathippatai lae Kanphatthana.

Alley, Kelly D. 2002. *On the Banks of the Ganga: When Wastewater Meets a Sacred River*. Ann Arbor: The University of Michigan Press.

Anderson, Benedict. 1978. "Studies of the Thai State". In *The Study of Thailand: Analyses of Knowledge, Approaches, and Prospects in Anthropology, Art History, Economics, History, and Political Science*, ed. Eliezer B. Ayal, 193–247. Athens: Ohio University Center for International Studies, Southeast Asia Program.

________. 1990. *Language and Power: Exploring Political Cultures in Indonesia*. Ithaca: Cornell University Press.

________. 1998. *The Spectre of Comparisons: Nationalism, Southeast Asia and the World*. New York: Verso.

________. 2006. *Imagined Communities: Reflections on the Origin and Spread of Nationalism*. London: Verso.

Assmann, Aleida. 2011. "Canon and Archive". In *The Collective Memory Reader*, ed. Jeffrey K. Olick, Vered Vinitzky-Seroussi, and Daniel Levy, 334–7. Oxford: Oxford University Press.

Assmann, Jan. 2011. *Cultural Memory and Early Civilization: Writing, Remembrance, and Political Imagination*. Cambridge: Cambridge University Press.

Bachelard, Gaston. 1983. *Water and Dreams: An Essay on the Imagination of Matter*, ed. Joanne H. Stroud, trans. Edith R. Farrell. Dallas: Pegasus Foundation.

Baker, Chris and Pasuk Phongpaichit. 2009. *A History of Thailand*. Cambridge: Cambridge University Press.

Barmé, Scot. 1993. *Luang Wichit Wathakan and the Creation of a Thai Identity*. Singapore: Institute of Southeast Asian Studies.

Barth, Fredrik, ed. 1998. *Ethnic Groups and Boundaries: The Social Organization of Culture Difference*. Prospect Heights: Waveland Press.

Basso, Keith H. 1996. *Wisdom Sits in Places: Landscape and Language Among the Western Apache*. Albuquerque: University of New Mexico Press.

Batson, Benjamin A. 2017. *อวสานสมบูรณาญาสิทธิราชย์ในสยาม* [The End of the Absolute Monarchy in Siam], trans. Kanjanee La-ongsri. Krungthep: Munnithi Khrongkan Tamra Sangkhomsat lae Manutsayasat.

Benda, Harry J. 1969. "The Structure of Southeast Asian History: Some Preliminary Observations". In *Man, State, and Society*, ed. Robert O. Tilman, 23–44. New York: Praeger.

Benedict, Ruth. 1952. *Thai Culture and Behavior: An Unpublished War-time Study, 1943*. Data Paper No. 4. Ithaca: Cornell University, Southeast Asia Program.

Boomgaard, Peter, ed. 2007. *A World of Water: Rain, Rivers and Seas in Southeast Asian Histories*. Leiden: KITLV Press.

Buddhadasa Phikkhu. n.d. *คู่มือมนุษย์* [Human Handbook]. Krungthep: Thammasapa.

Carter, Paul. 1987. *The Road to Botany Bay: An Exploration of Landscape and History*. Minneapolis: University of Minnesota Press.

Casey, Edward S. 1987. *Remembering: A Phenomenological Study*. Bloomington: Indiana University Press.

________. 1997. *The Fate of Place: A Philosophical History*. Berkeley: University of California Press.

Chaiwat Satha-Anand. 2005. *The Life of this World: Negotiated Muslim Lives in Thai Society*. Singapore: Marshall Cavendish.

Charnvit Kasetsiri. 1979. "Thai Historiography from Ancient Times to the Modern Period". In *Perceptions of the Past in Southeast Asia*, ed. Anthony Reid and David Marr, 156–70. Singapore: Heinemann Educational Books (Asia).

________. 1997. *อารยธรรมไทย: พื้นฐานทางประวัติศาสตร์* [Thai Civilization: Historical Foundation]. Krungthep: Ton O Grami.

________. 2008a. *มอญ-เขมรศึกษา* [Mon-Khmer Studies]. Krungthep: Munnithi Khrongkan Tamra Sangkhomsat lae Manutsayasat.

________. 2008b. *สยามหรือไทย* [Siam or Thai]. Krungthep: Munnithi Khrongkan Tamra Sangkhomsat lae Manutsayasat.

Chatri Prakitnonthakan. 2015. *การเมืองในสถาปัตยกรรมสมัยรัชกาลที่ ๑* [Politics in the Architecture of the First Reign]. Krungthep: Matichon.

Clark, Kenneth. 1979 [1949]. *Landscape into Art*. New York: Harper & Row.

Coedès, G. 1968. *The Indianized States of Southeast Asia*, ed. Walter F. Vella, trans. Susan Brown Cowing. Honolulu: University Press of Hawaii.

Connerton, Paul. 1989. *How Societies Remember*. Cambridge: Cambridge University Press.

Corkin, Suzanne. 2013. *Permanent Present Tense: The Unforgettable Life of the Amnesic Patient, H.M.* New York: Basic Books.

Cosgrove, Denis E. 1998. *Social Formation and Symbolic Landscape*. Madison: University of Wisconsin Press.

Desjarlais, Robert. 1997. *Shelter Blues: Sanity and Selfhood Among the Homeless*. Philadelphia: University of Pennsylvania Press.

Dhida Saraya. 1982. *ตำนานและตำนานประวัติศาสตร์กับการศึกษาประวัติศาสตร์ท้องถิ่น* [Tamnan and Historical Tamnan in the Study of Local History]. Krungthep: Samnakngan Khanakammakan Wathanatham haeng Chat.

Donner, Wolf. 1978. *The Five Faces of Thailand: An Economic Geography*. London: C. Hurst & Company.

Draaisma, Douwe. 2000. *Metaphors of Memory: A History of Ideas About the Mind*, trans. Paul Vincent. Cambridge: Cambridge University Press.

________. 2015. *Forgetting: Myths, Perils, and Compensations*, trans. Liz Waters. New Haven: Yale University Press.

Duncan, James S. 1990. *The City as Text: The Politics of Landscape Interpretation in the Kandyan Kingdom*. Cambridge: Cambridge University Press.

Erll, Astrid. 2011. *Memory in Culture*, trans. Sara B. Young. New York: Palgrave Macmillan.

Fabian, Johannes. 1996. *Remembering the Present: Painting and Popular History in Zaire*. Berkeley: University of California Press.

Feld, Steven. 2005. "Places Sensed, Senses Placed: Toward a Sensuous Epistemology of Environments". In *Empire of the Senses: The Sensual Culture Reader*, ed. David Howes, 179–91. New York: Berg Publishers.

Ferguson, James. 2006. *Africa in the Neoliberal World Order*. Durham: Duke University Press.

Fernández-Armesto, Felipe. 2002. *Civilizations: Culture, Ambition, and the Transformation of Nature*. New York: Touchstone Books.

Geertz, Clifford. 1973. *The Interpretation of Cultures*. New York: Basic Books.

________. 1995. *After the Fact: Two Countries, Four Decades, One Anthropologist*. Cambridge: Harvard University Press.

Gellner, Ernest. 1983. *Nations and Nationalism*. Oxford: Basil Blackwell.

Gilquin, Michel. 2005. *The Muslims of Thailand*, trans. Michael Smithies. Chiang Mai: Silkworm Books.

Goody, Jack. 1998. "Memory in Oral Tradition". In *Memory*, ed. Patricia Fara and Karalyn Patterson, 73–94. Cambridge: Cambridge University Press.

Halbwachs, Maurice. 1980 [1950]. *The Collective Memory*, trans. Francis J. Ditter and Vida Yazdi Ditter. New York: Harper & Row.

________. 1992 [1925]. *On Collective Memory*, trans. Lewis A. Coser. Chicago: University of Chicago Press.

Hansen, Thomas Blom. 2001. *Wages of Violence: Naming and Identity in Postcolonial Bombay*. Princeton: Princeton University Press.

Herzfeld, Michael. 1997. *Cultural Intimacy: Social Poetics in the Nation-State*. New York: Routledge.

________. 2002. "The Absent Presence: Discourses of Crypto-Colonialism". *The South Atlantic Quarterly* 101 (4): 899–926.

———. 2016. *Siege of the Spirits: Community and Polity in Bangkok*. Chicago: The University of Chicago Press.

Hobsbawm, Eric, ed. 1983. *The Invention of Tradition*. Cambridge: Cambridge University Press.

________. 1990. *Nations and Nationalism Since 1780: Programme, Myth, Reality*. Cambridge: Cambridge University Press.

Hoskins, W.G. 2013. *The Making of the English Landscape*. Toller Fratrum: Little Toller Books.

Ingold, Tim. 1993. "The Temporality of the Landscape". *World Archeology* 25 (2): 152–74.

________. 2000. *The Perception of the Environment: Essays on Livelihood, Dwelling and Skill*. London: Routledge.

________. 2007. *Lines: A Brief History*. London: Routledge.

________. 2011. *Being Alive: Essays on Movement, Knowledge and Description*. London: Routledge.

Ivarsson, Soren. 2008. *Creating Laos: The Making of a Lao Space between Indochina and Siam, 1860–1945*. Copenhagen: NIAS Press.

Ivarsson, Søren and Lotte Isager, eds. 2010. *Saying the Unsayable: Monarchy and Democracy in Thailand*. Copenhagen: NIAS Press.

Jackson, John Brinckerhoff. 1980. *The Necessity for Ruins and Other Topics*. Amherst: The University of Massachusetts Press.

________. 1984. *Discovering the Vernacular Landscape*. New Haven: Yale University Press.

Jackson, Michael. 1995. *At Home in the World*. Durham: Duke University Press.

Jackson, Peter A. 2007. "Autonomy and Subordination in Thai History: The Case for Semicolonial Analysis". *Inter-Asia Cultural Studies* 8 (3): 329–48.

________. 2010. "Virtual Divinity: A 21st-Century Discourse of Thai Royal Influence". In *Saying the Unsayable: Monarchy and Democracy in Thailand*, ed. Søren Ivarsson and Lotte Isager, 29–60. Copenhagen: NIAS Press.

Jit Phumisak. 1981 [1976]. *ความเป็นมาของคำว่า สยาม, ไทย ลาว และ ขอม และลักษณะทางสังคมของชื่อชนชาติ* [Origins of the Words Siam, Thai, Lao, and Khom and the Social Characteristics of the Names of Peoples]. Krungthep: Borisat Samnakphim Duang Kamon.

________. 1998 [1957]. *โฉมหน้าศักดินาไทย* [The Face of Thai Feudalism]. Krungthep: Samnakphim Sipanya.

________. 2009 [1957]. *ศิลปเพื่อชีวิต* [Art for Life]. Krungthep: Maekhamphang.

________. 2021 [1983]. *สังคมไทยลุ่มแม่น้ำเจ้าพระยาก่อนสมัยศรีอยุธยา* [Thai Society in the Chao Phraya Basin Before the Age of Ayutthaya]. Nonthaburi: Si Panya.

Kabir, Ananya Jahanara. 2009. *Territory of Desire: Representing the Valley of Kashmir*. Minneapolis: University of Minnesota Press.

Kakizaki Ichiro. 2014. *物語 タイの歴史:微笑みの国の真実* [Thai History: Truth of the Smiling Country]. Tokyo: Chuokoron-Shinsha.

Kampoon Boontawee. 1997. *ลูกอีสาน* [Child of Isan]. Krungthep: Samnakphim Bhannakij.

Kasian Tejapira. 1994. *แลลอดลายมังกร: รวมข้อเขียนว่าด้วยความเป็นจีนในสยาม* [Looking Through the Dragon Design: Collected Writings on Chineseness in Siam]. Krungthep: Khopfai.

________. 2001. *Commodifying Marxism: The Formation of Modern Thai Radical Culture, 1927–1958*. Kyoto: Kyoto University Press.

———. 2007. *รัฐประหารกับประชาธิปไตยไทย* [Coups and Thai Democracy]. Krungthep: Munnithi Khrongkan Tamra Sangkhomsat lae Manutsayasat.

Kermel-Torrès, Doryane. 2004. *Atlas of Thailand: Spatial Structures and Development*. Chiang Mai: Silkworm Books.

Keyes, Charles. 1967. *Isan: Regionalism in Northeastern Thailand*. Data Paper No. 65. Ithaca: Cornell University, Southeast Asia Program.

________. 1987. *Thailand: Buddhist Kingdom as Modern Nation-State*. Boulder: Westview Press.

________. 2002. "Presidential Adress: 'The Peoples of Asia'—Science and Politics in the Classification of Ethnic Groups in Thailand, China, and Vietnam". *The Journal of Asian Studies* 61 (4): 1163–203.

King, Ross. 2017. *Heritage and Identity in Contemporary Thailand: Memory, Place and Power*. Singapore: NUS Press.

Klima, Alan. 2002. *The Funeral Casino: Meditation, Massacre, and Exchange with the Dead in Thailand*. Princeton: Princeton University Press.

Kukrit Pramoj. 2009. *ไผ่แดง* [Red Bamboo]. Krungthep: Dokya 2000.

________. 2010. *หลายชีวิต* [Many Lives]. Krungthep: Dokya 2000.

________. 2011. *สี่แผ่นดิน* [Four Reigns]. Nonthaburi: Dokya 2000.

Leach, E.R. 1960. "The Frontiers of 'Burma'". *Comparative Studies in Society and History* 3 (1): 49–68.

Lefebvre, Henri. 1991. *The Production of Space*, trans. Donald Nicholson-Smith. Oxford: Blackwell.

London, Bruce. 1980. *Metropolis and Nation in Thailand: The Political Economy of Uneven Development*. Boulder: Westview Press.

Lubis, Mochtar. 1995. *Mochtar Lubis Bicara Lurus: Menjawab Pertanyaan Wartawan* [Mochtar Lubis Speaks Straight: Answering Questions from Journalists]. Jakarta: Yayasan Obor Indonesia.

________. 2008. *Nirbaya: Catatan Harian Mochtar Lubis dalam Penjara Orde Baru* [Nirbaya: Diary of Mochtar Lubis in a New Order Prison]. Jakarta: Yayasan Obor Indonesia.

Madjid, Nurcholish. 2018. *Indonesia Kita* [Our Indonesia]. Jakarta: Penerbit PT Gramedia Pustaka Utama.

Malinowski, Bronislaw. 1922. *Argonauts of the Western Pacific*. New York: E.P. Dutton & Co.

Matichon Online. 2021. "#เหตุเกิดที่ประตูแดง" [#Incident at the Red Gate]. September 24, 2021. Accessed June 22, 2024. https://www.matichon.co.th/politics/news_2956824#.

McNeill, J.R. and William McNeill. 2003. *The Human Web: A Bird's-Eye View of World History*. New York: W.W. Norton & Company.

Mead, Margaret, Frances Cooke Macgregor, and Gregory Bateson. 1951. *Growth and Culture: A Photographic Study of Balinese Childhood*. New York: G.P. Putnam's Sons.

Mitchell, W.J.T., ed. 1994. *Landscape and Power*. Chicago: University of Chicago Press.

Nakarin Mektrairat. 2010. *การปฏิวัติสยาม พ.ศ. 2475* [Siamese Revolution of the Buddhist Year 2475]. Krungthep: Fa Diaokan.

Nattapol Chaiching. 2020. *ขุนศึก ศักดินา และพญาอินทรี: การเมืองไทยภายใต้ระเบียบโลกของสหรัฐอเมริกา 2491–2500* [Military Chiefs, Feudalism, and the Great Eagle: Thai Politics Under the World Order of America, 1948–1957]. Nonthaburi: Fa Diaokan.

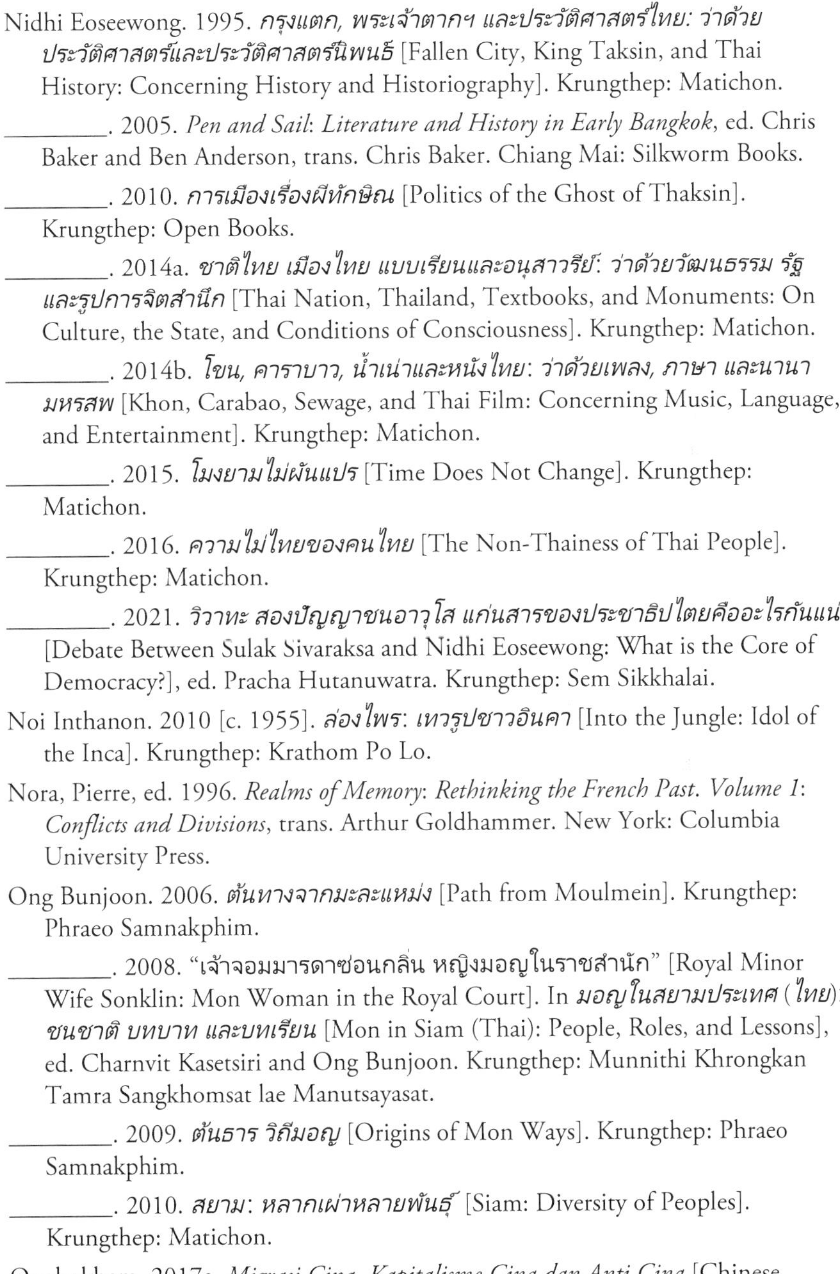

Nidhi Eoseewong. 1995. *กรุงแตก, พระเจ้าตากฯ และประวัติศาสตร์ไทย: ว่าด้วยประวัติศาสตร์และประวัติศาสตร์นิพนธ์* [Fallen City, King Taksin, and Thai History: Concerning History and Historiography]. Krungthep: Matichon.

________. 2005. *Pen and Sail: Literature and History in Early Bangkok*, ed. Chris Baker and Ben Anderson, trans. Chris Baker. Chiang Mai: Silkworm Books.

________. 2010. *การเมืองเรื่องผีทักษิณ* [Politics of the Ghost of Thaksin]. Krungthep: Open Books.

________. 2014a. *ชาติไทย เมืองไทย แบบเรียนและอนุสาวรีย์: ว่าด้วยวัฒนธรรม รัฐ และรูปการจิตสำนึก* [Thai Nation, Thailand, Textbooks, and Monuments: On Culture, the State, and Conditions of Consciousness]. Krungthep: Matichon.

________. 2014b. *โขน, คาราบาว, น้ำเน่าและหนังไทย: ว่าด้วยเพลง, ภาษา และนานามหรสพ* [Khon, Carabao, Sewage, and Thai Film: Concerning Music, Language, and Entertainment]. Krungthep: Matichon.

________. 2015. *โมงยามไม่ผันแปร* [Time Does Not Change]. Krungthep: Matichon.

________. 2016. *ความไม่ไทยของคนไทย* [The Non-Thainess of Thai People]. Krungthep: Matichon.

________. 2021. *วิวาทะ สองปัญญาชนอาวุโส แก่นสารของประชาธิปไตยคืออะไรกันแน่* [Debate Between Sulak Sivaraksa and Nidhi Eoseewong: What is the Core of Democracy?], ed. Pracha Hutanuwatra. Krungthep: Sem Sikkhalai.

Noi Inthanon. 2010 [c. 1955]. *ล่องไพร: เทวรูปชาวอินคา* [Into the Jungle: Idol of the Inca]. Krungthep: Krathom Po Lo.

Nora, Pierre, ed. 1996. *Realms of Memory: Rethinking the French Past. Volume 1: Conflicts and Divisions*, trans. Arthur Goldhammer. New York: Columbia University Press.

Ong Bunjoon. 2006. *ต้นทางจากมะละแหม่ง* [Path from Moulmein]. Krungthep: Phraeo Samnakphim.

________. 2008. "เจ้าจอมมารดาซ่อนกลิ่น หญิงมอญในราชสำนัก" [Royal Minor Wife Sonklin: Mon Woman in the Royal Court]. In *มอญในสยามประเทศ (ไทย): ชนชาติ บทบาท และบทเรียน* [Mon in Siam (Thai): People, Roles, and Lessons], ed. Charnvit Kasetsiri and Ong Bunjoon. Krungthep: Munnithi Khrongkan Tamra Sangkhomsat lae Manutsayasat.

________. 2009. *ต้นธาร วิถีมอญ* [Origins of Mon Ways]. Krungthep: Phraeo Samnakphim.

________. 2010. *สยาม: หลากเผ่าหลายพันธุ์* [Siam: Diversity of Peoples]. Krungthep: Matichon.

Onghokham. 2017a. *Migrasi Cina, Kapitalisme Cina dan Anti Cina* [Chinese Migration, Chinese Capitalism, and Anti-Chinese]. Depok: Komunitas Bambu.

________. 2017b. *Riwayat Tionghoa Peranakan di Jawa* [History of Peranakan Chinese in Java]. Depok: Komunitas Bambu.

Osborne, Milton. 2000. *The Mekong: Turbulent Past, Uncertain Future*. New York: Grove Press.

Paglia, Camille. 2013. *Glittering Images: A Journey Through Art from Egypt to Star Wars*. New York: Vintage Books.

Pamuk, Orhan. 2005. *Istanbul: Memories and the City*, trans. Maureen Freely. New York: Alfred A. Knopf.

Pandian, Anand. 2009. *Crooked Stalks: Cultivating Virtue in South India*. Durham: Duke University Press.

Pavin Chachavalpongpun. 2012. *ก้าวข้ามความกลัว* [Go Beyond Fear]. Publisher unknown.

Peleggi, Maurizio. 2002. *The Politics of Ruins and the Business of Nostalgia*. Bangkok: White Lotus Press.

________. 2007. *Thailand: The Worldly Kingdom*. London: Reaktion Books.

________. 2017. *Monastery, Monument, Museum: Sites and Artifacts of Thai Cultural Memory*. Honolulu: University of Hawaii Press.

Phra Paisal Visalo. 2011. *สุขเหนือสุข* [Happiness Above Happiness]. Krungthep: Nation Books.

________. 2018. *วิชาสุดท้ายที่ใช้ได้ตลอดชีวิต* [Knowledge Usable Throughout Life]. Krungthep: Amarin Dhamma.

Phya Anuman Rajthon. 1954. "The Loy Krathong". In *The Siam Society Fiftieth Anniversary Commemorative Publication: Selected Articles from The Siam Society Journal, Volume 2: 1929–1953*, 197–204. Bangkok: The Siam Society.

Pinyo Traisuriyathamma. 2013. *ตอบโจทย์ประเทศไทย* [Answering the Questions of Thailand]. Krungthep: Open Books.

Prapas Cholsaranont. 2011. *อภินิหารพระดิน* [Miracle of the Earth Buddha]. Pathum Thani: Workpoint.

Preecha Juntanamalaga. 1988. "Thai or Siam?" In *Names* 36 (1/2): 68–84.

Raffles, Hugh. 2002. *In Amazonia: A Natural History*. Princeton: Princeton University Press.

Reid, Anthony. 1988. *Southeast Asia in the Age of Commerce 1450–1680, Volume 1: The Lands Below the Winds*. New Haven: Yale University Press.

________. 1993. *Southeast Asia in the Age of Commerce 1450–1680, Volume 2: Expansion and Crisis*. New Haven: Yale University Press.

Rigg, Jonathan. 1991. *Southeast Asia: A Region in Transition*. London: Unwin Hyman.

Rodriguez, Richard. 2013. *Darling: A Spiritual Autobiography*. New York: Viking Press.

Said, Edward W. 1978. *Orientalism*. New York: Pantheon Books.

Sangkhit Chanthanaphothi. 2011. *ภาพเก่าในสยาม* [Old Pictures in Siam]. Krungthep: Sayam Banthuek.

Sathaporn Limmani et al. 2017. *รัฐธรรมนูญแห่งราชอาณาจักรไทย พุทธศักราช ๒๕๖๐* [Constitution of the Thai Kingdom, Buddhist Year 2560]. Krungthep: Winyuchon.

Schama, Simon. 1995. *Landscape and Memory*. New York: Alfred A. Knopf.

Sebald, W.G. 1998. *The Rings of Saturn*, trans. Michael Hulse. New York: New Directions Publishing.

Seksan Prasertkul. 2016. *ทาง: รวมเรื่องสั้นชุด "ซ้ายผ่านศึก"*. [Paths: Collected Short Stories about Leftist Combat Veterans]. Krungthep: Samanchon.

Skinner, G. William. 1957. *Chinese Society in Thailand: An Analytical History*. Ithaca: Cornell University Press.

Smith, Anthony D. 1986. *The Ethnic Origins of Nations*. Oxford: Basil Blackwell.

________. 2010. *Nationalism: Theory, Ideology, History*. Cambridge: Polity Press.

Solnit, Rebecca. 2000. *Wanderlust: A History of Walking*. New York: Viking Press.

________. 2001. *As Eve Said to the Serpent: On Landscape, Gender, and Art*. Athens: The University of Georgia Press.

Sombat Plainoi. 2001. *ชีวิตตามคลอง* [Life Along Canals]. Krungthep: Saithan.

________. 2010. *เกิดในเรือ บันทึกความทรงจำของ ส. พลายน้อย* [Born in a Boat: The Memories of So Plainoi]. Krungthep: Matichon.

Sopranzetti, Claudio. 2017. *Owners of the Map: Motorcycle Taxi Drivers, Mobility, and Politics in Bangkok*. Oakland: University of California Press.

Srisak Vallibhotama. 1990. *แอ่งอารยธรรมอีสาน: แฉหลักฐานโบราณคดีพลิกโฉมหน้าประวัติศาสตร์ไทย* [Cradle of Civilization in the Northeast: Archeological Evidence to Change the Face of Thai History]. Krungthep: Matichon.

________. 2008 *ความหมายของภูมิวัฒนธรรม* [The Meaning of Cultural Landscape]. Krungthep: Munnithi Lek-Prapai Wiriyaphan.

________. 2010 *กรุงศรีอยุธยาของเรา* [Our Ayutthaya]. Krungthep: Matichon.

________. 2013 *คนไทยไม่มีใครทำร้ายก็ตายเอง* [Even If No One Hurts Thai People, They Die on Their Own]. Krungthep: Munnithi Lek-Prapai Wiriyaphan.

________. 2014 *ความล้มเหลวในการศึกษาของชาติ* [Failure in National Education]. Krungthep: Munnithi Lek-Prapai Wiriyaphan.

________. 2017a. *ลุ่มเจ้าพระยา รากเหง้าแห่งสยามประเทศ* [Chao Phraya Basin: Roots of Siam], ed. Walailak Songsiri. Krungthep: Munnithi Lek-Prapai Wiriyaphan.

________. 2017b *สร้างบ้านแปงเมือง* [Building Villages and Cities]. Krungthep: Matichon.

Stilgoe, John R. 2015. *What is Landscape*? Cambridge: The MIT Press.

Streckfuss, David. 2011. *Truth on Trial in Thailand*: *Defamation*, *Treason*, *and Lèse-majesté*. London: Routledge.

________. 2012. "An 'Ethnic' Reading of 'Thai' History in the Twilight of the Century-old Official 'Thai' National Model". *South East Asia Research* 20 (3): 305–27.

Stuart-Fox, Martin. 1997. *A History of Laos*. Cambridge: Cambridge University Press.

Sucha Chulaphet. n.d. *ใครทำลายประเทศไทย* [Who Destroys Thailand?]. Krungthep: Ban Lek Thi 111.

Sujane Kanparit. 2012. *ตามรอยเจ้าอนุวงศ์: คลี่ปมประวัติศาสตร์ไทย-ลาว* [On the Trail of King Anuvong: Solve the Historical Problems of Thai and Lao]. Krungthep: Sarakhadi.

Sujit Wongthes. 1987. *เจ๊กปนลาว* [Chinese Mixed with Lao]. Krungthep: Samnakphim Sinlapa Wathanatham.

________. 1991. "คนไทยในอุษาคเนย์" [Thai People in Southeast Asia]. In *ไทยน้อย ไทยใหญ่ ไทยสยาม* [Little Thai, Big Thai, Siamese Thai], ed. Sujit Wongthes, 138–232. Krungthep: Matichon.

________. 2003. *วรรณกรรมการเมือง เรื่อง "อานุภาพพ่อขุนอุปถัมภ์": ศึกศิลาจารึกที่พ่อขุนรามคำแหงไม่ได้แต่งยุคสุโขทัย* ["Power of the Paternalistic King" as Political Literature: Conflict Over the Inscription Stone that was Not Written by King Ramkhamhaeng in the Sukhothai Era]. Krungthep: Matichon.

________. 2005. *กรุงเทพฯ มาจากไหน?* [Origins of Bangkok] Krungthep: Samnakphim Dream Catcher.

________. 2011. *พระแก้วมรกต มาจากไหน?* [Origins of the Emerald Buddha] Krungthep: Post Books.

________. 2016. *วัฒนธรรมร่วมอุษาคเนย์ในอาเซียน* [Shared Culture of ASEAN]. Krungthep: Samnakphim Natahaek.

________. 2017. *อาหารไทย มาจากไหน?* [Origins of Thai Food] Krungthep: Samnakphim Natahaek.

________. 2019. *เห่เรือ และ เรือพระราชพิธี มาจากไหน?* [Origins of the Royal Barges and Royal Barge Procession] Krungthep: Samnakphim Natahaek.

Sujit Wongthes and Puwadon Suwandi. 1999. *แม่น้ำเจ้าพระยา: มารดาแห่งสยามประเทศ* [Chao Phraya River: Mother of Siam]. Krungthep: Matichon.

Sulak Sivaraksa. 2016. *สถาบันพระมหากษัตริย์กับอนาคตของประเทศไทย* [Monarchy and the Future of Thailand], ed. Nibhondh Chamduang. Krungthep: Samnakphim Mai Khanrap?.

Sunait Chutintaranond. 2004. *พม่ารบไทย: ว่าด้วยการสงครามระหว่างไทยกับพม่า* [Burma Fights Thai: Concerning the Wars between Thai and Burma]. Krungthep: Matichon.

________. 2009. *ชาตินิยมในแบบเรียนไทย* [Nationalism in Thai Textbooks]. Krungthep: Matichon.

Surachai Chantimatorn. 2010. *ทางเส้นเก่า* [The Old Path]. Krungthep: Samanchon.

Suzuki Shunryu. 2003. *Not Always So: Practicing the True Spirit of Zen*, ed. Edward Espe Brown. New York: Quill.

Tambiah, Stanley J. 1976. *World Conqueror and World Renouncer: A Study of Buddhism and Polity in Thailand Against a Historical Background*. Cambridge: Cambridge University Press.

________. 1977. "The Galactic Polity: The Structure of Traditional Kingdoms in Southeast Asia". *Annals of the New York Academy of Sciences* 293: 69–97.

________. 1984. *The Buddhist Saints of the Forest and the Cult of Amulets: A Study in Charisma, Hagiography, Sectarianism, and Millennial Buddhism*. Cambridge: Cambridge University Press.

Tanabe Shigeharu. 1977. "Historical Geography of the Canal System in the Chao Phraya River Delta from the Ayutthaya Period to the Fourth Reign of the Ratanakosin Dynasty". *Journal of the Siam Society* 65 (2): 23–72.

Tanabe Shigeharu and Charles F. Keyes, ed. 2002. *Cultural Crisis and Social Memory: Modernity and Identity in Thailand and Laos*. Honolulu: University of Hawaii Press.

Teeraparb Lohitkun. 1993. *คืนความทรงจำสู่สายน้ำอันเป็นนิรันดร์: แม่น้ำเจ้าพระยา* [Remember the Eternal Waterway: Chao Phraya River]. Krungthep: Ban Wannakam.

Textor, Robert. 1961. *From Peasant to Pedicab Driver: A Social Study of Northeastern Thai Farmers Who Periodically Migrated to Bangkok and Became Pedicab Drivers*. Cultural Report Series No. 9. New Haven: Yale University, Southeast Asia Studies.

Thai Rath. 2014. "'ประยุทธ์' นำคสช.แถลงคุมอำนาจการปกครองประเทศเรียบร้อยแล้ว" ['Prayuth' leads the NCPO and Announces Taking Control of the Country]. May 22, 2014. Accessed May 31, 2014. http://www.thairath.co.th/content/424520.

Thak Chaloemtiarana. 1978. "Reflections on the Sarit Regime and the Process of Political Change in Thailand: Some Conceptual and Theoretical Reassessments". *South East Asian Studies* 16 (3): 400–10.

Thamrongsak Petchlertanan. 2014. Interview with author. In *ประชาธิป'ไทย* [Thai Democracy], ed. Pen-Ek Ratanaruang and Pasakorn Pramoolwong, 68–88. Krungthep: Matichon.

Thamsook Numnonda. 1978. "Pibulsongkram's Thai Nation-Building Programme during the Japanese Military Presence, 1941–1945". *Journal of Southeast Asian Studies* 9 (2): 234–47.

Thongchai Winichakul. 1994. *Siam Mapped: A History of the Geo-Body of a Nation*. Honolulu: University of Hawaii Press.

________. 1995. "The Changing Landscape of the Past". *Journal of Southeast Asian Studies* 26 (1): 99–120.

________. 2000. "The Others Within: Travel and Ethno-Spatial Differentiation of Siamese Subjects 1885–1910". In *Civility and Savagery: Social Identity in Tai Sates*, ed. Andrew Turton, 38–61. Richmond: Curzon Press.

Tilley, Christopher. 2008. *Body and Image: Explorations in Landscape Phenomenology 2*. Walnut Creek: Left Coast Press.

Trouillot, Michel-Rolph. 1995. *Silencing the Past: Power and the Production of History*. Boston: Beacon Press.

Tsing, Anna Lowenhaupt. 1993. *In the Realm of the Diamond Queen: Marginality in an Out-of-the-Way Place*. Princeton: Princeton University Press.

Tsuzuki Kyoichi. 2010. *Hell: 地獄の歩き方* [The Way of Walking in Hell]. Tokyo: Yosensha.

Tuan, Yi-Fu. 1977. *Space and Place: The Perspective of Experience*. Minneapolis: University of Minnesota Press.

Van Esterik, Penny. 2000. *Materializing Thailand*. Oxford: Berg Publishers.

Van Roy, Edward. 2017. *Siamese Melting Pot: Ethnic Minorities in the Making of Bangkok*. Singapore: Institute of Southeast Asian Studies.

Vella, Walter F. 1957. *Siam Under Rama III*. Locust Valley: J.J. Augustin.

Vichak Panich. 2015. *รัฐ-ธรรม-นัว* [State-Dharma-Engagement]. Krungthep: Matichon.

Walailak Songsiri, ed. 2017. *ลุ่มเจ้าพระยา รากเหง้าแห่งสยามประเทศ* [Chao Phraya Basin: Roots of Siam]. Krungthep: Munnithi Lek-Prapai Wiriyaphan.

Wales, H.G. Quaritch. 1931. *Siamese State Ceremonies: Their History and Function*. London: Bernard Quaritch.

Wanni W. Anderson. 2010. *Mapping Thai Muslims: Community Dynamics and Change on the Andaman Coast*. Chiang Mai: Silkworm Books.

Warren, William. 2002. *Bangkok*. London: Reaktion Books.

Waterson, Roxana. 2009. *Paths and Rivers: Sa'dan Toraja Society in Transformation*. Leiden: KITLV Press.

Wira Amphansuk. 2008. *ดำรงสยาม* [Sustain Siam]. Krungthep: Rongphim Samnakngan Phraphutthasatsana haeng Chat.

Wittfogel, Karl A. 1957. *Oriental Despotism: A Comparative Study of Total Power*. New Haven: Yale University Press.

Wolters, O.W. 1982. *History, Culture, and Region in Southeast Asian Perspectives*. Singapore: Institute of Southeast Asian Studies.

Wright, Michael. 1998. *ฝรั่งคลั่งสยาม* [Farang Enamored with Siam], ed. Sujit Wongthes. Krungthep: Matichon.

Wyatt, David K. 2003. *Thailand: A Short History*. New Haven: Yale University Press.

Index